Kobe University Monograph Series in Social Science Research

Series Editors

Yunfang Hu, Kobe University Graduate School of Economics, Kobe, Japan

Shigeyuki Hamori, Kobe University Graduate School of Economics, Kobe, Japan

Editorial Board

Masahiro Enomoto, Kobe University RIEB, Kobe, Japan

Yoshihide Fujioka, Kobe University Graduate School of Economics, Kobe, Japan

Yuka Kaneko, Kobe University Center for Social Systems Innovation, Kobe, Japan

Kazumi Suzuki, Kobe University Graduate School of Business Administration, Kobe, Japan

Kenji Yamamoto, Kobe University Graduate School of Law, Kobe, Japan

The Kobe University Monograph Series in Social Science Research is an exciting interdisciplinary collection of monographs, both authored and edited, that encompass scholarly research not only in the economics but also in law, political science, business and management, accounting, international relations, and other sub-disciplines within the social sciences. As a national university with a special strength in the social sciences, Kobe University actively promotes interdisciplinary research. This series is not limited only to research emerging from Kobe University's faculties of social sciences but also welcomes cross-disciplinary research that integrates studies in the arts and sciences.

Kobe University, founded in 1902, is the second oldest national higher education institution for commerce in Japan and is now a preeminent institution for social science research and education in the country. Currently, the social sciences section includes four faculties—Law, Economics, Business Administration, and International Cooperation Studies—and the Research Institute for Economics and Business Administration (RIEB). There are some 230-plus researchers who belong to these faculties and conduct joint research through the Center for Social Systems Innovation and the Organization for Advanced and Integrated Research, Kobe University. This book series comprises academic works by researchers in the social sciences at Kobe University as well as their collaborators at affiliated institutions, Kobe University alumni and their colleagues, and renowned scholars from around the world who have worked with academic staff at Kobe University. Although traditionally the research of Japanese scholars has been publicized mainly in the Japanese language, Kobe University strives to promote publication and dissemination of works in English in order to further contribute to the global academic community.

Yoichi Matsubayashi · Shigeto Kitano
Editors

Global Financial Flows in the Pre- and Post-global Crisis Periods

Editors
Yoichi Matsubayashi
Graduate School of Economics
Kobe University
Kobe, Japan

Shigeto Kitano 🆔
RIEB
Kobe University
Kobe, Japan

ISSN 2524-504X ISSN 2524-5058 (electronic)
Kobe University Monograph Series in Social Science Research
ISBN 978-981-19-3612-8 ISBN 978-981-19-3613-5 (eBook)
https://doi.org/10.1007/978-981-19-3613-5

© The Editor(s) (if applicable) and The Author(s), under exclusive license to Springer Nature
Singapore Pte Ltd. 2022
This work is subject to copyright. All rights are solely and exclusively licensed by the Publisher, whether
the whole or part of the material is concerned, specifically the rights of translation, reprinting, reuse
of illustrations, recitation, broadcasting, reproduction on microfilms or in any other physical way, and
transmission or information storage and retrieval, electronic adaptation, computer software, or by similar
or dissimilar methodology now known or hereafter developed.
The use of general descriptive names, registered names, trademarks, service marks, etc. in this publication
does not imply, even in the absence of a specific statement, that such names are exempt from the relevant
protective laws and regulations and therefore free for general use.
The publisher, the authors, and the editors are safe to assume that the advice and information in this book
are believed to be true and accurate at the date of publication. Neither the publisher nor the authors or
the editors give a warranty, expressed or implied, with respect to the material contained herein or for any
errors or omissions that may have been made. The publisher remains neutral with regard to jurisdictional
claims in published maps and institutional affiliations.

This Springer imprint is published by the registered company Springer Nature Singapore Pte Ltd.
The registered company address is: 152 Beach Road, #21-01/04 Gateway East, Singapore 189721,
Singapore

Preface

Excessive expansion of cross-border capital flows lies underneath the global financial crises that occurred in succession in the form of the subprime mortgage crisis, the collapse of Lehman Brothers, and the European debt crisis. Historically, the integration of the international financial market and the subsequent increase in international capital flow have been studied in terms of current and financial account, net and gross capital flow, and stocks of net foreign assets within the context of international macroeconomics and finance. In addition, it is also essential to obtain a broader picture of financial flows—including domestic and international credit activities of financial institutions around the world—and verify and examine the facts from different perspectives so as to comprehensively understand the series of global-scale financial crises and formulate new policy responses. This book fulfills the need and provides an in-depth and up-to-date integrated overview of the dynamics of today's globalized financial markets more appropriately. Chapter 1 introduces a recent concept of global liquidity that sheds a new light on global financial flows including the related historical overview. Chapters 2–4 discuss the international capital flow at the global level. Chapters 5 and 6 examine the effect of excess liquidity on key variables in international financial markets. Chapters 7–9 cover specific regions such as EU and emerging countries. More detailed explanations on each chapter of the book are as follows.

Chapter 1, by Yoichi Matsubayashi, is titled "Global Liquidity as a New Trend in International Capital Flows." First the author provides an historical overview of key concepts to understand international capital flows, and then explains the representative concepts such as international liquidity and dollar liquidity. The author also explains the recent concept of global liquidity including two representative indicators.

Chapter 2, by Shingo Iokibe, is titled "Destination of Global Liquidity Before the Global Financial Crisis: Role of Foreign Bank Presence and the EU Effect." The author elucidates that during the global liquidity surge period, global liquidity flooded more into countries in which foreign banks had already penetrated their banking systems. The author also shows that the destination of global liquidity flows before the global financial crisis was highly concentrated in EU members' banking systems. It is also shown that countries with less strictly regulated banking systems received larger inflows, which is in line with the regulatory arbitrage hypothesis.

Chapter 3, by Kimiko Sugimoto and Masahiro Enya, is titled "Global Liquidity and Reallocation of Domestic Credit." The chapter tackles an interesting but challenging problem of analyzing how global liquidity expansion affects the allocation of domestic credits in the recipient countries of capital inflows. For example, they examine the following problem: when capital inflow into banking sectors increases, does it increase domestic bank credit to business or household sector in the recipient countries? Their result suggests that there exists a heterogeneity among advanced and emerging countries.

Chapter 4, by Takeshi Hoshikawa and Kazuyuki Inagaki, is titled "Global Financial Crisis and Demand for the US Dollar as an International Currency." As the title says, the chapter focuses on demand of foreign financial institutions for the US dollar as an international currency. Although there exist many studies on the US currency demand function, few have specifically examined the demand of foreign countries. This differs the chapter from the previous related studies. The authors' analysis shows that global trade volume, US interest rates, appreciation of the US dollar, and financial market tightness are key variables for explaining the demand for the US dollar as an international currency.

Chapter 5, by Masahiro Inoguchi, is titled "Sovereign Credit Default Swaps and U.S. Economic Policy Uncertainty After the Global Financial Crisis." The chapter focuses on sovereign credit default swap (CDS) spreads. The author explores how the sovereign CDS spreads are affected by global factors such as US economic policy uncertainty and US financial market as well as domestic factors, comprehensively. The author's analysis suggests that the US financial market is more important as a global factor in influencing the sovereign credit risk in emerging economies compared to the US economic policy uncertainty.

Chapter 6, by Yukio Fukumoto, is titled "Global Liquidity and Uncovered Interest Rate Parity Puzzle." The chapter investigates how global liquidity is related to the uncovered interest rate parity (UIP) puzzle, which is one of the most important topics in international finance. The author's analysis suggests that there might be a stronger relationship between global liquidity and the UIP in developed countries rather than developing countries. It also implies that the relationship might be stronger when global liquidity is higher.

Chapter 7, by Agata Wierzbowska and Yoichi Matsubayashi, is titled "Bank Profitability in Europe Before and After the Global Financial Crisis: Leverage, Foreign Claims, and Monetary Policy." The chapter focuses on European banks that played an important role in the origination and channeling of the global gross capital flows and the boom in credit conditions prior to the global financial crisis. Against the background of the banks' heavy exposures to US assets prior to the crisis, the authors analyze the determinants of profitability of European banks before and after the global financial crisis. One of their interesting findings is that post-crisis bank deleveraging contributes to higher bank profitability, which implies the importance of the sound balance sheet and strong capital position for bank profitability in Europe in the post-crisis world.

Preface   vii

Chapter 8, by Shugo Yamamoto, is titled "Offshore Bond Issuance and Noncore Liability in BRICs Countries." In BRICs countries, to circumvent capital restrictions, the use of offshore affiliates as financing vehicles for accumulating low-yield US dollar liability has become widespread. Against this background, the chapter analyzes whether the increase of offshore bond issuance by offshore affiliates can be a source of the boom of noncore liability, which is an indicator of financial system vulnerability. Specifically, the author examines the relationship between offshore bond issuance and shadow banking in China, and points out potential but critical risks related to it.

Chapter 9, by Shigeto Kitano and Kenya Takaku, is titled "Recent Developments in the Adoption of Capital Controls in Emerging Economies: Theory and Practice." The large-scale quantitative easing measures implemented by developed countries after the global financial crisis leads to a rapid surge in capital inflows to emerging economies. In this context, policymakers and researchers have begun to discuss capital control policies—an option that attracted little attention in the past—as a real policy alternative for emerging economies to regulate capital flows properly. This chapter explains recent trends in theoretical research on these policies, and also outlines how emerging economies are using capital control policies.

We are grateful to Akira Kohsaka for his insightful comments and suggestions, which would surely make all the authors' future research more fruitful.

Kobe, Japan

Yoichi Matsubayashi
Shigeto Kitano

Contents

1 Global Liquidity as a New Trend in International Capital Flows 1
Yoichi Matsubayashi

2 Destination of Global Liquidity Before the Global Financial Crisis: Role of Foreign Bank Presence and the EU Effect 19
Shingo Iokibe

3 Global Liquidity and Reallocation of Domestic Credit 67
Kimiko Sugimoto and Masahiro Enya

4 Global Financial Crisis and Demand for the US Dollar as an International Currency 99
Takeshi Hoshikawa and Kazuyuki Inagaki

5 Sovereign Credit Default Swaps and U.S. Economic Policy Uncertainty After the Global Financial Crisis 113
Masahiro Inoguchi

6 Global Liquidity and Uncovered Interest Rate Parity Puzzle 143
Yukio Fukumoto

7 Bank Profitability in Europe Before and After the Global Financial Crisis: Leverage, Foreign Claims, and Monetary Policy 153
Agata Wierzbowska and Yoichi Matsubayashi

8 Offshore Bond Issuance and Noncore Liability in BRICs Countries 169
Shugo Yamamoto

9 Recent Developments in the Adoption of Capital Controls in Emerging Economies: Theory and Practice 183
Shigeto Kitano and Kenya Takaku

Index 222

Editors and Contributors

About the Editors

Yoichi Matsubayashi is a professor of economics at Kobe University in Japan, where he received his Ph.D. His main research interest is international macroeconomics, especially external imbalances in the recent world economy. He has published many papers in refereed journals, such as the *Japanese Economic Review* and *Japan and the World Economy*. He is also the co-author of *Financial Globalization and Regionalism in East Asia* (Routledge 2013).

Shigeto Kitano is a professor of economics at Kobe University. He received his Ph.D. from Nagoya University in Japan. His main research interest is international macroeconomics. He has published many papers in refereed journals, such as the *Journal of Macroeconomics, Economic Inquiry, Open Economies Review, Pacific Economic Review, International Review of Economics and Finance, Review of Development Economics, International Journal of Economic Theory, Journal of Economics,* and *Applied Economics Letters.*

Contributors

Enya Masahiro Faculty of Economics and Management, Kanazawa University, Kanazawa, Japan

Fukumoto Yukio Department of Economics, Osaka University of Economics, Osaka, Japan

Hoshikawa Takeshi Faculty of Economics, Kindai University, Higashi-Osaka, Japan

Inagaki Kazuyuki Department of Economics, Nanzan University, Nagoya, Japan

Inoguchi Masahiro College of Business Administration, Ritsumeikan University, Ibaraki, Osaka, Japan

Iokibe Shingo Faculty of Commerce, Doshisha University, Kyoto, Japan

Kitano Shigeto RIEB, Kobe University, Nada, Kobe, Japan

Matsubayashi Yoichi Graduate School of Economics, Kobe University, Kobe, Japan

Sugimoto Kimiko Hirao School of Management, Konan University, Nishinomiya, Japan

Takaku Kenya Faculty of International Studies, Hiroshima City University, Hiroshima, Japan

Wierzbowska Agata Graduate School of Economics, Kobe University, Kobe, Japan

Yamamoto Shugo Rikkyo University, Tokyo, Japan

List of Figures

Fig. 1.1	International capital flow 1994–2019	7
Fig. 1.2	Change of cross-border lending 1978Q4–2020Q2	10
Fig. 1.3	TED spread 1986 January–2020 December	12
Fig. 1.4	VIX and cross-border lending 1986 January–2020 December	14
Fig. 2.1	Quarterly change in cross-border bank claims to banks excluding central banks versus to non-banks (as a fraction of world GDP, five quarters moving average). *Source* Author's calculations using BIS' *Locational Banking Statistics* and IMF's *World Economic Outlook* database	20
Fig. 2.2	Patterns of international capital flows originated and/or transmitted by banks. *Source* Author	25
Fig. 2.3	Graphical image of how to calculate net cross-border bank-to-bank liabilities. *Source* Author's description	34
Fig. 2.4	Alternative measures of foreign bank penetration: Foreign bank asset share and foreign bank number share. *Source* Author. Data from Claessens and Van Horen [17]	35
Fig. 2.5	Bank inflows to offshore centres. *Source* Author's calculations using BIS' *Locational Banking Statistics* and IMF's *World Economic Outlook database*	64

xiii

Fig. 3.1	Total credit to government, households, and firms (average credit to GDP (%)). *Note* Advanced 20 economies include, Austria, Australia, Belgium, Canada, Switzerland, Germany, Denmark, Spain, Finland, France, United Kingdom, Greece, Ireland, Italy, Japan, Luxembourg, Netherlands, Norway, Portugal and Sweden. Emerging 9 economies include Korea, Thailand, Argentina, Brazil, Colombia, Mexico, Czech Republic, Hungary and Poland. Total credit is provided by domestic bank, all other sectors of the economy and non-residents. Credit covers loans and debt securities. *Source* BIS long series on total credit updated 6 June 2017	70
Fig. 3.2	Types and compositions of capital flows to emerging 9 economies in U.S. dollars. *Note* Emerging 9 economies include Korea, Thailand, Argentina, Brazil, Colombia, Mexico, Czech Republic, Hungary and Poland. The annual data is obtained by the annual average of quarterly data. Case 3 is the average value of three periods like before, during and after the global financial crisis. *Source* Balance of Payments statistics by IMF 2017	72
Fig. 4.1	Demand deposits due to Foreign Commercial Banks. *Source* Federal Reserve Bank of St. Louis. Billions of dollars, monthly, not seasonally adjusted	100
Fig. 4.2	Demand deposits due to Foreign Official Institutions. *Source* Federal Reserve Bank of St. Louis. Billions of dollars, monthly, not seasonally adjusted	101
Fig. 4.3	World trade volume	103
Fig. 4.4	US interest rates	104
Fig. 4.5	Effective US dollar exchange rate	104
Fig. 4.6	Tightness of financial markets	105
Fig. 4.7	US monetary base	106
Fig. 4.8	US dollar deposits-to-monetary base ratio held by foreign banks and foreign official institutions. Percentage in US monetary base (unit: %)	107
Fig. 5.1	Rate of change in CDS spreads in European and African emerging economies (monthly)	118
Fig. 5.2	Rate of change in CDS spreads in Asian and Middle-Eastern emerging economies (monthly)	119
Fig. 5.3	Rate of change in CDS spreads in Latin-American emerging economies (monthly)	120
Fig. 5.4	Rate of change in CDS spreads in advanced economies (monthly)	121
Fig. 5.5	Rates of change in sovereign CDS spreads and the U.S. stock index	122

Fig. 5.6	Rates of change in sovereign CDS spreads and the U.S. interest rate	123
Fig. 5.7	Rates of change in sovereign CDS spreads and changes in the VIX	124
Fig. 5.8	Rates of change in sovereign CDS spreads and the U.S. economic policy uncertainty index	125
Fig. 6.1	International claims expressed by growth rate. *Note* "Banks" and "Non-banks" denote international claims on the banking and non-banking sectors, respectively. The vertical axis represents the percentages	147
Fig. 6.2	Scatterplots for developed countries. *Note* Correlation_X in the horizontal axis is the correlation coefficient between global liquidity and deviation from UIP, and correlation_Y in the vertical axis is the correlation coefficient between the expected rate of change in the exchange rate and bilateral interest rate differentials. Former, Latter, Banks, and Non-banks indicate the former period, latter period, global liquidity based on the banking sector, and global liquidity based on the non-banking sector, respectively	148
Fig. 6.3	Scatterplots for developing countries. *Note* See note to Fig. 6.2	149
Fig. 7.1	Claims to US, index 2008Q2 $= 100$. *Source* BIS consolidated banking statistics, authors' estimations	155
Fig. 7.2	Total foreign claims, index 2008Q2 $= 100$. *Source* BIS consolidated banking statistics, authors' estimations	156
Fig. 7.3	Share of claims in US in total country claims. *Source* BIS consolidated banking statistics, authors' estimations	157
Fig. 7.4	Bank profit rates by country and year. *Source* Bankscope database, authors' estimations	158
Fig. 7.5	Bank leverage by country and year. *Source* Bankscope database, authors' estimations	159
Fig. 7.6	Total assets and total capital of European banks (million euro). *Source* Bankscope database, authors' estimations	159
Fig. 7.7	Overnight interbank interest rates. *Source* Eurostat, each country central bank	160
Fig. 8.1	Chinn–Ito Index of BRICs countries. *Note* Rising values represent increasing financial openness. *Source* Chinn and Ito (2016)	171
Fig. 8.2	Non-financial corporations as a surrogate intermediary. *Sources* [1 and 11]	172

Fig. 8.3	Nationality and residence of issuer with and without BRICs countries. *Note* The difference between "NATIONALITY" and "RESIDENCE" is offshore bond issuance: "with-BRICs" are economically developing countries including BRICs countries; and "without-BRICs" are economically developing countries, not including BRICs countries. *Source* BIS securities statistics	173
Fig. 8.4	Offshore US-dollar-denominated bond issuance by BRICs countries. *Source* BIS securities statistics	174
Fig. 8.5	China offshore bond issuance, within-company flow, and noncore liability. *Note* Because FDI represents a flow of a new investment, to unify the terms used, we calculate the backward difference of stock variables for both OFFSHORE and NONCORE. *Sources* OFFSHORE is from BIS securities statistics; FDI is from BOP of the IMF; and NONCORE is from IFS of the IMF	176
Fig. 8.6	Brazil offshore bond issuance, within-company flow, and noncore liability. *Note* Because FDI represents a flow of a new investment, to unify the terms used, we calculate the backward difference of stock variables of both OFFSHORE and NONCORE. *Sources* OFFSHORE is from BIS securities statistics; FDI is from BOP of the IMF; and NONCORE is from the Central Bank of Brazil	177
Fig. 8.7	Russia offshore bond issuance, within-company flow, and noncore liability. *Note* Because FDI represents a flow of a new investment, to unify the terms used, we calculate the backward difference of stock variables of both OFFSHORE and NONCORE. *Sources* OFFSHORE is from BIS securities statistics; FDI is from BOP of the IMF; and NONCORE is from IFS of the IMF	178
Fig. 8.8	India offshore bond issuance and within-company flow. *Note* NONCORE has a data limitation. We exclude this variable. Because FDI represents a flow of a new investment, to unify the terms used, we calculate the backward difference of stock variables of OFFSHORE. *Sources* OFFSHORE is from BIS securities statistics; FDI is from BOP of the IMF	179
Fig. 8.9	Noncore liability and core shadow banking activity in China (millions of yuan). *Sources* NONCORE represents data from domestic currency from IFS of the IMF; CORE_SHADOW represents data from the People's Bank of China	179

List of Figures

Fig. 9.1	Responses to an increase in the foreign interest rate: ω = 0.01, 0.5, 0.99 (Y, C, $E[R_k] - R$, e). *Source* Kitano and Takaku [43]	187
Fig. 9.2	Responses to an increase in the foreign interest rate, with and without capital controls: $\omega = 0.5$ ($E[R_k] - R_b$, Y, C, e). *Source* Kitano and Takaku [43]	188
Fig. 9.3	Welfare curves with varying τ: Different degrees of financial frictions. *Source* Kitano and Takaku [43]	189
Fig. 9.4	Maximum welfare gains of capital controls under different degrees of financial frictions (ω): Liability dollarization vs. no liability dollarization. *Source* Kitano and Takaku [43]	189
Fig. 9.5	Responses to a net worth shock (Y_H, $E[R_k] - R_b$, RER(e), C). *Source* Kitano and Takaku [44]	191
Fig. 9.6	Welfare curves with varying τ_b and τ_k. *Source* Kitano and Takaku [46]	194
Fig. 9.7	Maximum welfare gains under both capital controls and macroprudential regulation ($\chi = 0.43$). *Source* Kitano and Takaku [46]	195
Fig. 9.8	Maximum welfare gains from capital controls and macroprudential regulation under different degrees of financial frictions (χ). *Source* Kitano and Takaku [46]	195
Fig. 9.9	Maximum welfare gains from capital controls and macroprudential regulation under different degrees of financial frictions (χ): No-liability dollarization case. *Source* Kitano and Takaku [46]	196
Fig. 9.10	Fernández et al. [27]'s capital control measures on total inflows in India. *Note* India's overall inflow restrictions index (kai). *Data Source* Fernández et al. [27]	198
Fig. 9.11	Ahmed et al. [4]'s capital control measures on inflows in India. *Note* "CUM" denotes the cumulative number of capital control measures on inflows in each category. "DIF" denotes the first difference of the cumulative series, which indicates the number of new measures introduced in each quarter. *Data Source* Ahmed et al. [4]	198
Fig. 9.12	Fernández et al. [27]'s capital control measures on total inflows in Brazil. *Note* Brazil's overall inflow restrictions index (kai). *Data Source* Fernández et al. [27]	200
Fig. 9.13	Ahmed et al. [4]'s capital control measures on inflows in Brazil. *Note* "CUM" denotes the cumulative number of capital control measures on inflows in each category. "DIF" denotes the first difference of the cumulative series, which indicates the number of new measures introduced in each quarter. *Data Source* Ahmed et al. [4]	200

Fig. 9.14	Fernández et al. [27]'s capital control measures on total inflows in Thailand. *Note* Thailand's overall inflow restrictions index (kai). *Data Source* Fernández et al. [27]	201
Fig. 9.15	Ahmed et al. [4]'s capital control measures on inflows in Thailand. *Note* "CUM" denotes the cumulative number of capital control measures on inflows in each category. "DIF" denotes the first difference of the cumulative series, which indicates the number of new measures introduced in each quarter. *Data Source* Ahmed et al. [4]	202
Fig. 9.16	Total of the 19 countries. *Note* The 19 countries included in Table 9.3. "CUM" denotes the cumulative number of capital control measures on inflows in each category. "DIF" denotes the first difference of the cumulative series, which indicates the number of new measures introduced in each quarter. *Data Source* Ahmed et al. [4]	202
Fig. 9.17	Total number of capital control measures introduced in each quarter in different categories. *Note* The sample comprises the 19 countries over 2002Q1–2012Q4 as in Fig. 9.16	203
Fig. 9.18	Standard deviations of the capital control measures. *Note* The upper figure shows the standard deviations of DIF TOTAL in Table 9.4. The lower figure shows those of CUM TOTAL in Table 9.5	206
Fig. 9.19	Malaysia. *Note* "CUM" denotes the cumulative number of capital control measures on inflows in each category. "DIF" denotes the first difference of the cumulative series, which indicates the number of new measures introduced in each quarter. *Data Source* Ahmed et al. [4]	210
Fig. 9.20	Philippines. *Note* "CUM" denotes the cumulative number of capital control measures on inflows in each category. "DIF" denotes the first difference of the cumulative series, which indicates the number of new measures introduced in each quarter. *Data Source* Ahmed et al. [4]	211
Fig. 9.21	Poland. *Note* "CUM" denotes the cumulative number of capital control measures on inflows in each category. "DIF" denotes the first difference of the cumulative series, which indicates the number of new measures introduced in each quarter. *Data Source* Ahmed et al. [4]	211
Fig. 9.22	Argentina. *Note* "CUM" denotes the cumulative number of capital control measures on inflows in each category. "DIF" denotes the first difference of the cumulative series, which indicates the number of new measures introduced in each quarter. *Data Source* Ahmed et al. [4]	212

List of Figures xix

Fig. 9.23   Taiwan. *Note* "CUM" denotes the cumulative number of capital control measures on inflows in each category. "DIF" denotes the first difference of the cumulative series, which indicates the number of new measures introduced in each quarter. *Data Source* Ahmed et al. [4] 212

Fig. 9.24   Indonesia. *Note* "CUM" denotes the cumulative number of capital control measures on inflows in each category. "DIF" denotes the first difference of the cumulative series, which indicates the number of new measures introduced in each quarter. *Data Source* Ahmed et al. [4] 213

Fig. 9.25   Korea. *Note* "CUM" denotes the cumulative number of capital control measures on inflows in each category. "DIF" denotes the first difference of the cumulative series, which indicates the number of new measures introduced in each quarter. *Data Source* Ahmed et al. [4] 213

Fig. 9.26   Turkey. *Note* "CUM" denotes the cumulative number of capital control measures on inflows in each category. "DIF" denotes the first difference of the cumulative series, which indicates the number of new measures introduced in each quarter. *Data Source* Ahmed et al. [4] 214

Fig. 9.27   Colombia. *Note* "CUM" denotes the cumulative number of capital control measures on inflows in each category. "DIF" denotes the first difference of the cumulative series, which indicates the number of new measures introduced in each quarter. *Data Source* Ahmed et al. [4] 214

Fig. 9.28   Romania. *Note* "CUM" denotes the cumulative number of capital control measures on inflows in each category. "DIF" denotes the first difference of the cumulative series, which indicates the number of new measures introduced in each quarter. *Data Source* Ahmed et al. [4] 215

Fig. 9.29   Chile. *Note* "CUM" denotes the cumulative number of capital control measures on inflows in each category. "DIF" denotes the first difference of the cumulative series, which indicates the number of new measures introduced in each quarter. *Data Source* Ahmed et al. [4] 215

Fig. 9.30   Czech Republic. *Note* "CUM" denotes the cumulative number of capital control measures on inflows in each category. "DIF" denotes the first difference of the cumulative series, which indicates the number of new measures introduced in each quarter. *Data Source* Ahmed et al. [4] 216

Fig. 9.31	Hungary. *Note* "CUM" denotes the cumulative number of capital control measures on inflows in each category. "DIF" denotes the first difference of the cumulative series, which indicates the number of new measures introduced in each quarter. *Data Source* Ahmed et al. [4] 216
Fig. 9.32	Mexico. *Note* "CUM" denotes the cumulative number of capital control measures on inflows in each category. "DIF" denotes the first difference of the cumulative series, which indicates the number of new measures introduced in each quarter. *Data Source* Ahmed et al. [4] 217
Fig. 9.33	South Africa. *Note* "CUM" denotes the cumulative number of capital control measures on inflows in each category. "DIF" denotes the first difference of the cumulative series, which indicates the number of new measures introduced in each quarter. *Data Source* Ahmed et al. [4] 217
Fig. 9.34	Israel. *Note* "CUM" denotes the cumulative number of capital control measures on inflows in each category. "DIF" denotes the first difference of the cumulative series, which indicates the number of new measures introduced in each quarter. *Data Source* Ahmed et al. [4] 218

List of Tables

Table 1.1	International liquidity	5
Table 1.2	Development of Euromarket	6
Table 1.3	Balance sheets of financial institutions	8
Table 1.4	Types of credit extended by financial institutions	9
Table 2.1	Regional variabilities of net cross-border bank-to-bank capital inflows. Cumulative changes in net cross-border bank liabilities from 2004 Q2 to 2008 Q1	28
Table 2.2	Sample countries	31
Table 2.3	Descriptive statistics of the main variables	37
Table 2.4	Results of the traditional regressions with foreign banks' asset share	40
Table 2.5	Estimations with regional dummies	43
Table 2.6	Effect of regulatory variables	46
Table 2.7	Effect of other control variables	49
Table 2.8	Effect of foreign banks' number share	52
Table 2.9	Regressions on cumulative bank credit inflows through 2007 Q3	54
Table 2.10	Removing outliers' effect: excluding Estonia and Latvia	57
Table 2.11	Estimation results on non-OECD samples	59
Table 2.12	Data sources	63
Table 3.1	The effect of capital inflows classified by sectoral destination on the share of household credit	78
Table 3.2	The effect of capital inflows classified by sectoral destination on the ratio of household credit to GDP	80
Table 3.3	Regional differences in the effect of capital inflows classified by sectoral destination on the share of household credit	84
Table 3.4	Regional differences in the effect of capital inflows classified by sectoral destination on the ratio of household credit to GDP	88
Table 3.5	List of countries included in estimation	92

Table 3.6	Variable definitions and data sources	93
Table 4.1	Unit root test	109
Table 4.2	Cointegration test	109
Table 4.3	Estimation results	109
Table 4.4	Estimation results	110
Table 4.5	Estimation results	110
Table 5.1	Related studies	115
Table 5.2	Determinants of sovereign CDS spread: full sample period	129
Table 5.3	Determinants of sovereign CDS spread: subsample period of QE1	131
Table 5.4	Determinants of sovereign CDS spread: subsample period of QE2	133
Table 5.5	Determinants of sovereign CDS spread: subsample period of QE3	135
Table 5.6	Determinants of sovereign CDS spread: subsample period after the U.S. LSAPs	137
Table 6.1	Sample countries	146
Table 6.2	Regression results for developed countries	149
Table 6.3	Regression results for developing countries	150
Table 7.1	Number of bank-year observations for each country	158
Table 7.2	Determinants of bank profitability—summary	163
Table 7.3	Determinants of bank profitability—benchmark model estimations	164
Table 7.4	Impact of claims to US and monetary policy stance on bank profitability	166
Table 9.1	The welfare ranking of capital control and monetary policies	193
Table 9.2	Capital controls: Wall, gate, or open	204
Table 9.3	Changes in capital control measures before and after the financial crisis	205
Table 9.4	Standard deviations of the capital control measures introduced each quarter	207
Table 9.5	Standard deviations of the cumulative level of capital control measures	208

Chapter 1
Global Liquidity as a New Trend in International Capital Flows

Yoichi Matsubayashi

Abstract This chapter provides a comprehensive perspective on global liquidity, which has recently become a new trend in international capital flows. Global liquidity, in a broad sense, refers to the ease with which funds can be raised on a global scale, and a typical example is credit extended by private financial institutions. This chapter looks back at the history of international capital flows from the end of World War II to the present, and introduces the new trends in international capital flows that are attracting attention as global liquidity. In addition, we review representative indicators of global liquidity and outline their trends and characteristics.

Keywords Global liquidity · Dollar liquidity · LIBOR · VIX

1.1 Introduction

The globalisation of the financial markets has made remarkable progress due to the liberalisation of international capital flows. Along with these trends, funding procurement and fund management options across national borders have been expanding dramatically. However, the excessive expansion of these global capital flows may be a factor that could precipitate global financial crisis. For instance, the dramatic expansion of global capital flows was closely related to the deepening series of financial crises—namely, the United States subprime mortgage crisis, the Lehman crisis and the European financial crisis—that occurred during the early part of this century. Therefore, it is urgent that policy authorities and international organisations must accurately grasp the dynamism of international funds flows and how to monitor changes therein.

Accordingly, it has become increasingly imperative to realise which index is appropriate for grasping phenomena such as global fund flows and global financing. Therefore, in this chapter, we will attempt to create a comprehensive perspective

---

Y. Matsubayashi (✉)
Graduate School of Economics, Kobe University, 2-1, Rokkodai, Nada, Kobe 657-8501, Japan
e-mail: myoichi@econ.kobe-u.ac.jp

© The Author(s), under exclusive license to Springer Nature Singapore Pte Ltd. 2022
Y. Matsubayashi and S. Kitano (eds.), *Global Financial Flows in the Pre- and Post-global Crisis Periods*, Kobe University Monograph Series in Social Science Research,
https://doi.org/10.1007/978-981-19-3613-5_1

of the 'global liquidity', a concept that has recently begun to draw attention. This concept has been discussed since the beginning of the 2000s but has not yet been strictly defined. In this chapter, to further the understanding the global liquidity concept, we will consider the following two points. The first point will be to compare some clarifying concepts representing international funds flows in common usage. Simultaneously, the transition of the international financial markets since the 1950s must also be considered. We will examine the concepts appearing during that period. The second point is to carefully introduce the indices representing the new concept known as 'global liquidity' and clarify the surrounding implications.

The remainder of this chapter is organised as follows. Section 1.2 provides a brief overview of the history of international finance since the 1950s and explains representative concepts such as international liquidity and dollar liquidity. Section 1.3 provides a detailed introduction of the new concept of global liquidity and two representative indicators, and Sect. 1.4 discusses the fluctuations in, and controls for, global liquidity. A summary of this chapter is presented in Sect. 1.5.

1.2 The History of International Finance After World War II

The concept of global liquidity began attracting attention in the early 2000s. It is extremely useful for developing a deeper understanding of the characteristics of global liquidity by discussing how the concept came into being in the history of international finance following World War II. In the ensuing subsection, we delineate the appearance of this term within international financial markets since the 1950s.

In later sections of this paper, how the concept of global liquidity emerged in the history of international finance will be explained. In doing so, a brief introduction to the similar expressions 'international liquidity' and 'dollar liquidity' will be provided to clarify the differences between the two terms.

1.2.1 International Liquidity

The world economy was devastated by World War II. In retrospect, the United States, while leading the post-war economy, began learning that a blocked economy and currency devaluation were elements that formed the background of the pre-war Great Depression and thus constructed new and improved rules and systems. Two policies emerged regarding international financial systems—the establishment of the International Monetary Fund (IMF) and the International Recovery and Development Bank, along with the establishment of a system centred on these agencies. This system, known as the 'Bretton Woods regime', was an agreement made to link the currencies of each country with the U.S. dollar ($) at a fixed rate and exchange gold

1 Global Liquidity as a New Trend in International Capital Flows

at \$35 per ounce. The world currency was no longer linked directly to money but through the dollar.

Several efforts were made by the monetary policy authorities of each country to maintain this fixed exchange rate system. To maintain a fixed exchange rate, foreign exchange intervention had to be conducted daily in the foreign exchange market, particularly during periods when imports were markedly increasing since this is likely to cause a domestic currency to depreciate. In such cases, policy authorities must sell the foreign currency that they have in stock and purchase their own currency instead. At this point, foreign currency holdings become 'foreign exchange reserves'. A representative definition in an economics dictionary of the term 'international liquidity' as it was used during the fixed exchange rate system[1] is as follows:

> International liquidity may be defined as that stock of assets which is available to a country's monetary authorities to cover payments imbalances (when the exchange rate is fixed) or to influence the exchange value of the currency (when the exchange rate is flexible).
>
> —*New Palgrave Dictionary of Economics*

In the 1970s, two major changes occurred in the international financial markets that gradually forced the international liquidity concept to change: (1) there was a shift to a floating exchange rate regime and (2) the Eurocurrency market expanded.

By stopping the exchange of gold in dollars in August 1971 and shifting to a floating exchange rate system of the major currencies in the spring of 1973, the Bretton Woods regime collapsed. Under a floating exchange rate system, the balance of payments automatically adjusts according to fluctuations in the exchange rate such that policy authorities do not have to keep foreign exchange reserves (i.e. international liquidity).

However, due to the rapid economic growth in the 1950s and 1960s, countries that tended to have sustained current account deficits began to increase. Under these circumstances, policymakers needed some degree of international liquidity to cope with shortages of foreign currencies. In the 1970s, nevertheless, new mechanisms to raise foreign currency shortages in international financial markets began growing rapidly. This phenomenon came to be known as the 'Eurocurrency market'.

The Eurocurrency market (hereinafter, the 'euro market') refers to a local currency that is deposited in a financial institution outside of the home country, wherein the local currency is held by a non-resident. In the late 1950s, the fact that the former Soviet Union was concerned about assets being frozen by the United States and that its dollar deposits held in European financial institutions were regarded as falling under the 'euro market' was disconcerting. Later, the market began to show remarkable development. Especially through the two oil shocks of the 1970s, the huge foreign currency income (so-called 'oil money') garnered from oil-producing countries' crude oil sales began to flow into the euro market, leading to a dramatic increase in international foreign currency procurement and operations.

---

[1] Therefore, research on international liquidity mostly concerns the content of the foreign exchange reserves owned by policy authorities. For example, Altman [2], Brahmananda [3], Day [6], Fleming [9], Gowda [10], Hansen [11] and Reierson [14] considered international liquidity.

The structural changes in the international financial markets would gradually degenerate the concept of international liquidity. As previously mentioned, under a fixed exchange rate system, the demand for foreign currency was limited primarily to foreign exchange reserves by policy authorities. This foreign exchange reserve was called international liquidity. However, the acquisition and supply of foreign currency in the private sector, especially after the 1970s, would begin to expand dramatically in the new trading space of the euro market—the international financial market. In addition, the concept of international liquidity would be expanded beyond the base concept of foreign exchange reserves in the conventional public sector, thereby engendering a trend to embellish the category of foreign currency procurement and supply in the private sector.[2]

> International Liquidity refers to the availability of internationally accepted means of setting international debts relative to the demand or potential demand for such financial assets. The availability or supply of international liquidity depends on the stock of total reserve assets owned by world central banks or national monetary authorities, as well as the ability of these institutions from the International Monetary Fund (IMF), the Eurocurrency market and other financial institutions.
>
> —*Princeton Encyclopaedia of the World Economy*

Specifically, in the euro market, the expansion of deposits and loans by financial institutions, primarily banks, would begin to establish a new concept of international liquidity.[3] We will confirm this expansion of the international liquidity category on the basis of actual data.

Table 1.1 demonstrates the trends in international liquidity in a broad sense as well as a narrow sense (public preparations deposited in U.S. banks located in the United States and foreign currency deposits in the euro market).[4]

In 1970, deposits in the euro market totalled \$38 billion and increased rapidly thereafter. In 1976, they were \$173 billion, approximately four times greater. Meanwhile, the foreign exchange reserves held by the public sector—narrow liquidity—were increasing, but as of 1976, they comprised only about one-half of the deposits in the euro market. Thus, the enlargement of the euro market expanded the category of international liquidity in the 1970s, and its scale continued to grow rapidly.

---

[2] For example, the definition of international liquidity in the *Princeton Encyclopaedia of the World Economy* differs slightly from the one provided in the *New Palgrave Dictionary of Economics* (cited above) as it includes the expression 'borrowing from the euro market'.

[3] According to Yamamoto [17], 'Two structural changes, the floating exchange rate system that had a decisive influence on the world economy in the 1970s and the growth of the euro currency market, made "international liquidity" the former public preparation stock we have transformed it into an endogenous method of borrowing from the international banking industry set in the euro-currency market, that is, supply of flow, from the concept of the "Euro-currency market"'.

[4] The explanation of international liquidity in a broad sense based on Table 1.1 is modified in Table 6.2 in Aglietta [1].

1 Global Liquidity as a New Trend in International Capital Flows

Table 1.1 International liquidity

	1970	1974	1975	1976	1977	1978	1979	1980	1981	1982
Operations (in $bn) Deposits in Eurobanks										
Private	–	62	62	77	89	120	156	199	261	275
Official institutions	–	38	51	64	73	84	120	139	126	98
Various	–	25	34	32	51	65	95	62	67	107
Total	38	125	147	173	213	269	371	400	454	480
Private deposits in banks located in USA	4	8	10	11	12	14	16	17	23	41
Official reserves deposited in the USA	24	77	80	92	126	156	143	159	164	167
Overall total	66	210	237	276	351	439	530	576	641	688

Modified from Table 6.2 in Aglietta [1]

1.2.2 Dollar Liquidity

In the euro market, euro dollars, euro pounds and yen exist as transactional currencies. Compared to the other currencies in the euro market, the distribution of the U.S. dollar in the euro market is overwhelmingly large.

As shown in Table 1.2, from the 1970s to the 1980s, euro dollar transactions increased to keep pace with the expansion of the euro market. In 1984, nearly 87% of euro market transactions were considered U.S. dollar trading. Based on this trend, the U.S. dollar was traded worldwide (in both the euro market and in the United States), where it was expressed as dollar liquidity, especially by focusing on the dollar itself. The term 'dollar liquidity' was not strictly defined, but in real money markets and for policy authorities, it is frequently used as follows:

> The key variables which drive supply and demand for offshore *dollar liquidity* are how many rotations each of these various components of the system cycle through.
>
> —Andrew Norelli, JP. Morgan, May 2018
>
> *Examining Offshore Dollar Liquidity in Light of the Three Phases Model*
>
> During the recent crisis, financial markets in various countries run short of *dollar liquidity*, again indicating high demand for the dollar as a means of storing value and a means of payment.
>
> —Takehiko Nakao, Ministry of Finance, Japan, March 2010

Table 1.2 Development of Euromarket

	U.S. dollar	Mark	Pond	Swiss franc	Yen
1965	11.4	0.9	0.7	0.9	N.A
1966	14.8	1	0.7	1.2	N.A
1967	18.1	1.7	0.8	1.4	N.A
1968	26.9	3	0.8	2.3	N.A
1969	46.2	4.6	0.8	4	N.A
1970	58.7	8.1	0.9	5.7	N.A
1971	70.8	14.6	2.1	7.8	N.A
1972	96.7	19.5	2.2	8.8	N.A
1973	131.4	32	4.6	17.2	N.A
1974	222.9	35.4	3.8	18.7	N.A
1975	272.6	40.8	3.3	15.5	N.A
1976	339.9	48.3	4.1	16.2	N.A
1977	398.2	66.1	5.7	21.5	N.A
1978	404.2(0.74)	94.8(0.17)	10.4(0.02)	28.6(0.05)	6.2(0.01)
1979	499.7(0.72)	130.3(0.19)	15.3(0.02)	42.1(0.06)	10.3(0.01)
1980	630(0.74)	128.7(0.15)	24.4(0.03)	56.5(0.07)	11.2(0.01)
1981	782.9(0.77)	121.5(0.12)	19.6(0.02)	72.6(0.07)	16.1(0.02)
1982	935.5(0.82)	116.3(0.10)	16.2(0.01)	62.2(0.05)	16.9(0.01)
1983	1005.8(0.83)	111.7(0.09)	14.1(0.01)	61.8(0.05)	21.2(0.02)
1984	1387(0.87)	113.8(0.07)	15.9(0.01)	56.2(0.04)	21.7(0.01)

BIS: The figures in parentheses show the share of the five currencies in the total amount

1.3 The Concept of Global Liquidity

1.3.1 Indicators of Global Liquidity (1)

After the end of the Cold War and the collapse of the Berlin Wall in 1989, the interdependence of the global economy further deepened. In the expansion and deepening of global economic interdependence, the term 'globalisation' was frequently used rather than the traditional term 'internationalisation'. The progress of globalisation was particularly prominent in the international financial markets. International cross-border capital movements have significantly expanded since the 1990s.

Figure 1.1 shows the total capital flows of each country's direct investments, securities investments and derivative financial products (i.e. derivatives) from 1994 to 2019. The transaction amounts, which were approximately one trillion dollars in 1994, increased nearly tenfold by 2007. This can be confirmed by the rapid expansion of the international financial markets that occurred in the 1990s. The Lehman shock

1 Global Liquidity as a New Trend in International Capital Flows

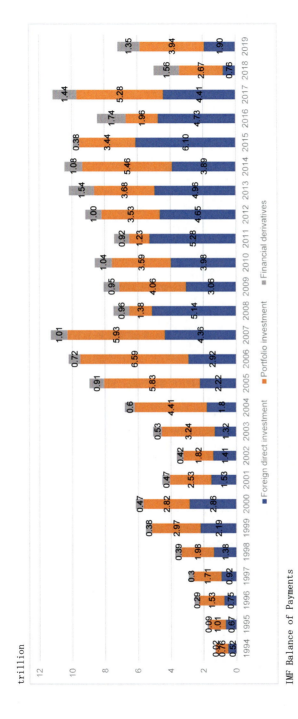

Fig. 1.1 International capital flow 1994–2019

Table 1.3 Balance sheets of financial institutions

Assets	Liabilities
Lending (For financial institutions)	Deposit
	Other liabilities
Lending (For non-financial institutions)	
Other assets	Net worth

in 2008 caused a significant decline in international capital transactions. Since then, however, trading has gradually recovered, and they returned to 2007 levels by 2017.

Internationally funded transactions with these characteristics differ from the traditional expressions of international liquidity and are now referred to as 'global liquidity'. As explained earlier, international liquidity initially meant foreign exchange reserves held by policy authorities, but due to the subsequent expansion of capital flows, it meant financial transactions by financial institutions in the euro market. In addition, since most deals were done in dollars, it came to be expressed in terms of dollar liquidity. Moreover, with the progress of financial market globalisation, it began to be used in tandem with the term 'global liquidity' by adding the adjective 'global' to liquidity rather than using international adjective phrases.[5]

Initially, the term 'global liquidity' was used in the sense of the aggregate money supply in the major countries.[6] However, as recently pointed out by Eickmeier et al. [8], the role of bank credit in international financial markets has become emphasised and global liquidity is beginning to be used in the context of financial institutions' international credit.[7]

Therefore, the Committee on the Global Financial System (CGFS) [5] defined global liquidity as a descriptor for the 'ease of global financing'. Although this expression is slightly difficult to understand, the situation in which global financing is easy refers to an expansion of global credit by private financial institutions considering the supply of funds (i.e. the credit side).

Sorting out the meaning of global credit in terms of financial institutions' balance sheets is important. In Table 1.3, a simple picture of a financial institution's balance sheet is depicted. The lending of assets (hereinafter, 'credit') is divided between financial and non-financial institutions. Taking the global actions of financial institutions into consideration, credit may be classified more precisely, as shown in Table 1.4.

In the case of Japanese financial institutions, 'domestic local currency-denominated credit' means lending to Japanese domestic financial institutions (non-financial institutions) in yen. However, it is possible to lend dollars to

---

[5] The term 'international liquidity' is still in use today.

[6] For example, Sousa and Zaghini [16] focused on the euro area, the United Kingdom, the United States, Canada and Japan as the target countries for money supply aggregation, and Rueffer and Stracca [15] focused on the United States, Japan, the United Kingdom, Canada and China. India, South Korea, Thailand, Taiwan, Brazil, Mexico, Australia, New Zealand and South Africa are targeted to G7 countries in D'Agostino and Surico [7].

[7] For example, Bruno and Shin [4], Domanski et al. [18] and the CGFS [5].

1 Global Liquidity as a New Trend in International Capital Flows

Table 1.4 Types of credit extended by financial institutions

	Credit for non-financial institutions	Credit for financial institutions
Local currency for domestic use	Case A	Case D
Foreign currency for domestic use	Case B	Case E
For overseas	Case C	Case F

The bold part corresponds to global liquidity

foreign-owned companies in Japan. This action creates 'domestic foreign currency-denominated credit'. Lending overseas is also carried out across national borders, which corresponds to 'credit going overseas'.[8]

As seen in the above arrangement, 'the situation in which global funding is easy' means that the bold part of Table 1.4 expands in terms of the supply of funds (i.e. the credit side). Here we refer to the word 'liquidity'. Thus far, the vocabulary of liquidity—such as 'international liquidity' and 'dollar liquidity'—is used in the nuance of a 'noun' such as the dollar or the euro. However, the CGFS [5] sets the meaning of an abstract noun called the 'ease of financing' against liquidity.[9]

Such considerations suggest that global liquidity can be understood not only according to quantitative variables such as those used in the past but also by price-related variables such as interest rates. For example, the situation in which global financing is easy means that the interest rate, which is the cost of procuring funds, is relatively low in terms of price. To clarify the global liquidity picture, the trend in global credit worldwide is shown in Fig. 1.2, which depicts global credit transitions for bank and non-bank sectors from the fourth quarter of 1978 to the second quarter of 2020.

The periods during which global credit is rising are (1) the latter half of the 1970s to the early 1980s, (2) the latter half of the 1980s, (3) the early 2000s and (4) the end of 2010s. In particular, the rise in the first half of the 2000s continued to raise the sustained growth rate for about six years after 2002.

---

[8] Japanese financial institutions have established branches abroad. The cross-border credit going to those branches is considered credit going overseas.

[9] According to Hicks [12], the term liquidity began to be used in the field of economics in 1930, apparently stemming from resolutions made by the United Kingdom's Macmillan committee. However, according to Keynes [13], the term explicitly used in the field of economics is 'money theory'. Moreover, the reason that 'the degree of possibility that assets can be converted into money immediately without capital loss' was clearly given the meaning used in today's financial world in Keynes' *General Theory of Employment Interest and Money* (apparently in 1936). Since currency is 100% considered to be *cash*, the term *liquidity* means money itself.

Furthermore, this term is used as the substance of the noun it denotes. The term *liquidity*, as used in the vocabulary of international liquidity and dollar liquidity, is as strong in the meaning of money itself. In modern financial markets, the terms 'funding liquidity' and 'market liquidity' express the ease of investment with investors' assets, wherein the term liquidity is often used. Global liquidity can be interpreted as having a relatively similar meaning to fund liquidity among these terms.

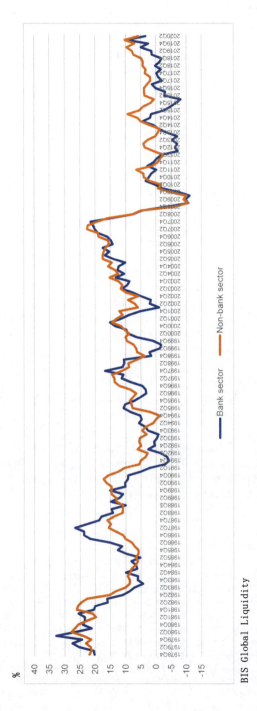

Fig. 1.2 Change of cross-border lending 1978Q4–2020Q2

Conversely, credit declines substantially (1) during the early 1990s, (2) in 1998 and 1999 and (3) in 2009, which is especially noteworthy given that this is the year after the 2008 Lehman shock. As can be seen from the figure, the credit for financial institutions is more varied than for non-financial ones, and fluctuations in cross-border credit occur mainly due to cross-border loans to financial institutions. From a financing perspective (i.e. the liability side), this implies that cross-border funds procurement deployed by financial institutions is likely to fluctuate due to various factors.

1.3.2 Indicators of Global Liquidity (2)

The concept of global liquidity introduced above is viewed from a quantitative perspective, but it can also be understood indirectly from a price perspective. A situation in which global funding is *easy* means that the interest rate—the cost of funds procurement—is low in terms of price. The London Interbank Offered Rate (LIBOR), a representative index, is the interest rate used in short-term transactions between banks in the London market. As interest rates are offered by lenders, various interest rates on interbank lending are determined based on LIBOR, so it has become the benchmark for the representative short-term interest rate in the international financial markets.

In fact, LIBOR quotations exist for interbank transactions with dollars, yen and euros (to be precise, euro dollar, euro–euro and euro–yen trades) in the London market. In financial institutions that have difficulty procuring dollar liquidity, it is likely that any movement to convert euros and yen into dollars in the foreign exchange market and convert to dollars in the foreign exchange swap market (so-called dollar movements) will also be active. Therefore, a dollar liquidity shortage crisis seems to simultaneously influence, to some extent, the euro money market and the yen funding market. Therefore, the situation of insufficient dollar liquidity during a global financial crisis should be more clearly characterised by comprehensively examining the movements in the dollar-denominated LIBOR rate, along with those in the euro- and yen-denominated LIBOR rates.

In addition, to measure the tightness of the actual money market, the value obtained by subtracting the 'three-month U.S. Treasury bill' (T-bill) rate from the U.S. dollar LIBOR rate is often indicated in many cases. The U.S. T-bill rate can be interpreted as reflecting the market view on the future of monetary policy. Therefore, discrepancies between the U.S dollar LIBOR rate and the T-bill rate (hereinafter, the 'TED spread') represent the difference between the interest rate forecast by the bank and the future interest rate.

Figure 1.3 shows trends in daily TED spreads from January 1986 to December 2020. In the first half of 2007, the TED spread remained at extremely low levels. However, in the latter half of 2007, it began to rise and sustained a nearly 2% level. It seemed to fall shortly after the beginning of 2008, but after October 2008, it showed a significant rise and a particularly high value of 4.6% at its peak on 10 October 2008.

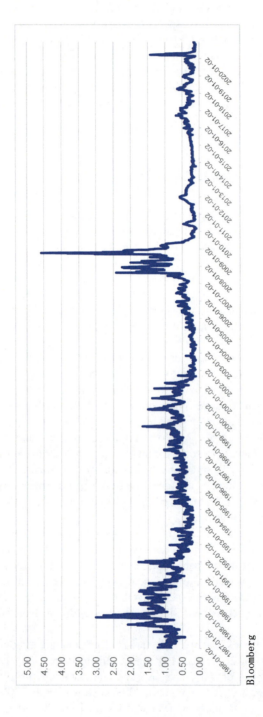

Fig. 1.3 TED spread 1986 January–2020 December

1 Global Liquidity as a New Trend in International Capital Flows

About three weeks after 15 September 2008, when Lehman Brothers failed, the value of this indicator indicates that international financial markets were suffering from an unprecedented shortage in dollar liquidity.

1.4 Fluctuation and Control of Global Liquidity

1.4.1 Fluctuation of Global Liquidity

Clarifying policy responses and factors of global liquidity is important because they will change depending on the factors involved. As introduced in Sect. 1.2, the most straightforward image of global liquidity is the total amount of cross-border credit (i.e. loans) given. The situation is easy to understand by dividing this factor into the side receiving the credit (i.e. the demand side of the funding) and the side giving the credit (i.e. the supply side of the funding). An important factor for the side receiving credit is the cost of financing represented by interest rates. Therefore, global banking liquidity will expand under circumstances in which the central bank of each country reduces policy-mandated interest rates, and worldwide interest rates are generally low. In international financial markets, if investors' risk appetites are increasing, the tendency to invest in stocks and other risky products will increase by means of loans (i.e. credit) from financial institutions. This side of the credit equation, when affected by a sudden financial crisis, must find a remedy in the financial markets. If instability rapidly increases, global liquidity will decline as countries refrain from cross-border borrowing.

When considering fluctuations in global liquidity, risk recognition in the market becomes a crucial factor. Therefore, we will examine the relationship between global credit dynamics and the volatility index (VIX) as an indicator of risk perception in international financial markets. The VIX is a widely used indicator that is measured by the Chicago Options Exchange based on information pertaining to price movements in option transactions targeting the Standard & Poor's (S&P) 500.

Figure 1.4 shows changes in global liquidity by overlaying the VIX. This graph illustrates the relationship between global liquidity availability and investor psychology. For example, in the 1990s, the VIX and global credit show similar movement. This point is highlighted by the fact that the VIX is also rising, and the risk appetite is high in a situation in which credit increases remarkably. However, after the Lehman crisis in 2008, the rise in the VIX, conversely, reduced the global credit supply. This suggests that the market psychology of investors deteriorated, and cross-border credit was stymied.

Consequently, the relationship between the market psychology of investors and global liquidity varies over time, so policy responses must also be formulated based on a flexible viewpoint. Since global credit may rise or decline with the market's risk appetite, one must consider measures that are assumed in advance of any phase of global liquidity expansion or contraction. Two points are especially important to

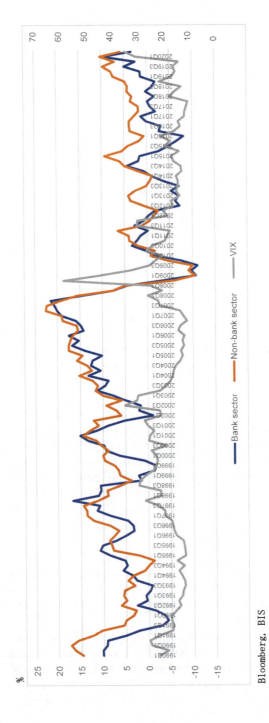

Bloomberg, BIS

Fig. 1.4 VIX and cross-border lending 1986 January–2020 December

consider: (1) as market psychology rapidly deteriorates, so does global liquidity, and (2) measures do exist that can flexibly provide liquidity when credit becomes depleted.

The excessive expansion of global credit could also destabilise the global economy by precipitating surges in asset prices in various countries. Therefore, it is quite important that such situations be detected in advance so that measures can be taken. This perspective is being considered for implementation as macroprudential policy in a single-country economy. The most distinctive feature of macroprudential policies is that they not only regulate and supervise each individual financial institutions' (micro) prudential policies, but they also uniformly regulate and adjust overall credit to financial institutions as a whole. At present, however, macroprudential policies are based on the premise that each country should take its own measures; global prudential policies that consider cross-border credit trends have not yet been developed.

1.4.2 Control of Global Liquidity

Individual responses are gradually being formed for prudential policies based on a global perspective. The following examples will be categorised into ex-ante and ex-post prescriptions.

The global financial crisis that began in the summer of 2007 prompted a review of the Basel Accord, which has been under review since, and a final agreement on a new regulatory framework (known as 'Basel III') was reached in 2017. Basel III introduced measures such as leverage ratio regulation, the liquidity coverage ratio and the stable funding ratio. These measures can be positioned as ex-ante prescriptions for global liquidity.

The discussion on capital controls at the IMF is also worthy of attention. Traditionally, the IMF has taken the liberalisation of international capital flows as its principle and has consistently taken a negative view of capital controls. However, the IMF (2012) pointed out that unrestricted capital flows can be a risk factor, especially in emerging market countries, and suggests that capital controls should be considered as an option. In terms of cross-border credit, capital controls have ex-ante prudential implications for controlling excessive transactions from a global perspective.

The depletion of global liquidity in the wake of a sudden financial crisis calls for the need for global liquidity supply during a crisis. In this regard, the IMF has already secured foreign exchange reserves in each country, established a system for mutual use of foreign exchange reserves between countries (e.g. the Chiang Mai Initiative) and provided various types of support for providing liquidity (e.g. strengthening the so-called Flexible Credit Line and creating the so-called Precautionary Credit Line (PCL) and its successor, the Precautionary and Liquidity Line (PLL)).

While these measures are effective for the ex-post management of global liquidity, they would not necessarily have been a sufficient response to the global financial crisis that began in 2008. This led to the creation of a new policy response, the so-called 'dollar swap agreement'. Under this agreement, the central bank of each country swaps their currency for U.S. dollars, thereby providing a plentiful supply of dollars. The dollar swap agreement is an innovative method of controlling global liquidity (or dollar liquidity) after the fact, and it is hoped that this system will evolve further.

1.5 Conclusion

Cross-border capital flows expanded rapidly with the growth of the world economy after World War II. The concept of international liquidity initially referred to the foreign exchange reserves held by the official sector of each country. However, with the expansion of international trade in goods and funds, the opportunities for trading in national currencies outside of the home country began to increase dramatically, and the concept of international liquidity became more broadly defined. In particular, with the overwhelming dominance of the U.S. economy in the post-war world, the global circulation of U.S. dollars became prominent, and the term 'dollar liquidity' was introduced.

The huge amount of cross-border credit extended by financial institutions, especially banks, is a prominent feature of the enormous international flow of funds occurring today. This feature, collectively known as global liquidity, has been attracting attention since the global financial crisis of 2008. There is still insufficient agreement on the scope and concept of global liquidity, so further elaboration and a more detailed examination is required in the future. In addition, how to control global liquidity from a policy standpoint is still unknown, so detailed study is essential. The term 'liquidity', introduced by John Maynard Keynes over 50 years ago, is currently undergoing a remarkable evolution in the torrent of today's global economy.

References

1. Aglietta, M. (1985). The creation of international liquidity. In L. Tsoukais (Ed.), *The political economy of international money*. R.I.I.A., London.
2. Altman, O. L. (1964). The management of international liquidity. In *IMF staff papers* (Vol. 11, No. 2, pp. 216–247).
3. Brahmananda, P. R. (1969). *The gold money rift: A CLASSICAL THEORY OF INTERNATIONAL LIQUIDITY*. Humanities Press.
4. Bruno, V., & Shin, S. (2013). Capital flows, cross-border banking global liquidity. NBER working paper, No.19038.
5. Committee on the Global Financial System. (2011). Global liquidity–concept, measurement, and policy implications. CGF papers, No.45.
6. Day, A. C. L. (1959). *International liquidity problem*. Manchester, Norbury, Lockwood
7. D'Agostino, A., & Surico, P. (2009). Does global liquidity help to forecast U.S. inflation? *Journal of Money Credit and Banking, 41*(2–3), 479–489.
8. Eickmeier, S., Gambacorta, L., & Hofmann, B. (2013). Understanding global liquidity. *European Economic Review, 68*, 1–18.

9. Fleming, J. M. (1964). The fund and international liquidity. In *IMF staff papers* (Vol. 11, pp. 177–215).
10. Gowda, K. V. (January 1962). Keynes-triffin plans and international liquidity. *Kautilya.*
11. Hansen, B. (1962). *International liquidity.* Central Bank of Cairo.
12. Hicks, J. R. (1962). Liquidity. *The Economic Journal, 72*(228), 787–802.
13. Keynes, J. M. (1930). *Treatise on money.* London: Macmillan and Co., Ltd.
14. Reierson, R. L. (1965). *The question of international liquidity.* New York: Bankers Trust Co.
15. Rueffer, R., Stracca, L. (2006). What is global excess liquidity and does it matter? ECB working paper, No.696.
16. Sousa, J., & Zaghini, A. (2008). Monetary policy shocks in the euro area and global liquidity. *International Journal of Finance and Economics, 13*(3), 205–218.
17. Yamamoto, E. (1988). *Dollar with replacement of key currency,* Yuhikaku.
18. Domanski, D., Fender, I., McGuire, P. (2011). Assessing Global Liquidity, *BIS Quarterly Review*, December, 2011.

Yoichi Matsubayashi is a professor of economics at Kobe University in Japan, where he received his Ph.D. His main research interest is international macroeconomics, especially external imbalances in the recent world economy. He has published many papers in refereed journals, such as the *Japanese Economic Review* and *Japan and the World Economy*. He is also the co-author of *Financial Globalization and Regionalism in East Asia* (Routledge 2013).

Chapter 2
Destination of Global Liquidity Before the Global Financial Crisis: Role of Foreign Bank Presence and the EU Effect

Shingo Iokibe

Abstract The global liquidity cycle, or extraordinary supply and acute retrenchment of cross-border bank flows before and after the global financial crisis, was one of the major factors of the crisis. While the cause and development of the post-crisis retrenchment of bank flows have been examined, we have less understood the development of the pre-crisis over-expansion of bank flows and the status of the cross-country distribution of global liquidity during its surge period before the crisis. We explore the determinants of cross-country variabilities in global liquidity inflows between 2004 Q2 and 2008 Q1 by running cross-country regressions on 97 countries and defining cross-border bank-to-bank credit inflows as global liquidity. Our empirical results highlight the presence of foreign banks in host banking systems at the beginning of the global liquidity surge period is a significant pull factor of global liquidity inflows. In addition, the volume of global liquidity inflow to a country is affected by the region to which the country belongs. Before the global financial crisis, global liquidity flows were highly concentrated in EU members' banking systems. Banks located in EU member countries have received cross-border bank credit (relative to the 2004 GDP) by 20–30 percentage points larger than banks outside the EU. This EU effect cannot explain other possible determinants of cross-border bank inflows, such as the development of institutions and banking system stability. Countries with less strictly regulated banking systems received larger inflows of global liquidity, in line with the predictions of the regulatory arbitrage hypothesis.

Keywords Cross-border bank flows · Destination of capital flows · Foreign banks' penetration · European Union · Regulatory arbitrage

---

S. Iokibe (✉)
Faculty of Commerce, Doshisha University, Karasuma Higashi-iru, Imadegawa-dori, Kamigyo-ku, Kyoto 602-8580, Japan
e-mail: siokibe@mail.doshisha.ac.jp

© The Author(s), under exclusive license to Springer Nature Singapore Pte Ltd. 2022
Y. Matsubayashi and S. Kitano (eds.), *Global Financial Flows in the Pre- and Post-global Crisis Periods*, Kobe University Monograph Series in Social Science Research,
https://doi.org/10.1007/978-981-19-3613-5_2

2.1 Introduction

Financial globalization accelerated in the early 2000s. The volume of portfolio flows across the globe quadrupled from that in the 1990s.[1] The growth of other investment flows was much higher. Its volume in the early 2000s was six times larger than that in the 1990s. In particular, internationally active banks have accumulated their cross-border claims (Fig. 2.1) and the local claims of their foreign affiliates. This global banking boom was synchronized by trade and economic booms, and in some countries, housing booms. From 2002 to 2007, world merchandise trade and world GDP grew at the highest rate since 1990, by 17% and 4% per annum, respectively.[2] During the same period, house price indexes in Ireland and Spain, for example, rose by 11% and 15% per annum, respectively, higher than the Organisation for Economic Co-operation and Development (OECD) average of 6%.[3] However, the global financial crisis (GFC), culminating in the collapse of Lehman Brothers in September 2008, changed the tide. After the GFC and the following European sovereign debt crisis,

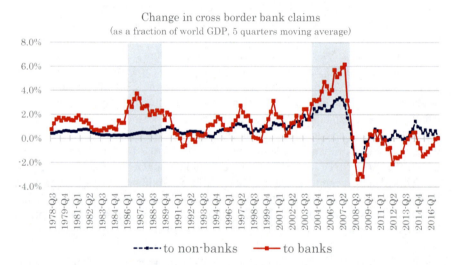

Fig. 2.1 Quarterly change in cross-border bank claims to banks excluding central banks versus to non-banks (as a fraction of world GDP, five quarters moving average). *Source* Author's calculations using BIS' *Locational Banking Statistics* and IMF's *World Economic Outlook* database

---

[1] According to our calculation using the International Monetary Funds' (IMF's) balance of payments data, the averages of the sum of net acquisition of portfolio equity and foreign debt assets by all countries were 597 and 1065 trillion US dollars between 2000 and 2007, respectively, while the corresponding averages during the 1990s were 154 and 245 trillion US dollars.

[2] The growth rates are calculated by the author using the series "Merchandise exports (current US$)" and "GDP (constant 2010 US$)" from World Bank's *World Development Indicators* database (World Development Indicators | DataBank (worldbank.org)).

[3] Author's calculation using the housing price data from OECD (Prices—Housing prices—OECD Data).

financial globalization has stopped deepening and retrenched across the globe; in particular, the contraction of cross-border bank lending has been the most massive and protracted (Fig. 2.1).[4]

The surge and stop in cross-border bank credit flows can be interpreted as expansion and contraction of liquidity supply across borders by banks. European banks' liquidity supply to the United States banks and financial institutions has played a significant role in accelerating bubbles in the US housing market before the GFC, and the US dollar liquidity shortage for European banks was the main conduit of international transmission of financial crises [33, 38]. Therefore, the massive contraction of cross-border bank claims after the GFC should be interpreted as the opposite side of the same coin as the overflow of cross-border bank lending before the GFC.

Considering the *post*-crisis development, the decrease in bank flows resulted from supply factors. Shrinkage of cross-border credit supply by crisis-inflicted global banks was the main driver of the decrease. In crisis-affected countries, tightening funding conditions in the money market made it difficult for banks to supply and/or rollover credits on foreign borrowers. The subsequent economic downturn increased the non-performing loan share in the banks' loan portfolios, deteriorated their capital to asset ratio, and thus further cut their ability to supply cross-border loans.[5] Banks dependent on non-deposit liabilities before the GFC met more severe funding conditions, and thus declined cross-border claims to a larger extent.[6] The supply factors also played an important role when global liquidity expanded rapidly before the GFC. Global push factors, such as vigorous investors' risk appetite reflected in the low VIX and the loose monetary policy of the United States and Euro Area, were the main drivers of the surge in cross-border bank flows.[7] Therefore, global banks are both the culprits and the victims of the crisis because they are stimulated by the global push factors, excessively expanded supplies of global liquidity before the GFC, and faced severe deterioration of their balance sheets and liquidity shortages after the GFC.

This study focuses on the other global liquidity boom and bust cycle victims. Which country was most damaged by the surge and retrenchment of cross-border bank flows? In other words, in a period when global liquidity expands, what direction global liquidity take? What are the significant determinants of global liquidity inflows to an individual country? To our knowledge, relatively little attention has been paid to the destination of global liquidity before the GFC than to the development of cross-border bank deleveraging after the GFC. However, disentangling the destination of global liquidity before the GFC is important because understanding who had acquired the foreign banks' credit before the crisis equals to understanding who most suffered from global bank deleverage after the crisis. Suppose we detect the

---

[4] Thus, the deleverage of cross-border banking has generated tremendous interest among researchers [5, 7–11, 13, 20, 21, 37, among others].

[5] See Emter et al. [20] and Kapan and Minoiu [31, 30] for the positive correlation between the non-performing loan ratio and the post-crisis bank deleverage. See Reinhardt and Riddiough [37], McGuire and von Peter [34], and Amiti et al. [2] for the positive correlation between a decline in bank's capital-to-asset ratio and the post-crisis bank deleverage.

[6] See Kapan and Minoiu [31, 30] and Amiti et al. [2].

[7] See Bruno and Shin [6] and Cerutti et al. [9].

characteristics of the destination countries of global liquidity supply before the crisis, we can distinguish which countries or areas will be susceptible to future global liquidity overflows, particularly in the form of bank flows and we can advise them on policies to prevent the harmful effects of global liquidity cycles.

Considering the geographical distribution of the global liquidity supply, we can assume several scenarios. First, international banks might easily extend cross-border credit to countries where they already have many branches or affiliated banks and have a record of extending a substantial amount of credit. For example, parent banks of multinational banking groups met by easy access to liquidity in their domestic funding markets increased their exposure to foreign borrowers, not by direct cross-border lending to foreign entities, but by cross-border intra-group lending to foreign affiliates who, in turn, increase lending to local borrowers. This implies that global liquidity flows unevenly to countries in which foreign banks occupy a larger share of the total bank assets.

Second, the extent of information asymmetry, cultural, and linguistic proximities between creditors and borrowers are the critical determinants of the volume and direction of international financial flows. At the onset of the global liquidity surge period, banks located in Europe supplied approximately 60% of cross-border bank credit worldwide.[8] The fifth enlargement of the European Union (EU) in 2004 and 2007 offered a chance for global banks in the EU to expand their cross-border banking networks. Therefore, we can guess that global liquidity has been distributed unevenly among EU member states, the closest borrowers from European global banks.

Finally, differences in banking regulations may determine the destinations of global liquidity. As the regulatory arbitrage hypothesis [28] tells us, global banks might extend a larger volume of credit to countries where the banking sector is regulated less strictly than the home country bank.

To test these three hypotheses empirically, we run cross-sectional regressions on net inflows of bank-to-bank cross-border credit to an individual country accumulated during the period preceding the GFC with several host country characteristics, including foreign banks' penetration rate. Our empirical strategy is similar to Lane and McQuade [32] in having an interest in medium-term developments. We ran cross-country regressions using variables averaged over five years to examine the determinants of *medium-term* bank inflows before the GFC.

We confirm the hypothesis that the higher the foreign banks' penetration in the domestic banking system, as captured by the share of foreign banks' assets to total bank assets, the larger the cross-border bank-to-bank credit inflows during the global liquidity surge period in the mid-2000s. We also confirm that the destination of global liquidity flows was highly concentrated in EU members' banking systems. Banks in EU members have received cross-border bank credit by 20–30 percentage points (relative to their 2004 GDP) larger than banks outside the area. This EU effect cannot

---

[8] According to Bank for International Settlement's *Locational Banking Statistics*, the BIS-reporting banks located in the EU, Norway, and Switzerland held 60.5% of the cross-border bank claims worldwide at the end of the 4th quarter in 2002.

explain other possible determinants of cross-border bank inflows, such as the development of institutions, capital openness, and expected population growth. Finally, we found evidence of regulatory arbitrage in medium-term cross-border bank-to-bank flows in the mid-2000s; that is, cross-border bank credit in the medium-term tended to flow into banking systems where banking activities are regulated more loosely.

This study contributes to the existing bank flow literature in three main ways. First, we add new evidence supporting the view highlighting increasing importance of global banking groups and their intra-group cross-border lending and funding activities [11–14, 15–17, 22, 23]. By econometrically detecting the positive effect of foreign banks' presence in the domestic banking system on global liquidity inflows during the mid-2000s, we indirectly show the growing importance of intra-group lending and funding activities in understanding capital flows. To the best of our knowledge, this study is the first to directly examine the effect on capital flows of the share of foreign banks' assets to total bank assets in a banking system by utilizing the estimated shares compiled by Claessens and Van Horen [17].[9]

Second, we present new evidence on strong *regional* patterns of cross-border liquidity inflows, in particular, extremely large cross-border bank credit inflows to EU members' banking systems. This result indirectly shows an origin of the "financial de-globalization" observed in cross-border banking since the GFC, especially among EU member countries [10, 20]. Emter et al. (20) examined the determinants of contraction of cross-border bank-to-bank (and bank-to-non-bank) loans in the EU since 2008, and found that an increase in the ratio of non-performing loans to total loans in the host banking system dampens inflows of cross-border bank loans. However, the higher development of institutional quality in the host banking system partially offsets the negative effect. In the period preceding the GFC, Hale and Obstfeld [26] highlight the specific role of intra-euro bank flows. They presented evidence that after the introduction of the euro, "core European Monetary Union (EMU)" countries increased their lending to "the EMU periphery" and suggested the possibility that large core EMU banks' lending to periphery borrowers might have spurred their borrowing from outside the euro area. Our empirical finding on the significant role of EU dummy variables presents additional evidence on the special role of Europe in accumulating cross-border bank liabilities during the period before the GFC.

The above two contributions, findings on the importance of foreign banks' presence and the regional (EU) bias, also support the view that the level of informational asymmetry between lenders and borrowers is a crucial factor in the volume of cross-border bank lending [8, 20].[10]

Third, by examining cross-border bank flows from medium-term and borrowers' perspectives, we introduce an insight into the existing literature, which examines

---

[9] Cull and Pería [19] highlight a negative effect of foreign-owned banks on local lending since the GFC in Eastern Europe. Combined with this paper's finding of the positive effect of ex-ante foreign banks' presence on global liquidity inflows before the GFC, their result implies that Eastern European economies whose banking system had been already largely occupied by foreign banks in the early 2000s suffered from larger contraction in local lending after the GFC.

[10] Cerutti et al. [8] and Emter et al. [20] found negative effects of distance between lender country and borrower country on cross-border lending in their panel regression analyses.

how cross-border bank credit turned around before and after the GFC [7, 8, 13, 14, among others].[11] To our knowledge, few studies have explored what type of borrowers benefit the most when the supply of global liquidity surges over the medium-run of five years. For example, Giannetti and Laeven [23], found that foreign leader banks of internationally syndicated loans increase the share of foreign loans in their total loan portfolio when funding conditions in their domestic money market improve. However, their analysis did not say anything about which country received most of the increased foreign loans by leader banks. In addition, they focused on the syndicated loan market, which occupies only a part of or less than half of the global cross-border loan market [8].[12] By using BIS locational banking statistics, our analysis covers a larger fraction of cross-border bank lending. Numerous studies detect several significant pull factors of cross-border bank inflows: institutional quality highlighted by Houston et al. [28], Bremus and Fratzscher [5], and Emter et al. [20], and lagged real GDP growth and lagged CPI inflation rate by Cerutti et al. [9], among others. However, most of these existing studies run panel regressions using quarterly or annual data, so their analyses can only explain the short-run fluctuations of cross-border bank flows. On the contrary, because our focus (and our dependent variable) is cumulative capital flows over nearly five years, our analysis can explain the determinants of medium-term movement of cross-border bank flows.

The remainder of this chapter is organized as follows. Section 2.2 describes our conjecture about the pull factors of cross-border bank-to-bank credit flows during a surge period of global liquidity. Section 2.3 explains the empirical methodology and the data. Section 2.4 presents the main empirical results and their implications. Section 2.5 presents robustness checks, and Sect. 2.6 concludes.

2.2 Definition and Hypothesis

2.2.1 Patterns of International Capital Flows and Our Definition of "Global Liquidity"

In this paper, we will focus on cross-border credit flows from banks to banks, or bank-to-bank flows. Before explaining our analysis, let us present reasons why we look at bank-to-bank lending flows among various types of capital flows.

We can classify international capital flows originated and/or transmitted by banks into five patterns as shown in Fig. 2.2. Country C in Fig. 2.2 represents a country where final borrowers, firms or government, who utilize capital originated in country A for real investment, reside. In patterns (a) and (b), the final borrower borrows money from domestic bank C who in turn borrows from foreign banks either in the

---

[11] Bremus and Fratzscher [5] show that a monetary easing in source countries has increased cross-border bank lending after the GFCs.

[12] According to Cerutti et al. [8], estimations from 1995 to 2012, the share of syndicated lending in total cross-border loan claims fluctuated between 17 and 41%.

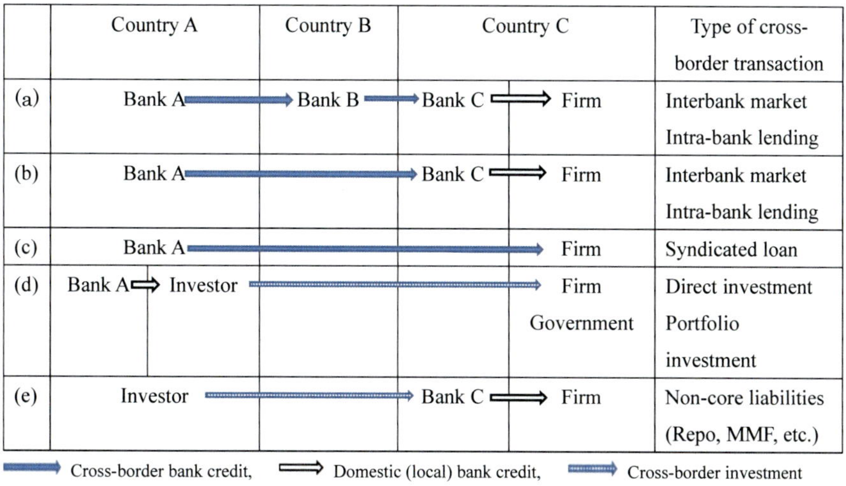

	Country A	Country B	Country C		Type of cross-border transaction
(a)	Bank A ⟶	Bank B ⟶	Bank C ⟹	Firm	Interbank market Intra-bank lending
(b)	Bank A ⟶		Bank C ⟹	Firm	Interbank market Intra-bank lending
(c)	Bank A ⟶			Firm	Syndicated loan
(d)	Bank A ⟹ Investor ⟶			Firm	Direct investment
				Government	Portfolio investment
(e)	Investor ⟶		Bank C ⟹	Firm	Non-core liabilities (Repo, MMF, etc.)

⟶ Cross-border bank credit, ⟹ Domestic (local) bank credit, ⟶ Cross-border investment

Fig. 2.2 Patterns of international capital flows originated and/or transmitted by banks. *Source* Author

international interbank market or by cross-border intra-group lending. In pattern (c), the final borrower acquires money directly from foreign banks (mainly in the form of a syndicated loan). Patterns (d) and (e) depict two types of cross-border capital flows extended by investors other than banks. In pattern (d), investor in country A, who borrows funds from domestic bank A, supplies capital to firm or to government in country C by purchasing equities or debt securities. This pattern of capital flows is recorded as direct investment or portfolio investment in the balance of payment statistics. Pattern (e) highlights cross-border funding by bank C in country C from a foreign investor in the form of "non-core liabilities" such as repo transactions and money market funds [25]. In the period preceding the GFC, international capital flows like pattern (d) (especially in portfolio debt investments) and (e) have expanded massively and their turnaround played an important role in spreading the crisis across the globe (see Bruno and Shin [6]). To focus on how and to which countries banks supplied global liquidity in that period, this paper focuses on patterns (a) to (c) and puts aside patterns (d) and (e) in the analysis below.

In addition, as shown in Fig. 2.2, international bank lending has two forms: bank-to-bank lending (patterns (a) and (b)) and bank-to-non-bank-institution lending (pattern (c)). The latter includes not only cross-border credit extended to non-financial enterprises but also non-depository financial institutions such as investment banks and non-banks.

This paper focuses on bank-to-bank capital flows like patterns (a) and (b) in Fig. 2.2. The reason why we focus on bank-to-bank flows is the much higher volatility of bank-to-bank flows relative to bank-to-non-bank flows as shown in Fig. 2.1. The standard deviation of five quarters moving average of quarterly changes in cross-border bank-to-bank claims of BIS reporting banks as a fraction of world GDP is

1.66%, more than double for bank-to-non-bank claims, 0.81%, between 1978 and 2016. Although cross-border bank claims on non-banks have increased sharply in the mid-2000s, the size of the increment was about half for bank-to-bank claims, and the magnitude of shrinkage after the Lehman shock has been much smaller for bank-to-non-bank claims as compared with bank-to-bank claims. In addition, growth in bank-to-non-bank cross-border claims had been modest and stable during the second half of the 1980s when bank-to-bank cross-border claims showed a massive and sustained growth suggesting a surge in global liquidity. All these facts imply that the quarterly change in cross-border bank-to-non-bank claims is not an appropriate measure of global liquidity.

According to this reason, we will examine determinants of cross-border bank-to-bank inflows, or "global liquidity" inflows, as our definition.[13]

2.2.2 The Period of Global Liquidity Expansion

Credit cycle can be asymmetric in length between its expansion phase and contraction phase; expansions are moderate and long-stretched, while contractions are acute and occurring only over a short period. Though numerous literature explored how negative funding shocks in global banks' home markets transmitted across borders during a crisis in a relatively short period, relatively few studies explored how and to which countries large sustained positive funding shocks are transmitted to banks across the globe.

Here, we will define the period of global liquidity expansion as a period with extraordinary high growth of cross-border bank credit to banks across the globe. More concretely, we define the period during which five-quarters-moving-average of increase in cross-border bank claims to private banks was not less than 2% of world GDP for more than four consecutive quarters. Following this criterion, as shown in Fig. 2.1, we found two periods as a global liquidity expansion period; one is the period from 2004 Q2 to 2008 Q1, and another is from 1986 Q1 to 1989 Q3.

In the econometric analysis below, we focus on the global liquidity surge period from 2004 Q2 to 2008 Q1 because for the period in the 1980s, data are limited or nil for some variables utilized in Sects. 2.3 and 2.4.

2.2.3 Hypothesis

Our first conjecture on the determinants of the destination of global liquidity flows is as follows: *The degree of foreign bank penetration in the host country's banking*

---

[13] Our definition of "global liquidity" in this paper follows BIS's definition that "global liquidity" can be defined as the degree of easiness for banks to fund money from foreign banks, including their subsidiaries [3].

system at the beginning of the global liquidity surge period might have a positive correlation with the volume of global liquidity inflows to that country. The reason is threefold.

First, global banks in developed economies might easily extend cross-border credit to countries where they already have many branches or affiliated banks and have a record of extending a large amount of cross-border credit. However, it must be more difficult for global banks to lend money to countries where they have few affiliates and to which they have not extended cross-border credit.

Second, *positive* funding shocks in the home banking system of parent banks of global banking groups *increase* their cross-border internal lending to their foreign affiliates. Numerous literature stress extensive use of internal cross-border funding from their affiliated banks or branches overseas by parent banks in a crisis period. Cetorelli and Goldberg [12], using a long-run bank-level data from 1980 to 2005, showed that US global banks, especially those with a low liquidity-to-asset ratio, have increased cross-border internal funding from affiliates outside US and reduced local lending from their foreign offices when the US monetary policy is tightened. Global banks outside US also showed the same funding-lending pattern before and after the GFC during 2007 and 2008; parent banks outside US who are hit by negative funding shocks during the crisis have increased internal capital inflows from their large branches in the U.S., which resulted in a decrease in local loan growth by the US branches [13]. As for syndicated loan data from 1997 to 2009, Giannetti and Laeven [22] found that a negative funding shock in the home banking system of the parent bank of a global banking group decreases the share of foreign loans as a fraction of total loans originated by the parent bank, and they named this "flight home effect."

According to these empirical results, *negative* funding shocks in the home country of parent banks *decrease* cross-border internal lending from those parent banks to their foreign affiliates. So, a simple analogy suggests that *positive* funding shocks in the home banking system of parent banks *increase* their cross-border internal lending to their foreign affiliates. Along this conjecture, Giannetti and Laeven [23] detected "flight abroad effect"; that is, an improvement in funding conditions in the home banking system of the parent bank of the leader bank of syndicated loans increases the foreign loan share of the parent bank.[14] This implies that when the flight abroad effect appears, parent banks extend cross-border credit to countries where their affiliates or branches are founded, but do not extend to countries where their affiliates or branches do not exist. In other words, if the flight abroad effect comes out when global liquidity surges, the flight abroad effect will be larger in banking systems where foreign banks' penetration rate is already high.

Third, when banks enter into a foreign country, establish a new affiliate bank, or open a new branch for the first time in a foreign country, they might prefer a country whose banking system is largely occupied by foreign banks because higher

---

[14] The proxy of banks' funding conditions in country i in Giannetti and Laeven's analysis is either the median value of the market-to-book ratio of equity of banks in country i in the previous year or the average spread in the interbank market over the overnight swap rate in country i during the corresponding period (month). Higher value of market-to-book ratio of equity or lower interest rate spread means looser funding conditions, and vice versa.

foreign banks' penetration might reflect looser regulation on banking activity. As Claessens and Van Horen [17] show, the number of net entries of foreign banks increased rapidly between 2004 and 2007, the period during which the supply of global liquidity expanded rapidly. Although we cannot deny a causality from an increase in cross-border finance by the domestic banking system to an increase in foreign banks' entry to the banking system, it seems to be more reasonable to interpret that an increase in cross-border credit inflows to the domestic banking system takes place as a result of a growth in foreign banks' entry.

Overall, all these conjecture support our first hypothesis that the larger the penetration rate of foreign banks in a domestic banking system at the beginning of the surge period of global liquidity, the larger the inflow of cross-border bank credit to the banking system during the corresponding period.

Our second conjecture is as follows: *Global liquidity was distributed unevenly between regions, especially to EU member banking systems during the global liquidity surge period in the mid-2000s.* This conjecture comes from a glance at descriptive statistics. As shown in Table 2.1, the cumulative net increase in bank-to-bank cross-border liabilities as a fraction of 2004 GDP shows large discrepancies

Table 2.1 Regional variabilities of net cross-border bank-to-bank capital inflows. Cumulative changes in net cross-border bank liabilities from 2004 Q2 to 2008 Q1

Region		Number of observations	Median	Average	Standard deviation
(1) Main regions	EU	24	0.24	0.25	0.31
	Central and Eastern Europe (CEE) ex EU-member countries	14	0.08	0.11	0.11
	East and South Asia	13	0.02	0.04	0.05
	Latin America	19	0.01	0.02	0.04
	Sub-Saharan Africa	26	0.01	0.01	0.02
	Other	16	0.05	0.07	0.19
	Tax havens and financial centers	8	0.68	0.66	0.96
	Whole sample	120	0.03	0.13	0.33
(2) Sub-regions	Euro area	12	0.24	0.16	0.29
	CEE all	23	0.18	0.23	0.26
	EU and CEE all	38	0.19	0.20	0.26

Note Author's calculation. "Central & Eastern Europe ex EU-member countries" includes all Central and Eastern European countries excluding EU members, while "CEE all" includes all Central and Eastern European countries. The countries included in "Tax havens & financial centers" are Bahrain, Barbados, Cyprus, Luxemburg, Mauritius, Panama, Seychelles, and Singapore. The sub-categories in the last three rows are the European sub-regions overlapping with the EU and each other

2 Destination of Global Liquidity Before the Global Financial Crisis … 29

between regions. Banking systems in EU members as well as tax havens and financial center countries[15] have experienced large inflows of international bank credit, while those in most of emerging economies and developing countries except in Central and Eastern Europe received fairly small volume of net cross-border bank-to-bank credit as a fraction of 2004 GDP. This fact suggests that destination of cross-border bank-to-bank credit might tend to be concentrated in one region. Significance of informational asymmetry in cross-border banking can explain this uneven regional distribution of global liquidity. A gravity-type empirical analysis using micro banking data has found a significant negative relationship between the distance between lender and borrower countries and the volume of cross-border bilateral credit [8]. Because a large fraction of global liquidity in the mid-2000s was supplied directly by and/or through European banking systems (U.K., Germany, France, and Netherlands), it flowed into countries most proximate to those banking systems, that is, other EU members.

The third conjecture follows the regulatory arbitrage hypothesis [28]. Global banks should extend a larger volume of credit to countries where the banking sector is regulated less strictly than the home country banks. Consequently, the differences in banking regulation determine the destination of global liquidity; the less strict the regulation on banking, the more the country acquires bank inflows.

2.3 Empirical Methodology and Data

2.3.1 Empirical Model

Our cross-sectional model for ordinary least squares (OLS) regressions is expressed in Eq. (2.1).

$$\Delta NCBL_{i,04Q2-08Q1} = \alpha + \beta FB_{i,04} + \gamma GR_{i,99Q1-04Q1} + \delta RD^{j}_{i,04-07} + \theta X_{i,00-04} + \varepsilon_i \tag{2.1}$$

$\Delta NCBL_{i,04Q2-08Q1}$ is the cumulative change in *net* cross-border bank liabilities of banks in country i from the start to the end of the global liquidity surge period between the second quarter in 2004 and the first quarter in 2008; α is a constant, β and γ are coefficients, and δ and θ are coefficient vectors; $FB_{i,04}$ is foreign bank penetration rate in country i's banking system at the beginning of the global liquidity surge period[16]; $GR_{i,99Q1-04Q1}$ is average annual growth rate of real GDP over five years preceding the global liquidity surge period (i.e., growth rate between 1999 Q1 and 2004 Q1); $RD^{j}_{i,04-07}$ is a matrix of regional dummies which take the value 1 if

---

[15] Bahrain, Barbados, Cyprus, Luxemburg, Mauritius, Panama, Seychelles, and Singapore.

[16] Thus, we should use the FB variable at 2004, but for foreign banks' assets to total bank assets ratio we use variables at 2005 supplemented by variables at 2006 and 2007 if needed for some countries, due to data availability. See Sect. 2.3.2.2 below.

country i belongs to region j, and 0 otherwise. As for the EU dummy, it takes the value 1 if country i has joined EU until 2007; $X_{i,00-04}$ is a matrix of proxies for extensive factors affecting credit demand in borrower country i at the beginning of the expansion period of global liquidity. We use five-year-average between 2000 and 2004 for most of these credit demand proxies; and ε_i is the error term. β and δ are the coefficients we are most interested in.

As for the foreign bank penetration, $FB_{i,04}$, we utilize two proxies, the share of foreign bank assets to total bank assets ("foreign banks' asset share") and the share of the number of foreign banks to total number of banks ("foreign banks' number share"), both from Claessens and Van Horen [16]. We prefer the asset share to the number share as a proxy for foreign banks' penetration rate according to the reason described in Sect. 2.3.2.2 below.

We include average real GDP growth rate as a main control variable, as a simple proxy for the average prospect of economic growth of country i investors across the globe hold. In theory, capital flows into faster growing economies as textbook-type perfect-foresight intertemporal open macro models depict. A straightforward interpretation is that a country with relatively higher real economic growth prospect attracts more foreign capital[17]; thus, when global liquidity expands, it might flow more into countries whose real GDP is expected to grow more rapidly. Cerutti et al. [9] and Reinhardt and Riddiough [37], in fact, found significant and positive coefficients on lagged GDP growth of host countries in their panel regressions on quarterly changes in cross-border bank claims on banks.[18] Here, we will test this relation from a more medium-term perspective. If a bank economist follows adaptive expectation on a country's future economic growth rate, the average real GDP growth rate in preceding five years before the global liquidity surge period is a good proxy of the macroeconomic growth expectation.

To capture the uneven distribution of global liquidity between regions found in Table 2.1, we add regional dummies to our control variables; dummies for EU members, Central and Eastern Europe excluding EU members, Sub-Saharan Africa, East and South Asia, and Latin America. The EU dummy takes the value 1 if country i has joined EU no later than 2008 and 0 otherwise, and the other regional dummies are defined similarly. Table 2.2 exhibits our classification of the regions.

A host of credit demand proxies $X_{i,00-04}$ consists of four dimensions; institutional development and capital openness, macroeconomic conditions, banking system characteristics, and regulations on banking. Extensive literature has shown that the degree of institutional development in the host countries affects volume of capital inflows to those countries [1, 35, 36, 39, among others[19]]. Papaioanou [36], in particular,

---

[17] Of course, the textbook real economic models, which do not incorporate money and the banking sector, should be applied to a specific type of capital flows like foreign direct investment flows and portfolio debt flows.

[18] Reinhardt and Riddiough [37] found a positive effect of lagged GDP growth on interbank capital inflows, but did not detect the same effect on intra-group cross-border bank flows.

[19] Papaioannou [36] analyzes covariates with bank credit flows as this paper does, while Alfaro et al. [1] and other authors analyze covariates with foreign direct investment and portfolio equity investment flows.

Table 2.2 Sample countries

Region	Countries	Number
EU members	OECD: Austria, Belgium, Denmark, Finland, France, Germany, Greece, Italy, Ireland, Netherlands, Portugal, Spain, Sweden, United Kingdom (UK) Non-OECD: Bulgaria, Czech Republic, Estonia, Hungary, Latvia, Lithuania, Poland, Romania, Slovenia, Slovakia	24
Other OECD	Australia, Canada, Japan, New Zealand, Norway, Switzerland, United States	7
East and South Asia	Bangladesh, China, India, Indonesia, Malaysia, Mongolia, Pakistan, Philippines, South Korea, Thailand, Vietnam	11
Latin America	Argentina, Bolivia, Brazil, Chile, Colombia, Costa Rica, Dominican Republic, Ecuador, El Salvador, Guatemala, Honduras, Jamaica, Mexico, Nicaragua, Paraguay, Peru, Uruguay, Venezuela	18
Central and Eastern Europe (not EU)	Albania, Armenia, Azerbaijan, Belarus, Croatia, Kazakhstan, Russia, Turkey, Ukraine	9
Sub-Saharan Africa	Angola, Botswana, Burkina Faso, Cameroon, Cote d'Ivoire, Ghana, Kenya, Mozambique, Mali, Madagascar, Malawi, Namibia, Niger, Nigeria, South Africa, Senegal, Sudan, Togo, Uganda, Zambia	20
Other Non-OECD	Algeria, Egypt, Hong Kong SAR, Kuwait, Jordan, Lebanon, Morocco, Tunisia	8
Total		97

detects positive effects of host country's institutional quality on bank capital inflows to all sectors in that country (see also Houston et al. [28], Bremus and Fratzscher [5]). Foreign investors must feel more ease to invest their capital in a country where property rights are protected by the law, business rules are well-established, and corruption and bribery are not widespread. In the same manner, we can conjecture that during a global liquidity flood across the globe, cross-border bank credit flows more into countries with higher institutional quality. The degree of capital account openness is also a possible covariate with the cumulative net bank credit inflows because banks can extend less cross-border credit to banks in countries with stricter barriers to capital account transactions [8]. To address endogeneity issues, we use both the degree of the development of economic institution and of capital openness at the beginning of global liquidity surge period as control variables.

The host country's macroeconomic conditions and characteristics, like trade openness, population growth prospect, stage of economic development, CPI inflation rate, real effective exchange rate, and development of capital and credit markets, can also influence demand for cross-border bank credit. A higher trade linkage between lender and borrower countries tends to increase cross-border bank claims between the same two countries [8]. In the same manner, a banking system in a country with higher trade openness, measured by export and import as a fraction of GDP, might tend to receive larger bank-to-bank flows. Both higher growth prospects of population and lower stage of economic development, which can be interpreted as higher potential for economic growth, can attract larger foreign bank credit. We use lagged (5-year-average) population growth rate and GDP per capita in current US dollar as proxies for the growth prospects of population and economic development, respectively.

A record of high inflation rate in a host country implies that there exist financial and macroeconomic instability in that country; thus, higher inflation rate in a country in the preceding 5 years may discourage cross-border bank inflows to that country.[20] Currency appreciation to the US dollar can increase cross-border bank credit inflows to local banks, because it revaluates the dollar value of local loan assets (or collaterals for foreign lenders), held by local banks, denominated in domestic currency terms [6].

Stability and profitability of the host country's banking system can also affect volumes of cross-border bank inflows. Bank credit might tend to flow into more profitable banking systems with higher return of equity (ROE) [37], or to more stable banking systems where banks on average sustain higher capital to asset ratio [5]. Net interest margin and non-performing loan ratio can also affect cross-border bank inflows by changing volumes of intra-group cross-border funding. Reinhardt and Riddiough [37] showed that affiliate banks in host banking systems with lower net interest margin, or tighter funding conditions, have accepted larger intra-group cross-border funding. Higher non-performing loan ratio to total loan in the domestic banking system may hinder cross-border bank inflows, if subsidiary banks of foreign banking groups cut their local lending when they hold a large amount of non-performing loans [29]. We also add five banks' concentration ratio in the domestic banking system to our control variables, because it may deter cross-border bank inflows [28].

The final set of the credit demand proxies are those related to regulatory arbitrage. Capital might move across borders from banking systems where regulations on banking are strict to those where regulations on banking are relatively weak. As Houston et al. [28] and Bremus and Fratzscher [5] highlighted, this regulatory arbitrage has significant effects on cross-border bank flows in terms of various aspects of banking regulation identified and indexed by Barth et al. [4]. In particular, cross-border bank credit tends to flow into a "recipient" country by a larger extent, if banking regulation in the "recipient" country is looser in either overall banking activity restrictions, or strength of external audit, or financial statement transparency, or independence of supervisory authority, or official supervisory power. Banking systems where a smaller fraction of banks are owned by their governments also tend to accept larger

---

[20] Cerutti et al. [9] found a statistically significant negative effect of lagged inflation on quarterly changes in BIS locational cross-border claims on banks in panel regressions using data on 77 countries over the period 1990–2014.

2 Destination of Global Liquidity Before the Global Financial Crisis ... 33

cross-border bank inflows [28]. We thus add these regulatory indexes to our control variables.

2.3.2 Data

2.3.2.1 Net Cross-Border Bank Liabilities

One of the main variables in our analysis is the cumulative changes in *net* cross-border bank liabilities of (or claims to) country j during the global liquidity surge period. Because we analyze the *economic* distribution of global liquidity, we do not focus on *gross* cross-border liabilities of country j, but do on *net* cross-border liabilities of country j. From a perspective of *financial* distribution of global liquidity, financial center and tax haven countries tend to absorb a large volume of global liquidity inflows just in order to pass them to other countries where the funds are credited to enterprises or households for the sake of real investment. So, the net cross-border liabilities of banks in financial center and tax haven countries might be smaller, while their gross cross-border liabilities tend to be large, or sizable. Because our focus is on to which country global liquidity flooded for the purpose of economic-growth-motive investment, we analyze cross-country distribution of the *net* cross-border bank liabilities.

Changes in net cross-border liabilities of banks in country *j* are calculated from *BIS Locational Banking Statistics (LBS)*. This statistics compiles claims and liabilities of 48 LBS reporting countries; thus, we can directly calculate the net cross-border liabilities of banks in an LBS reporting country by subtracting their gross cross-border assets from their gross cross-border liabilities. This data covers 48 countries, a large fraction of the world,[21] but in order to expand our sample size we add countries whose gross cross-border bank liabilities can be taken from *BIS LBS. BIS LBS* reports LBS-reporting banks' cross-border claims on destination country *k,* which includes non-LBS reporting countries. Because the coverage of this destination countries is much larger than that of the LBS-reporting countries, the sample size can be more than doubled by adding these data on non-LBS reporting countries. Figure 2.3 illustrates our methodology of calculating the net cross-border liabilities.

Note that in the analysis below, we exclude financial center countries that have a tremendously large financial sector relative to their real GDP to avoid the confusing effect of these countries' role as liquidity pass-through. In fact, Table 2.1 shows financial center countries exhibited tremendously large net inflows of bank-to-bank cross-border credit as a fraction of their GDP at 2004. However, cross-border bank claims to financial center countries have occupied fairly a small fraction of the total cross-border claims across the world (see Fig. 2.5 in Appendix). We also exclude

---

[21] The LBS-reporting countries include numerous tax haven countries such as the Netherlands Antilles, Bermuda, The Bahamas, Curacao, Guernsey, Isle of Man, Jersey, Cayman Islands, and Panama, all of which are omitted from our sample as discussed below in the text.

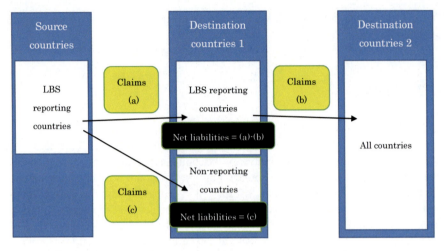

Fig. 2.3 Graphical image of how to calculate net cross-border bank-to-bank liabilities. *Source* Author's description

tax havens because net cross-border liabilities of these countries can grow rapidly during a global liquidity surge period due to an increasing motive to escape taxes all over the world.

2.3.2.2 Foreign Banks' Penetration Rate

The second key variable in our analysis is foreign banks' penetration rate, or the degree of foreign banks' presence in a host country's banking system. Data on foreign banks' penetration rate are taken from Claessens and Van Horen [17]. They compile bank ownership database covering 138 countries for the years 1995–2013.[22] Their database covers commercial banks, saving banks, cooperative banks, and bank holding companies, active or inactive (exit) in Bankscope during the sample years. It includes subsidiaries of foreign banks, but not branches. By defining a bank being foreign owned when 50% of more of its shares are held by foreigners, they calculate two proxies for foreign banks' penetration rate in an individual country; percentage of foreign banks among total banks (*foreign banks' number share*) and percentage of foreign bank assets among total bank assets (*foreign banks' asset share*).

An increase in cross-border bank credit inflows might occur with new entries of foreign banks. In fact, the number of foreign banks' entry has tripled from 40 in 2004 to 120 in 2007. To avoid endogeneity issues, we will examine the effect of the ex-ante degree of foreign banks' penetration on cross-border bank credit inflows during the global liquidity surge period.

---

[22] The database is an updated version of Claessens and Van Horen [16].

2 Destination of Global Liquidity Before the Global Financial Crisis … 35

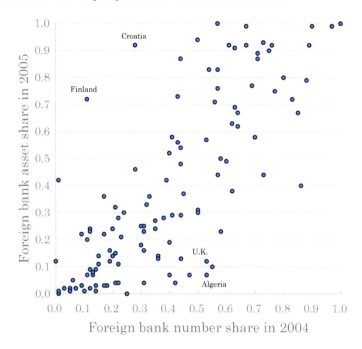

Fig. 2.4 Alternative measures of foreign bank penetration: Foreign bank asset share and foreign bank number share. *Source* Author. Data from Claessens and Van Horen [17]

In the regression analysis below, we prefer foreign banks' asset share to foreign banks' number share as our main control variable. Figure 2.4 depicts scatter plots of foreign banks' number share (horizontal axis) and foreign banks' asset share (vertical axis), showing a remarkably high positive correlation between the two shares. In fact, correlation index between these two variables is 0.78.[23] However, a close look at the data reveals that there exists some divergence between these variables. In some banking systems, the foreign banks' number share is small, but the foreign banks' asset share is extremely large; for example, the number share is 0.28 and 0.11, while the asset share is 0.92 and 0.72 for Croatia and Finland, respectively. In such a banking system, though foreign banks seem not to be significant in terms of numbers, they in fact dominate over local banks in the domestic lending market. On the contrary, there are banking systems where the foreign banks' asset share is extremely low relative to its number share; for example, the foreign banks' asset share in the U.K. and Algeria is 0.12 and 0.07, respectively, while the foreign banks' number share in both countries is 0.53. Though these banking systems seem to be occupied by foreign banks in terms of numbers, they are in fact not dominated by foreign banks because their domestic assets are only a small fraction of total banking

---

[23] This correlation coefficient between the foreign banks' asset share and the foreign banks' number share is slightly different from that in Table 2.3a (0.79), because the sample size of Fig. 2.2 is 120, larger than that of Table 2.1 (97).

assets. This is why we use the foreign banks' asset share as the main proxy variable of foreign banks' penetration rate in our regression analysis.

In addition, prior to 2005, the balance sheet information in the current Bankscope database had been limited [17]. So, some countries do not have data on foreign banks' asset share in 2005. In order to expand our observations as large as possible, we will use an "extended foreign banks' asset share in 2005" which includes foreign banks' asset share reported for the first time between 2006 and 2008 for the countries for which the Claessens and Van Horen database do not report foreign banks' asset share in 2005.[24] We believe that this modification does not matter because the foreign banks asset shares show a high invariability between 2005 and 2008 for most of the sample countries.

2.3.2.3 Other Control Variables

The sources of other control variables are summarized in the Appendix (Table 2.12). Average annual growth rate of real GDP between 1999 Q1 and 2004 Q1 is calculated from quarterly real GDP index data from IMF's *International Financial Statistics* (IFS). Institutional index is the index of "law & order" from International Country Risk Guide (ICRG) political index series. Because the original law and order index data is monthly, we use its twelve-month-average in 2004 as the ex-ante degree of development of institution. The institutional index takes values from 1 (least developed) to 6 (most developed). We also use alternative institutional indexes from World Bank's *Worldwide Governance Indicators* following Bremus and Fratzscher [5]. Capital openness index is from Chinn and Ito [15]. We adjust the original Chinn-Ito index so as to take value from 0 (strictest restriction on capital mobility) to 4.28 (full capital mobility). We use the adjusted Chinn-Ito index in 2004 as the ex-ante degree of capital openness. All of the other macroeconomic indicators— trade openness, population growth, GDP per capita, stock market capitalization, and domestic credit to private sector—are taken from World Bank's *World Development Indicators*. Variables on profitability and stability of banking system, such as ROE and net interest margin for example, are from World Bank's *World Financial Development Database*. Lastly, bank regulatory indexes like overall restrictions on banking activity and independence of supervisory authority are taken from survey data compiled by Barth et al. [4].

Table 2.3a presents correlations matrix between the selected (main) variables and Table 2.3b presents basic statistics on the main variables.

---

[24] We add 13 country data to our sample of foreign banks' asset share following this criterion; observations in 2006 are utilized for Australia, New Zealand, Turkey, Nigeria, Sudan, and Singapore. Observations for 2007 are for Japan, China, Albania, Ghana, Morocco, and Lebanon. Observations for 2008 is Chile, though we drop Singapore from our regression analysis.

Table 2.3 Descriptive statistics of the main variables

(a) Correlation matrix

	(1)	(2)	(3)	(4)	(5)	(6)	(7)	(8)	(9)	(10)	(11)	(12)	(13)	(14)
(1) Cum. B-to-B inflows 04Q208Q1	1													
(2) FB asset share	0.20	1												
(3) FB number share	0.08	0.79	1											
(4) RGDP growth 99–04	0.30	−0.04	−0.09	1										
(5) EU dummy	0.45	0.05	0.04	−0.14	1									
(6) Sub-Sahara Africa dummy	−0.22	0.32	0.31	0.03	−0.29	1								
(7) Law and order 04	0.25	−0.09	−0.15	0.02	0.46	−0.33	1							
(8) Chinn-Ito index 04	0.21	0.07	−0.01	−0.28	0.46	−0.41	0.43	1						
(9) Trade openness 00–04	0.23	0.13	0.18	0.23	0.17	−0.13	0.18	0.07	1					
(10) Population growth 00–04	−0.41	−0.04	0.07	−0.09	−0.54	0.63	−0.41	−0.33	−0.20	1				
(11) GDP per capita 00–04	0.04	−0.21	−0.25	−0.30	0.46	−0.34	0.69	0.57	0.10	−0.31	1			
(12) ROE 00–04	−0.01	0.26	0.21	0.17	−0.12	0.43	−0.08	−0.15	0.16	0.27	−0.17	1		
(13) Net interest margin 00–04	−0.14	0.25	0.25	0.06	−0.41	0.48	−0.51	−0.37	−0.09	0.30	−0.60	0.39	1	
(14) Bank assets per GDP 00–04	−0.03	−0.31	−0.28	−0.23	0.30	−0.43	0.56	0.44	0.20	−0.20	0.70	−0.26	−0.70	1

(b) Basic statistics on the main variables

Variables	Median	Average	Standard deviation	Max	Min
Net bank inflows 2004Q2-08Q1	3.2	9.5	19.5	99.7	−52.0
Foreign banks' asset share 2005	25.0	37.3	32.1	100.0	0.0

(continued)

Table 2.3 (continued)

(b) Basic statistics on the main variables

Variables	Median	Average	Standard deviation	Max	Min
Foreign banks' number share 2004	35.0	38.0	25.2	100.0	0.0
Real GDP growth 1999–2004	4.0	4.2	2.3	10.9	−1.2
Law and order index	4.0	3.8	1.3	6.0	1.0
Chinn-Ito index	3.0	2.7	1.5	4.3	0.7
Trade openness	66.3	76.4	38.3	272.8	21.2
Population growth	1.2	1.2	1.2	4.0	−1.2
GDP per capita	2.5	8.8	12.0	45.5	0.2
ROE	12.4	13.8	12.0	62.2	−23.6
Net interest margin	4.5	5.0	3.0	14.5	0.3
Bank assets per GDP	43.0	54.4	42.2	171.0	2.8

Source Author's calculation

2.4 Empirical Results

2.4.1 Results with Standard Covariates

Table 2.4 shows results of cross-sectional regressions on cumulative changes in net cross-border bank liabilities from the second quarter in 2004 to the first quarter in 2008 using *standard* independent variables in the related literature. Column (1) is the result of the regression on foreign banks' asset share coupled with ex-ante five-year-average real GDP growth rate, institutional index, and capital openness index as control variables. The estimated coefficient on the foreign banks' asset share is statistically significant and positive, suggesting that the foreign banks' asset share in a host country had a positive effect on the cumulative net inflows of foreign bank credit to the corresponding country. This implies that a country with a banking system in which foreign banks had occupied a larger share of assets at the start of the global liquidity surge period in the mid-2000s has experienced larger inflows of global liquidity, as we conjectured in Sect. 2.2.3.

The ex-ante five-year-average real GDP growth rate also has a statistically significant positive effect on the cumulative net inflows of cross-border bank credit. In line with the existing literature, global liquidity has flooded into countries with higher degree of institution and countries more open in regards to capital accounts. The estimated coefficients for the law and order index and Chinn-Ito index are both positive and statistically significant. However, the significance of coefficients for both indexes disappear once we control the regional effect of the European Union and Sub-Sahara Africa as shown in Sect. 2.4.2.

From columns (2) to (4), we show results of the regressions when one of the macroeconomic conditions are added to the controls, and column (5) shows the result when all the macroeconomic variables are included. Ex-ante population growth has a significant negative effect on the cumulative net inflows of bank-to-bank credit (columns (2) and (4)). That is, a banking system in a country with expected higher population growth received less cross-border bank credit during the global-liquidity boom period. Though this result contradicts with our conjecture, this may reflect the fact that Sub-Sahara African countries, the ones with the highest population growth prospects,[25] are the region that accepted the least cross-border bank-to-bank credit in the mid-2000s. The degree of trade openness and the level of per-capita GDP do not have a statistically significant effect.[26]

From columns (6) to (9), we show the results when we include banking system related variables as controls. Neither return on equity (ROE), net interest margin, nor

---

[25] As for the Sub-Sahara Africa sample, the average of the average annual growth rate of population between 2000 and 2004 is 2.6%. On the other hand, the corresponding average for the other countries is 0.9%.

[26] The per-capita GDP has a significant effect if we use as control variables foreign banks' asset share, real GDP growth rate, and per-capital GDP only. However, the coefficient on GDP per-capita becomes insignificant if we add to the independent variables either of the EU dummy, institutional index, or Chinn-Ito index.

Table 2.4 Results of the traditional regressions with foreign banks' asset share

	The dependent variable: cumulative net changes in cross-border bank liabilities from 2004 Q2 to 2008 Q1									
	(1)	(2)	(3)	(4)	(5)	(6)	(7)	(8)	(9)	(10)
Foreign bank asset share 2005	0.133**	0.125*	0.123**	0.117*	0.098*	0.149**	0.143**	0.110*	0.126*	0.083
	[0.063]	[0.064]	[0.057]	[0.062]	[0.057]	[0.067]	[0.065]	[0.066]	[0.069]	[0.065]
Real GDP growth 1999–04	3.037***	2.861**	2.664**	2.763***	2.200**	3.152***	3.051***	2.832***	2.790**	1.879*
	[1.074]	[1.113]	[1.033]	[1.042]	[1.055]	[1.115]	[1.073]	[1.053]	[1.08]	[1.096]
Law and order 2004	2.556**	2.359**	1.219	3.662**	2.395	2.552**	2.125*	3.387**	3.141**	2.695
	[1.079]	[1.045]	[1.239]	[1.768]	[1.722]	[1.096]	[1.121]	[1.319]	[1.273]	[1.745]
Capital openness 2004	2.837*	2.768*	1.913	3.343**	2.473*	2.680*	2.645*	3.204**	2.976**	2.639
	[1.476]	[1.453]	[1.3]	[1.66]	[1.398]	[1.491]	[1.434]	[1.554]	[1.495]	[1.407]
Trade openness 2000–04		0.042			0.034					0.055
		[0.046]			[0.047]					[0.052]
Population growth 2000–04			−4.990***		−4.932***					−4.443***
			[1.556]		[1.557]					[1.656]
GDP per capita 2000–04				−0.223	−0.266					−0.241
				[0.312]	[0.303]					[0.302]
ROE 2000–04						−0.156			−0.118	−0.004
						[0.131]			[0.145]	[0.145]
Net interest margin 2000–04							−0.471		−0.968	−1.063
							[0.595]		[0.779]	[0.761]
Bank assets per GDP 2000–04								−0.059	−0.105	−0.097
								[0.06]	[0.073]	[0.066]

(continued)

2 Destination of Global Liquidity Before the Global Financial Crisis … 41

Table 2.4 (continued)

	(1)	(2)	(3)	(4)	(5)	(6)	(7)	(8)	(9)	(10)
The dependent variable: cumulative net changes in cross-border bank liabilities from 2004 Q2 to 2008 Q1										
Constant	−25.468***	−26.752***	−10.137	−27.284***	−13.157*	−23.963***	−21.416***	−24.640***	−14.520*	−4.903
	[7.646]	[7.563]	[6.601]	[8.533]	[7.174]	[7.637]	[8.444]	[7.582]	[8.517]	[7.645]
Observations	97	97	97	97	97	97	97	97	97	97
Adjusted R^2	0.208	0.206	0.272	0.206	0.269	0.208	0.203	0.208	0.212	0.263

Note The dependent variable in all the regressions is the cumulative changes in net cross-border bank-to-bank liabilities of individual countries from 2004 Q2 to 2008 Q1 relative to its nominal GDP in current US dollar in 2004. Foreign banks' asset share 2005 is the ratio of foreign banks' assets to total bank assets in 2005, from Claessens and Van Horen [17]. Average real GDP growth rates between 1999 and 2004 are calculated from the real GDP index of *International Financial Statistics* (IMF). Law and order is the sub-index of ICRG political risk index compiled by the Political Risk Services (PRS) Group. Capital openness is the updated version of Chinn-Ito index from Chinn and Ito [15]. The other macroeconomic and banking system variables are 5-year average over the period from 2000 to 2004 and taken from the World Bank databases. ***, **, and * indicate that the estimated coefficient is statistically significant in 1%, 5%, and 10%, respectively. The robust standard errors are in parenthesis.

bank assets as a fraction of GDP had a statistically significant effect on the cumulative net bank credit inflows in the mid-2000s.[27]

The most striking result in Table 2.4 is the robustness of the positive coefficient on foreign banks' asset share, which is statistically significant in all regressions except column (10) where all independent variables are included. That is, the positive effect of foreign banks' asset share on bank-to-bank credit inflows during the global liquidity surge period in the mid-2000s were not affected by other major macroeconomic and banking system variables. This effect of foreign banks' asset share is also economically significant. The point estimate in column (1), 0.133, implies that one standard deviation increase in foreign banks' asset share spurred net bank-to-bank inflows between 2004 Q2 and 2008 Q1 as a percent of 2004 GDP by 4.3 percentage points. Compared with the sample average of the cumulative net inflows of bank-to-bank credit, 9.5%, the pull effect of foreign banks' asset share is economically significant. This result supports our conjecture that global liquidity flowed by a larger extent into banking systems characterized with high foreign banks' penetration.

Another notable result in Table 2.4 is that the coefficients on ex-ante real GDP growth rate are always positive and statistically significant, suggesting that a larger fraction of global liquidity floods into banking systems in countries whose real output growth prospect was higher at the beginning of the global liquidity surge period, consistent with predictions from a standard intertemporal open economy macro models. This effect is also economically significant. The estimated coefficient on real GDP growth in column (1), 3.037, implies that one standard deviation increase in the ex-ante 5-year real GDP growth rate augment net bank-to-bank inflows between 2004 Q2 and 2008 Q1 as a percent of 2004 GDP by 7.0 percentage points, which can be seen as economically significant compared with the sample average of the cumulative net bank-to-bank inflows, 9.5%.

2.4.2 Regional Effects

Since the size of net cross-border bank flows shows a large regional variability (as shown in Table 2.1), we next examine whether some regional effect existed or not. First, we run a regression using our two baseline covariates (foreign banks' asset share and real GDP growth rate) as well as two regional dummies; the EU dummy and Sub-Saharan Africa dummy. Column (1) of Table 2.5 shows the result. Both coefficients for the foreign banks' asset share and the ex-ante real GDP growth are statistically significant and have positive signs again. Estimated coefficients for the EU and Sub-Saharan Africa dummies are statistically significant, though the signs are opposite with each other. The coefficient for the EU dummy is 19.9, while those

---

[27] ROE and net interest margin have significant effects if we use as control variables foreign banks' asset share, real GDP growth rate, and either ROE or net interest margin, only. However, the coefficients on both variables become insignificant if we add to the independent variables either of the EU dummy, institutional index, or Chinn-Ito index.

2 Destination of Global Liquidity Before the Global Financial Crisis … 43

for the Sub-Saharan Africa dummy is −8.8. This means that the cumulative changes in net cross-border bank capital inflows during the global liquidity surge period as a percentage of the initial GDP in 2004 is 20 percentage points larger for EU

Table 2.5 Estimations with regional dummies

Variables	The dependent variable: cumulative net changes in cross-border bank liabilities from 2004 Q2 to 2008 Q1						
	(1)	(2)	(3)	(4)	(5)	(6)	(7)
Foreign bank asset share 2005	0.154^{**}	0.152^{**}	0.132^{**}	0.141^{**}	0.113^{*}	0.132^{*}	0.104
	[0.062]	[0.06]	[0.06]	[0.067]	[0.067]	[0.068]	[0.073]
Real GDP growth 1999–04	3.145^{***}	3.184^{***}	2.805^{***}	3.016^{***}	2.658^{***}	2.986^{***}	2.539^{**}
	[0.823]	[0.938]	[0.851]	[0.841]	[0.946]	[0.979]	[1.012]
EU dummy	19.923^{***}	19.485^{***}	20.313^{***}	20.958^{***}	18.923^{***}	19.350^{***}	18.551^{***}
	[5.589]	[5.872]	[6.769]	[5.651]	[6.455]	[5.801]	[6.374]
Sub-Saharan Africa dummy	-8.791^{***}	-8.335^{***}	-7.519^{*}	-9.909^{***}	−5.717	-8.944^{***}	−6.422
	[3.175]	[3.106]	[3.882]	[3.013]	[4.363]	[2.902]	[4.766]
Law and order 2004		0.078			1.482	1.099	1.88
		[1.143]			[1.348]	[1.332]	[1.47]
Capital openness 2004		0.307			1.142	0.659	1.248
		[1.066]			[1.21]	[1.106]	[1.259]
Trade openness 2000–04			0.014		0.016		0.03
			[0.803]		[0.057]		[0.059]
Population growth 2000–04			−1.039		−1.12		−0.707
			[0.539]		[1.776]		[1.974]
GDP per capita 2000–04			−0.151		−0.325		−0.248
			[0.231]		[0.306]		[0.323]
ROE 2000–04				−0.034		−0.05	−0.046
				[0.808]		[0.717]	[0.128]
Net interest margin 2000–04				0.096		0.14	−0.134
				[0.606]		[0.59]	[0.658]
Bank assets per GDP 2000–04				−0.042		−0.064	−0.061
				[0.06]		[0.072]	[0.068]
Constant	-12.598^{**}	-13.788^{**}	−9.208	−9.327	-15.063^{**}	-13.336^{*}	-13.463^{*}
	[5.13]	[5.664]	[5.883]	[7.825]	[6.323]	[7.424]	[8.015]
Observations	97	97	97	97	97	97	97

(continued)

Table 2.5 (continued)

	The dependent variable: cumulative net changes in cross-border bank liabilities from 2004 Q2 to 2008 Q1						
Variables	(1)	(2)	(3)	(4)	(5)	(6)	(7)
Adjusted R^2	0.376	0.363	0.363	0.363	0.357	0.354	0.341

Note The dependent variable in all the regressions is the cumulative changes in net cross-border bank-to-bank liabilities of individual countries from 2004 Q2 to 2008 Q1 relative to its nominal GDP in current US dollar in 2004. Foreign banks' asset share 2005 is the ratio of foreign banks' assets to total bank assets in 2005, from Claessens and Van Horen [17]. Average real GDP growth rates between 1999 and 2004 are calculated from the real GDP index of *International Financial Statistics* (IMF). The EU dummy takes the value of 1 if the country observation has joined EU until the end of 2007 and 0 otherwise. Law and order is the sub-index of ICRG political risk index compiled by the Political Risk Services (PRS) Group. Capital openness is the updated version of Chinn-Ito index from Chinn and Ito [15]. The other macroeconomic and banking system variables are 5-year average over the period from 2000 to 2004 and taken from the World Bank databases. ***, **, and * indicate that the estimated coefficient is statistically significant in 1%, 5%, and 10%, respectively. The robust standard errors are in parenthesis

member countries than the sample mean, while 9 percentage points smaller for Sub-Saharan African countries. That is, EU members were the largest beneficiaries of the exuberance of global liquidity, while Sub-Saharan African economies were the least beneficiaries. On the other hand, other regional dummies have no statistically significant effect on the net cross-border inflows of bank credit.[28]

These regional effects are strong enough that they diminish the explanatory power either of institutional quality or of capital openness on the cross-country variability in cumulative changes in net cross-border bank inflows as shown in Table 2.5. In column (2), we ran a regression including both for law and order and Chinn-Ito index as well as for EU and Sub-Saharan Africa dummies as control variables. While the coefficients for the regional dummies are totally the same in their sign and magnitude as in column (1) and statistically significant, those for the law and order index and capital openness index turn to be insignificant and much smaller in their magnitude relative to those in Table 2.4. This result did not qualitatively change even if we add macroeconomic variables (trade openness, population growth, and per capita GDP) and/or banking system variables (ROE, net interest margin, and bank assets per GDP ratio) as control variables (columns (2) to (7)).

The sizes of point estimates on EU dummy in Table 2.5 imply a strong and economically significant effect of EU membership on cumulative net inflows of bank-to-bank credit during the mid-2000s. If a country had joined EU before the end of 2007, that country's banking system has received 18.6% to 21.0% larger net inflows of cross-border bank credit during the global liquidity surge period. The magnitude of this EU effect more than doubles the above-mentioned positive effect of foreign banks' asset share and of ex-ante real GDP growth rate.

---

[28] Although we also run a regression by adding Central and Eastern Europe (excluding EU members), East and South Asia, and Latin America dummies to the controls, the estimated coefficients on these regional dummies are not statistically significant and the results on other controls are not totally different from column (1) in Table 2.5.

In addition, the explanatory power of the regression models jumps up if the EU and Sub-Sahara Africa dummies are included in the control variables. The adjusted R-squared are much higher in the regressions in Table 2.5 than those in Table 2.4. The adjusted R-squared of column (2) in Table 2.5, our baseline regression hereafter, is 0.36, 0.15 higher than that of column (1) in Table 2.4.

These results imply that the apparent positive relationships between both institutional quality and capital openness, and cumulative net inflows of bank credit during the global liquidity boom period found in Table 2.4 merely capture the *regional discrepancy* in volume of cross-border bank-to-bank inflows during the corresponding period. As Table 2.3 shows, both the law and order and capital openness indexes are highly and positively correlated with the EU dummy (the corresponding correlation coefficients are 0.46 for both), and highly and negatively correlated with the Sub-Saharan Africa dummy (the correlation coefficients are -0.33 and -0.43, respectively). That is, EU member countries, on the average, established more developed institutional environment relative to the other countries, on the average, where foreign investors feel easy to invest. However, in Sub-Saharan African countries, the institutional quality is poorer than the world average, which made foreign banks hesitate to extend cross-border credits. In the same manner, as to capital account openness, EU members are the most open due to its regulation, but Sub-Saharan African countries are more closed relative to the world average. So, once we control the regional effect of EU and Sub-Saharan Africa, we cannot detect any correlation between either institutional quality or capital openness and volume of net inflows of cross-border bank credit for the whole sample.

2.4.3 Regulatory Arbitrage

Table 2.6 shows the regression results that test whether stringency of banking regulation in the capital "recipient" country influenced the volume of global liquidity inflows. We use various indexes constructed by Barth et al. [4] as control variables.[29] The coefficient for overall restrictions on banking activity is statistically significant and negative (column (1)). Banking systems under looser overall restriction on banking activity accepted larger inflows of cross-border bank credit, or regulatory arbitrage transpired, during the global liquidity surge period. Any coefficient on the other regulation indexes—independence of supervisory authority, supervisory power, strength of external audit, financial statement transparency, limitation on foreign bank operations, and capital regulatory stringency—are insignificant and in most cases are incompatible with regulatory arbitrage (columns (2) to (7)). A larger share of government ownership seems to deter cross-border bank inflows, but the estimated coefficient in not significant (column (8)).

---

[29] Note that number of observation decreases (by a large extent in some regressions) in Table 2.6 due to the low availability of data on bank regulation indexes of Barth et al. [4].

Table 2.6 Effect of regulatory variables

Variable	The dependent variable: cumulative net changes in cross-border bank liabilities from 2004 Q2 to 2008 Q1								
	(1)	(2)	(3)	(4)	(5)	(6)	(7)	(8)	(9)
Foreign bank asset share 2005	0.154**	0.174**	0.168*	0.179***	0.183***	0.180**	0.173**	0.183**	0.151**
	[0.063]	[0.075]	[0.092]	[0.066]	[0.069]	[0.076]	[0.069]	[0.073]	[0.065]
Real GDP growth 1999–04	3.653***	3.675***	3.439***	3.715***	4.133***	3.315***	2.731**	3.766***	3.686***
	[0.899]	[1.053]	[1.068]	[0.917]	[0.895]	[1.054]	[1.267]	[1]	[0.981]
EU dummy	17.718***	19.110***	21.235***	18.837***	18.724***	21.472***	16.983**	19.018***	18.725***
	[5.414]	[5.702]	[6.769]	[5.388]	[5.453]	[6.368]	[7.161]	[5.89]	[5.248]
Sub-Saharan Africa dummy	−7.977**	−8.515**	−6.014	−10.271***	−8.224**	−10.427**	−11.146**	−7.462*	−8.752*
	[3.234]	[3.834]	[4.857]	[3.612]	[3.553]	[4.449]	[4.599]	[3.871]	[4.627]
Bank activity restriction	−1.838*								−2.424**
	[0.996]								[1.18]
Independence of authority		0.895							
		[2.159]							
Supervisory power			−0.887						
			[0.962]						
Strength of external audit				1.829					
				[1.74]					
Financial statement transparency					2.315				
					[1.97]				
Limit on foreign banks' Operation						1.273			
						[2.786]			

(continued)

Table 2.6 (continued)

Variable	(1)	(2)	(3)	(4)	(5)	(6)	(7)	(8)	(9)
	The dependent variable: cumulative net changes in cross-border bank liabilities from 2004 Q2 to 2008 Q1								
Capital regulatory stringency							1.7		
							[1.44]		
Government bank ownership								−0.195	
								[0.073]	
Bank capital to total assets									1.227
									[0.792]
Constant	−0.611	−17.141***	−23.108	−26.128**	−27.754**	−17.852	−19.167	−16.101	−0.683
	[8.853]	[6.094]	[12.793]	[12.618]	[12.785]	[12.697]	[11.986]	[6.071]	[13.483]
Observations	85	78	61	88	82	63	41	77	67
Adjusted R^2	0.406	0.395	0.36	0.398	0.417	0.388	0.373	0.388	0.417

Note The dependent variable in all the regressions is the cumulative changes in net cross-border bank-to-bank liabilities of individual countries from 2004 Q2 to 2008 Q1 relative to its nominal GDP in current US dollar in 2004. Foreign banks' asset share 2005 is the ratio of foreign banks' assets to total bank assets in 2005, from Claessens and Van Horen [17]. Average real GDP growth rates between 1999 and 2004 are calculated from the real GDP index of *International Financial Statistics* (IMF). The EU dummy takes the value of 1 if the country observation has joined EU until the end of 2007 and 0 otherwise. The indexes for strictness of banking regulation, from "bank activity restrictions" to "government bank ownership" are taken from Barth et al. [4]. Bank capital to total assets is from World Bank's *Global Financial Development Database*. ***, **, and * indicate that the estimated coefficient is statistically significant in 1%, 5%, and 10%, respectively. The robust standard errors are in parenthesis

In sum, regulatory arbitrage was weakly detected in cross-border bank-to-bank lending during the period of global liquidity expansion in the mid-2000s. Note also that in Table 2.6, the coefficients for ex-ante foreign banks' asset share and real GDP growth rate are both significant and positive again in all regressions.

2.5 Robustness Checks

In this section, let us explain the results of several robustness tests. First, we check whether the regression models above are too parsimonious in selecting control variables. Second, we will examine whether the positive effect of ex-ante foreign banks' penetration rate can be found if we use foreign banks' number share instead of foreign banks' asset share as a proxy for foreign banks' penetration rate. Third, the results above are driven by cross-border bank flows after the BNP Paribas shock in summer of 2007. Fourth, we test robustness by excluding outliers from the sample. Finally, we will run regressions on the subsample of non-OECD countries.

Other controls

Because the regression analysis above might be too parsimonious, we check some other plausible independent variables. We test the following control variables which are supposed to have an effect on cross-border bank-to-bank flows as described in Sect. 2.3.1; CPI inflation rate, real effective exchange rate appreciation, stock market capitalization, domestic credit to private sector, bank's regulatory capital to risk-weighted asset ratio, bank's total capital to total asset ratio, non-performing loans to total loans ratio, top five banks' concentration rate, bank's credit to deposit ratio, and the regulatory quality index from World Bank's *Worldwide Governance Indicators.*

As shown in columns (1) and (2), in line with our conjecture, the coefficient for ex-ante inflation rate is negative and that for the real exchange rates is positive, but both of them are statistically insignificant contrary to the existing literature [9, 6, respectively]. This may imply that while inflation rate and exchange rate have effects on quarterly changes in cross-border bank flows, both do not have any explanatory power on the large cross-country variability of medium-term cross-border bank inflows in the mid-2000s.

None of other control variables tested in Table 2.7, except bank capital to total asset ratio, have a statistically significant effect. Positive and significant coefficient for bank capital to total assets is consistent with the view that cross-border bank credit flows more into more stable banking system in which banks on average hold a larger buffer to loss.

Coefficients for ex-ante foreign banks' asset share, real GDP growth rate, and the EU dummy are all positive and significant again in all regressions in Table 2.7, while coefficients for the Sub-Sahara Africa dummy are negative and significant again. Note that these results are robust to changes in sample size because numbers of observation are smaller in some of the regressions in Table 2.7 due to data availability

Table 2.7 Effect of other control variables

Variables	The dependent variable: cumulative net changes in cross-border bank liabilities from 2004 Q2 to 2008 Q1									
	(1)	(2)	(3)	(4)	(5)	(6)	(7)	(8)	(9)	(10)
Foreign bank asset share 2005	0.163^{**}	0.147^{**}	0.198^{***}	0.155^{**}	0.210^{**}	0.149^{**}	0.178^{**}	0.226^{***}	0.162^{**}	0.152^{**}
	[0.064]	[0.066]	[0.073]	[0.065]	[0.086]	[0.07]	[0.077]	[0.076]	[0.066]	[0.063]
Real GDP growth 99–04	3.454^{***}	2.837^{**}	3.707^{***}	3.159^{***}	4.298^{***}	3.367^{***}	3.767^{***}	3.750^{***}	3.135^{***}	3.169^{***}
	[0.936]	[1.076]	[0.959]	[0.825]	[1.062]	[0.927]	[1.184]	[0.955]	[0.821]	[0.813]
EU dummy	20.403^{***}	16.102^{**}	19.101^{***}	19.867^{***}	17.220^{***}	21.598^{***}	17.798^{***}	19.653^{***}	19.286^{***}	19.442^{***}
	[5.638]	[6.918]	[5.607]	[5.765]	[5.463]	[5.372]	[5.854]	[5.577]	[5.881]	[6.384]
S–S Africa dummy	-7.165^{**}	-5.913	-9.330^{**}	-8.697^{***}	-14.658^{**}	-13.635^{***}	-14.304^{**}	-11.561^{***}	-8.664^{***}	-8.494^{***}
	[3.139]	[4.127]	[3.956]	[3.023]	[3.595]	[6.378]	[6.072]	[4.11]	[3.137]	[3.131]
CPI inflation 1999–04	-0.029									
	[0.038]									
REER appreciation		0.02								
		[1.632]								
Stock mkt capitalization			-0.003							
			[0.042]							
Domestic. credit to private sector				0.004						
				[0.037]						
Regulatory capital to risk asset					-0.861					
					[0.542]					
Bank capital to total asset						1.307^{*}				

(continued)

Table 2.7 (continued)

Variables	The dependent variable: cumulative net changes in cross-border bank liabilities from 2004 Q2 to 2008 Q1									
	(1)	(2)	(3)	(4)	(5)	(6)	(7)	(8)	(9)	(10)
						[0.781]				
Non-performing loan							−0.355			
							[0.271]			
5 banks' concentration								−0.109		
								[0.106]		
Loans to deposit									0.015	
									[0.025]	
Regulatory quality 2004										0.456
										[2.305]
Constant	−14.452**	−10.727**	−15.471***	−12.900**	−4.372	−24.447**	−11.585*	−8.187	−14.245**	−12.699**
	[5.724]	[6.371]	[5.777]	[5.494]	[7.478]	[10.109]	[6.205]	[7.463]	[6.344]	[5.022]
Observations	91	62	79	97	73	72	72	86	96	97
Adjusted R^2	0.374	0.229	0.384	0.37	0.386	0.387	0.37	0.409	0.368	0.37

Note The dependent variable in all the regressions is the cumulative changes in net cross-border bank-to-bank liabilities of individual countries from 2004 Q2 to 2008 Q1 relative to its nominal GDP in current US dollar in 2004. Foreign banks' asset share 2005 is the ratio of foreign banks' assets to total bank assets in 2005, from Claessens and Van Horen [17]. Average real GDP growth rates between 1999 and 2004 are calculated from the real GDP index of *International Financial Statistics* (IMF). The EU dummy takes the value of 1 if the country observation has joined EU until the end of 2007 and 0 otherwise. The other macroeconomic and banking system variables are 5-year average over the period from 2000 to 2004 and taken from IMF's or the World Bank's databases. ***, **, and * indicate that the estimated coefficient is statistically significant in 1%, 5%, and 10%, respectively. The robust standard errors are in parenthesis

2 Destination of Global Liquidity Before the Global Financial Crisis ... 51

on the additional variables. Summing up Table 2.5 to Table 2.7, the estimated result of our baseline regression (column (1) in Table 2.5) is remarkably robust by adding various other control variables covering other macroeconomic, banking system, and regulatory conditions.

In addition, overall restrictions on the banking activity index have a significant negative effect on the net cross-border bank-to-bank inflows from 2004 Q2 to 2008 Q1, because we keep getting a negative and significant coefficient whenever we add overall restrictions on banking activity index as well as bank capital to total loans to the control variables (see column (9) in Table 2.6). This suggests that regulatory arbitrage has (weakly) transpired in cross-border bank-to-bank flows over 5 years in the mid-2000s.

Foreign banks' asset share versus foreign banks' number share

Table 2.8 shows the results of the regressions on foreign banks' number share in place of foreign banks' asset share. In the first three regressions the coefficients for foreign bank' number share at 2004 are significant, but the levels of statistical significance are lower (10%) and the fit of the models is worse (or adjusted R-squared is lower) than the corresponding regressions in Tables 2.4 and 2.5. In the other five regressions in Table 2.8, coefficients on foreign banks' number share are not significant. These results imply the number of foreign banks as a fraction of the number of total banks is inferior to the share of foreign banks' assets as a fraction of total bank assets as an indicator of foreign bank penetration rate, as discussed above. Even though foreign banks' number share is high, the local branches of foreign banks may not have incentives to increase cross-border internal funding by a substantial amount because they cannot find many borrowers to whom they can extend loans if they have only a small share in the total bank assets in the banking system.

Repeatedly, the robustness of the other estimated coefficients is confirmed in Table 2.8. Real GDP growth rate in 5 years before 2004 consistently has a statistically significant and positive effect in the all regressions. The coefficients for the law and order index and capital openness index in 2004 are significant in a regression without regional dummies (column (1)), but turn out to be insignificant once we add the EU and Sub-Saharan Africa dummies as controls (columns (3), and (6) to (8)). The coefficient for the EU dummy is consistently positive and significant, while that for Sub-Saharan Africa dummy are always negative and significant except the regressions including macroeconomic variables. Coefficients for other macroeconomic and banking system variables are not significant at all again.

Cross-border bank flows until the BNP Paribas shock

The surge in global liquidity in the mid-2000s, or quarterly increases in cross-border bank claims on banks around the globe, has peaked out on the third quarter of 2007 (Fig. 2.1). The suspension of three investment funds related with BNB Paribas bank in August 2007 was supposed to be the turning point. Table 2.9 shows the results of regressions on cumulative changes in cross-border bank liabilities from 2004 Q2 to

Table 2.8 Effect of foreign banks' number share

Variables	The dependent variable: cumulative net changes in cross-border bank liabilities from 2004 Q2 to 2008 Q1							
	(1)	(2)	(3)	(4)	(5)	(6)	(7)	(8)
Foreign bank number share 2004	0.114*	0.111*	0.108*	0.07	0.088	0.047	0.082	0.033
	[0.061]	[0.062]	[0.058]	[0.056]	[0.07]	[0.056]	[0.068]	[0.06]
Real GDP growth 1999–04	3.138***	3.183***	3.313***	2.626***	2.943***	2.505***	2.977***	2.297**
	[1.134]	[0.868]	[1.015]	[0.798]	[0.844]	[0.92]	[1.013]	[0.936]
EU dummy		20.833***	19.841***	20.262***	22.031***	18.346***	19.564***	17.759***
		[5.866]	[6.157]	[7.187]	[5.926]	[6.796]	[6.013]	[6.669]
Sub-Saharan Africa dummy		−6.767**	−5.724***	−3.668	−8.800***	−1.464	−7.285***	−2.72
		[2.649]	[2.618]	[3.147]	[2.857]	[3.654]	[2.851]	[4.152]
Law and order 2004	2.415**		−0.049			1.651	1.254	2.095
	[1.072]		[1.186]			[1.318]	[1.33]	[1.447]
Capital openness 2004	3.167**		0.913			1.862	1.267	1.955
	[1.569]		[1.156]			[1.27]	[1.209]	[1.316]
Trade openness 2000–04				0.022		0.025		0.042
				[0.058]		[0.059]		[0.061]
Population growth 2000–04				−2.241		−2.219		−1.735
				[1.748]		[1.793]		[1.903]
GDP per capita 2000–04				−0.195		−0.417		−0.328
				[0.243]		[0.311]		[0.326]
ROE 2000–04					0.006		−0.021	−0.014
					[0.131]		[0.129]	[0.11]

(continued)

Table 2.8 (continued)

Variables	The dependent variable: cumulative net changes in cross-border bank liabilities from 2004 Q2 to 2008 Q1							
	(1)	(2)	(3)	(4)	(5)	(6)	(7)	(8)
Net interest margin 2000–04					0.045		0.09	−0.3
					[0.586]		[0.562]	[0.618]
Bank assets per GDP 2000–04					−0.06		−0.088	−0.078
					[0.065]		[0.077]	[0.071]
Constant	−25.625***	−11.877**	−14.549**	−5.791	−6.944	−13.881**	−12.957	−10.742
	[7.673]	[5.456]	[5.785]	[5.649]	[8.598]	[6.306]	[7.881]	[7.511]
Observations	97	97	97	97	97	97	97	97
Adjusted R^2	0.181	0.337	0.325	0.332	0.328	0.335	0.325	0.322

Note The dependent variable in all the regressions is the cumulative changes in net cross-border bank-to-bank liabilities of individual countries from 2004 Q2 to 2008 Q1 relative to its nominal GDP in current US dollar in 2004. Foreign banks' number share 2004 is the ratio of the number of foreign banks to total banks in 2004, from Claessens and Van Horen [17]. Average real GDP growth rates between 1999 and 2004 are calculated from the real GDP index of *International Financial Statistics* (IMF). The EU dummy takes the value of 1 if the country observation has joined EU until the end of 2007 and 0 otherwise. Law and order is the sub-index of ICRG political risk index compiled by the Political Risk Services (PRS) Group. Capital openness is the updated version of Chinn-Ito index from Chinn and Ito (2006). The other macroeconomic and banking system variables are 5-year average over the period from 2000 to 2004 and taken from the World Bank's databases. ***, **, and * indicate that the estimated coefficient is statistically significant in 1%, 5%, and 10%, respectively. The robust standard errors are in parenthesis

Table 2.9 Regressions on cumulative bank credit inflows through 2007 Q3

Variables	The dependent variable: cumulative net changes in cross-border bank liabilities from 2004 Q2 to 2007 Q3								
	(1)	(2)	(3)	(4)	(5)	(6)	(7)	(8)	(9)
Foreign bank asset share 2005	0.111**	0.132**	0.127**	0.114*	0.118**	0.097	0.107*	0.132**	0.132**
	[0.054]	[0.056]	[0.054]	[0.06]	[0.059]	[0.062]	[0.059]	[0.066]	[0.061]
Real GDP growth 99–04	2.388**	2.394***	2.487***	2.199***	2.218***	2.176**	2.246**	2.575***	2.818***
	[0.931]	[0.736]	[0.848]	[0.747]	[0.735]	[0.861]	[0.876]	[0.827]	[0.883]
EU dummy		14.485***	13.833**	13.187**	15.146***	12.076*	13.506**	15.594***	12.887***
		[5.042]	[5.496]	[6.527]	[5.216]	[6.22]	[5.61]	[5.184]	[4.984]
S-Sahara Africa dummy		−7.308**	−6.489***	−4.243	−8.649***	−2.425	−7.397***	−11.307**	−7.479*
		[2.824]	[2.723]	[3.359]	[2.717]	[3.777]	[2.631]	[5.627]	[4.093]
Law and order 2004	1.723		−0.058			0.58	0.82		
	[1.044]		[1.247]			[1.238]	[1.421]		
Capital openness 2004	2.503**		0.646			1.214	0.966		
	[1.24]		[0.948]			[1.11]	[1.011]		
Trade openness 2000–04				−0.013		−0.011			
				[0.043]		[0.044]			
Population growth 2000–04				−2.078		−2.268			
				[1.481]		[1.559]			
GDP per capita 2000–04				−0.06		−0.171			
				[0.249]		[0.315]			
ROE 2000–04					0.018		0.002		
					[0.111]		[0.109]		

(continued)

Table 2.9 (continued)

Variables	The dependent variable: cumulative net changes in cross-border bank liabilities from 2004 Q2 to 2007 Q3								
	(1)	(2)	(3)	(4)	(5)	(6)	(7)	(8)	(9)
Net interest margin 2000–04					−0.071		−0.047		
					[0.565]		[0.535]		
Bank assets per GDP 2000–04					−0.044		−0.066		
					[0.05]		[0.063]		
Overall restrictions on bank activity									−2.369**
									[1.16]
Bank capital to total asset 2000–04								1.062*	1.023
								[0.632]	[0.634]
Constant	−20.173***	−9.847**	−11.580**	−4.714	−5.987	−8.471	−9.931	−19.429	−2.31
	[6.794]	[4.695]	[5.414]	[5.292]	[7.044]	[5.611]	[6.188]	[8.786]	[12.916]
Observations	97	97	97	97	97	97	97	72	67
Adjusted R^2	0.176	0.295	0.282	0.283	0.38	0.274	0.272	0.302	0.342

Note The dependent variable in all the regressions is the cumulative changes in net cross-border bank-to-bank liabilities of individual countries from 2004 Q2 to 2008 Q1 relative to its nominal GDP in current US dollar in 2004. Foreign banks' asset share 2005 is the ratio of foreign banks' assets to total bank assets in 2005, from Claessens and Van Horen [17]. Average real GDP growth rates between 1999 and 2004 are calculated from the real GDP index of *International Financial Statistics* (IMF). The EU dummy takes the value of 1 if the country observation has joined EU until the end of 2007 and 0 otherwise. Law and order is the sub-index of ICRG political risk index compiled by the Political Risk Services (PRS) Group. Capital openness is the updated version of Chinn-Ito index from Chinn and Ito [15]. The other macroeconomic and banking system variables are 5-year average over the period from 2000 to 2004 and taken from the World Bank's databases. The overall restrictions on bank activity index is from Barth et al. [4]. ***, **, and * indicate that the estimated coefficient is statistically significant in 1%, 5%, and 10%, respectively. The robust standard errors are in parenthesis

2007 Q3. The results are robust to those of the corresponding regressions of column (1) in Table 2.4 and columns (1) to (7) in Table 2.5. Note that the absolute values of the estimated coefficients in Table 2.9 are smaller than those in Tables 2.4 and 2.5 because the dependent variable is the *cumulative* net changes in cross-border bank liabilities during a shorter period and thus smaller than the baseline regressions. We also found cross-border bank-to-bank credit flowed into more stable banking systems, where banks keep larger capital to asset ratios (column (8)), as well as into less-regulated banking systems consistent with regulatory arbitrage (column (9)).

In sum, our baseline empirical results are not qualitatively affected by developments in cross-border bank credit flows after the BNP Paribas shock.

Outliers: Estonia and Latvia

In our sample, Estonia and Latvia are two outliers in terms of the size of cumulative net changes in cross-border bank liabilities during 2004 Q2 and 2008 Q1 as a percentage of GDP in 2004. The cumulative net changes per 2004 GDP of Estonia and Latvia are 0.997 and 0.929, respectively, much higher than the rest of the sample average 0.087 (standard deviation is 0.203). In addition, the shares of foreign banks' assets to total bank assets in 2005 in these countries are large (1.00 in Estonia and 0.58 in Latvia). These facts imply that the baseline results of positive effect of ex-ante foreign bank penetration on the global liquidity inflows during its boom before 2008 might be driven by these two countries' data.

Table 2.10 shows the results of regressions where Estonia and Latvia are dropped from the sample. In the regression without regional dummies, as shown in column (1), coefficients for foreign banks' asset share are positive, but not significant, suggesting the two outliers might have a non-negligible effect on the estimation results in Table 2.4. However, once we add regional dummies as controls, the coefficients for foreign banks' asset share has a significance as in Table 2.5 in most of the regressions in columns (2) to (9). Note that the value of the coefficient for foreign banks' asset share is much smaller in Table 2.10 than in Tables 2.4 and 2.5 because the outliers of net bank credit inflows are omitted from the sample. The main results in the previous section are qualitatively unchanged and robust if we exclude Estonia and Latvia from our sample.

Non-OECD countries

Finally, we will run the key regressions above for a smaller sample of 76 non-OECD countries. Table 2.11 shows the estimated results. The coefficient for foreign banks' asset share is positive but not significant except for column (1) where only ex-ante real GDP growth rate, and institutional and capital openness indexes are included as control variables. However, once the EU and Sub-Saharan Africa dummies are added in the controls, the coefficient for foreign banks' asset share becomes much smaller in its size and turns to be insignificant. This result suggests that the degree of foreign banks' penetration primarily affected OECD countries by accelerating global liquidity inflows during its boom.

2 Destination of Global Liquidity Before the Global Financial Crisis …

Table 2.10 Removing outliers' effect: excluding Estonia and Latvia

Variables	The dependent variable: cumulative net changes in cross-border bank liabilities from 2004 Q2 to 2008 Q1								
	(1)	(2)	(3)	(4)	(5)	(6)	(7)	(8)	(9)
Foreign bank asset share 2005	0.071	0.094**	0.098**	0.084*	0.088*	0.079	0.085	0.100*	0.086
	[0.046]	[0.046]	[0.046]	[0.049]	[0.053]	[0.051]	[0.055]	[0.066]	[0.056]
Real GDP growth 99–04	1.896***	2.247***	2.143***	2.703***	2.221***	1.869***	2.050***	2.649***	2.404***
	[0.664]	[0.574]	[0.591]	[0.628]	[0.619]	[0.631]	[0.659]	[0.645]	[0.68]
EU dummy		14.461***	13.955***	14.426**	15.468***	14.060**	14.164***	13.585***	16.212***
		[4.705]	[5.092]	[6.165]	[4.817]	[5.956]	[5.087]	[4.906]	[4.491]
S–S Africa dummy		−7.123***	−7.228***	−6.622**	−7.694***	−6.414**	−7.535***	−6.747**	−10.242**
		[2.508]	[2.783]	[3.066]	[2.323]	[3.252]	[2.34]	[2.683]	[4.84]
Law and order 2004	2.540***		0.71			1.486	1.555		
	[0.914]		[0.973]			[1.029]	[1.114]		
Capital openness 2004	1.316		−0.426			0.009	−0.162		
	[0.983]		[0.803]			[0.743]	[0.776]		
Trade openness 2000–04				0.016		0.015			
				[0.055]		[0.057]			
Population growth 2000–04				−0.64		−0.21			
				[1.382]		[1.428]			
GDP per capita 2000–04				−0.064		−0.177			
				[0.224]		[0.282]			
ROE 2000–04					−0.06		−0.077		
					[0.117]		[0.117]		

(continued)

Table 2.10 (continued)

Variables	The dependent variable: cumulative net changes in cross-border bank liabilities from 2004 Q2 to 2008 Q1								
	(1)	(2)	(3)	(4)	(5)	(6)	(7)	(8)	(9)
Net interest margin 2000–04					0.255		0.335		
					[0.538]		[0.524]		
Bank assets per GDP 2000–04					−0.02		−0.041		
					[0.057]		[0.068]		
Overall restrictions on bank activity								−0.858	
								[0.829]	
Bank capital to total asset									1.117
									[0.696]
Constant	−15.753***	−6.915**	−11.580**	−6.188	−6.019	−9.797*	−9.393	−1.99	−16.786*
	[4.132]	[3.615]	[5.414]	[4.762]	[6.852]	[5.119]	[6.254]	[8.702]	[8.5]
Observations	95	95	95	95	95	95	95	83	70
Adjusted R^2	0.127	0.275	0.282	0.254	0.258	0.244	0.252	0.28	0.274

Note The dependent variable in all the regressions is the cumulative changes in net cross-border bank-to-bank liabilities of individual countries from 2004 Q2 to 2008 Q1 relative to its nominal GDP in current US dollar in 2004. Foreign banks' asset share 2005 is the ratio of foreign banks' assets to total bank assets in 2005, from Claessens and Van Horen [17]. Average real GDP growth rates between 1999 and 2004 are calculated from the real GDP index of *International Financial Statistics* (IMF). The EU dummy takes the value of 1 if the country observation has joined EU until the end of 2007 and 0 otherwise. Law and order is the sub-index of ICRG political risk index compiled by the Political Risk Services (PRS) Group. Capital openness is the updated version of Chinn-Ito index from Chinn and Ito [15]. The other macroeconomic and banking system variables are 5-year average over the period from 2000 to 2004 and taken from the World Bank's databases. The overall restrictions on bank activity index is from Barth et al. [4]. ***, **, and * indicate that the estimated coefficient is statistically significant in 1%, 5%, and 10%, respectively. The robust standard errors are in parenthesis

Table 2.11 Estimation results on non-OECD samples

Variables	The dependent variable: cumulative net changes in cross-border bank liabilities from 2004 Q2 to 2008 Q1							
	(1)	(2)	(3)	(4)	(5)	(6)	(7)	(8)
Foreign bank asset share 2005	0.117*	0.041	0.024	0.064	0.026	0.032	0.047	0.015
	[0.066]	[0.056]	[0.055]	[0.057]	[0.05]	[0.054]	[0.067]	[0.074]
Real GDP growth 1999–2004	2.184**	2.132**	1.910***	2.233***	2.251***	2.525***	2.814***	2.930***
	[1.079]	[0.829]	[0.703]	[0.732]	[0.81]	[0.708]	[0.9]	[0.874]
EU dummy		30.676***	28.462***	33.264***	30.620***	30.112***	30.982***	30.367***
		[8.15]	[8.848]	[8.27]	[8.094]	[7.494]	[8.481]	[7.706]
S–S Africa dummy		−3.739	−0.043	−5.928**	−1.953	−5.016*	−6.502	−6.135**
		[2.922]	[3.394]	[2.257]	[2.691]	[2.653]	[4.572]	[2.843]
Law and order 2004	4.566***	1.622			0.639			
	[1.544]	[1.099]			[1.099]			
Capital openness 2004	3.187**	1.505			1.214			
	[1.534]	[1.088]			[1.077]			
Trade openness 2000–04			0.035					
			[0.025]					
Population growth 2000–04			−1.977					
			[1.49]					
GDP per capita 2000–04			0.736***		0.734**	0.503	0.836**	0.477
			[0.221]		[0.356]	[0.368]	[0.352]	[0.411]
ROE 2000–04				0.071				
				[0.099]				

(continued)

Table 2.11 (continued)

Variables	The dependent variable: cumulative net changes in cross-border bank liabilities from 2004 Q2 to 2008 Q1							
	(1)	(2)	(3)	(4)	(5)	(6)	(7)	(8)
Net interest margin 2000–04				0.119				
				[0.785]				
Bank assets per GDP 2000–04				0.051				
				[0.056]				
Overall restrictions on bank activity						-2.626^{**}		-3.058^{**}
						[1.23]		[1.497]
Bank capital to total asset							0.663	0.292
							[0.626]	[0.576]
Constant	-27.661^{***}	-13.692^{**}	-6.229	-9.952	-12.474^{**}	12.592^{**}	-17.030^{*}	12.027
	[8.613]	[5.199]	[5.89]	[6.308]	[4.857]	[9.579]	[9.136]	[14.662]
Observations	76	76	76	76	76	64	52	47
Adjusted R^2	0.302	0.585	0.606	0.567	0.601	0.652	0.577	0.627

Note The dependent variable in all the regressions is the cumulative changes in net cross-border bank-to-bank liabilities of individual countries from 2004 Q2 to 2008 Q1 relative to its nominal GDP in current US dollar in 2004. Foreign banks' asset share 2005 is the ratio of foreign banks' assets to total bank assets in 2005, from Claessens and Van Horen [17]. Average real GDP growth rates between 1999 and 2004 are calculated from the real GDP index of *International Financial Statistics* (IMF). The EU dummy takes the value of 1 if the country of observation has joined EU until the end of 2007 and 0 otherwise. Law and order is the sub-index of ICRG political risk index compiled by the Political Risk Services (PRS) Group. Capital openness is the updated version of Chinn-Ito index from Chinn and Ito [15]. The other macroeconomic and banking system variables are 5-year average over the period from 2000 to 2004 and taken from the World Bank's databases. The overall restrictions on bank activity index is from Barth et al. [4]. ***, **, and * indicate that the estimated coefficient is statistically significant in 1%, 5%, and 10%, respectively. The robust standard errors are in parenthesis

The coefficient for the EU dummy is consistently positive and significant, and much larger in value, around 30, than the correspondent coefficients in the regressions on full sample, around 20 (Tables (5) to (8)). Thus, the EU bias in the direction of global liquidity is not driven by more developed countries in the EU. This result is also consistent with the "collateral effects" of political integration in new member countries of the EU [27]. The entry to the EU of Central and Eastern European economies were regarded as collaterals by banks in the old EU-member countries, which massively increased cross-border credit to the new member states of the EU.

As shown in column (1), among emerging and developing economies, countries with more developed institution and those who are more open to capital transactions seemed to have accepted larger inflows of cross-border bank-to-bank credit in the mid-2000s. However, the significance of the coefficients for the law and order index and Chinn-Ito index disappears again once regional dummies are included in the independent variables (columns (2) and (5)).

We also test whether other selected control variables have a significant effect. Interestingly, the "allocation puzzle" among developing economies [24] seems to present in the global liquidity flows in the mid-2000s. The coefficient for ex-ante GDP per capita is positive and significant at 1% level (column (3)), and the coefficient remains significant even if the institution and capital openness indexes are added as controls (column (5)). Though the neoclassical growth theory predicts that capital flows from countries with lower marginal rate of return on capital to countries with higher marginal rate of return on capital, Gourinchas and Jeane [24] found the inverse holds among developing countries and named the phenomenon the "allocation puzzle." The positive coefficient for GDP per capita in columns (3) and (5) implies that cross-border bank flows tended to flow in the medium run to more developed economies, or economies with lower marginal rate of capital, among emerging and developing countries in the mid-2000s, consistent with the allocation puzzle.

Quite remarkably, regulatory arbitrage might solve this allocation puzzle. As shown in columns (6) and (8), the significant effect of GDP per capita disappears once we add overall restrictions on bank activity index to the set of control variables. The strictness of overall restrictions on bank activity has a negative effect on cross-border bank inflows, suggesting that regulatory arbitrage functioned among emerging and developing economies during the global liquidity surge period. R-squared also improves a lot in these regressions. Though we cannot reject the possibility that this result is driven by the effect of a smaller sample, it might be fruitful to explore the relation between the allocation puzzle and regulatory arbitrage.

2.6 Conclusions

This chapter explores the major factors determining the destination of global liquidity flows during the period preceding the GFC. Our empirical findings from the cross-sectional analysis are threefold. First, during the global liquidity surge period, global liquidity flooded more into countries whose banking systems had already been penetrated by foreign banks. This empirical finding is consistent with our conjecture that because information asymmetry between lenders and borrowers is much larger for cross-border lending, banks prefer to extend cross-border credit to borrowers in countries where the banks have established their affiliates or branches. Those affiliates have had a good record of lending in the local markets. In addition, this finding is consistent with the "flight abroad effect" in the international syndicated loan market [23] and with the massive utilization of internal cross-border funding by parent banks of global banking groups during the GFC [13, 14].

Second, the destinations of global liquidity during the mid-2000s are unevenly distributed in a specific region; EU member states, including new entrants between 2004 and 2007, were the main receivers of global liquidity, while Sub-Saharan Africa received the least global liquidity. This finding suggests that the expression of "global" liquidity might be misleading. The easiness for banks to fund money across borders during the period preceding the GFC was pervasive not globally but regionally among EU member states; thus, it might be appropriate to call it "regional" liquidity. This result is not driven by developed countries because it is robust to a smaller sample restricted to non-OECD countries.

Third, we detected weak evidence that regulatory arbitrage between banking systems occurred on cross-border bank-to-bank flows during the global liquidity surge period. Our empirical result on the non-OECD sample suggests that the existence of regulatory arbitrage might be a key factor in solving the "allocation puzzle" concerning capital flows among emerging and developing economies.

In addition, we also found that the real GDP growth rate in the five years preceding the global liquidity surge period is consistent and the most significant covariate with inflows of global liquidity. Suppose we can see the preceding five-year average of real GDP growth rate as investors' expectations of the real GDP growth rate in the following five years or more. This result implies that global liquidity flows into countries with higher output growth prospects as simple intertemporal-endowment-economy open macro models predict.

Appendix

See Table 2.12 and Fig. 2.5.

2 Destination of Global Liquidity Before the Global Financial Crisis … 63

Table 2.12 Data sources

Data	Sources and notes
Net change in cross-border credit from banks in country i to banks in country j	BIS' *Locational Banking Statistics*
Share of foreign banks' assets to total bank assets	Claessens and Van Horen [17]
Share of foreign banks to total banks	
Real GDP index	IMF's *International Financial Statistics*
Capital openness index	Chinn-Ito index from Chinn and Ito [15]
Law and order index	ICRG political risk index of the Political Risk Services Group
CPI Inflation rate	IMF's *International Financial Statistics*
Trade openness	World Bank's *World Development Indicators* Sum of exports and imports as a fraction of GDP
Population growth rate (percent)	World Bank's *World Development Indicators*
GDP per capita (at current US dollars)	
Stock market capitalization (percent of GDP)	
Domestic credit to private sectors (percent of GDP)	
Return on equity (ROE, percent)	World Bank's *Global Financial Development Database*
Net interest margin (percent)	
Bank assets per GDP (percent)	World Bank's *Global Financial Development Database* Depository banks' assets per GDP
Bank's regulatory capital to risk asset (percent)	World Bank's *Global Financial Development Database*
Bank capital to total asset (percent)	
Non-performing loan ratio to total loan (percent)	
Five banks' concentration	
Loans to deposit ratio	
Regulatory quality	World Bank's *Worldwide Governance Indicators*
Political stability	World Bank's *Worldwide Governance Indicators*. "Political Stability and Absence of Violence" series
Corruption	World Bank's *Worldwide Governance Indicators*. "Control of Corruption" series
Overall restrictions on banking activities	Barth et al. [4]. Higher values indicate greater stringency
Independence of supervisory authority	Barth et al. [4] Higher values indicate greater independence
Official supervisory power	Barth et al. [4]. Higher values indicate greater power

(continued)

Table 2.12 (continued)

Data	Sources and notes
Strength of external audit	Barth et al. [4] Higher values indicate better strength of external audit
Financial statement transparency	Barth et al. [4]. Higher values indicate better transparency
Government bank ownership	Barth et al. [4]
Capital regulatory stringency	
Limit on foreign bank operation	Barth et al. [4], limitation on foreign bank entry or ownership. Lower values indicate greater stringency

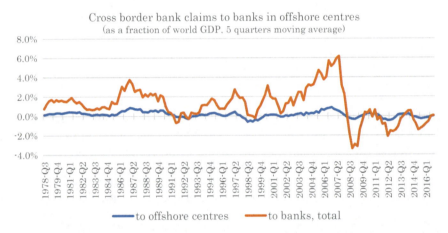

Fig. 2.5 Bank inflows to offshore centres. *Source* Author's calculations using BIS' *Locational Banking Statistics* and IMF's *World Economic Outlook database*

References

1. Alfaro, L., Kalemli-Ozcan, S., & Volosovych, V. (2008). Why doesn't capital flow from rich to poor countries? An empirical investigation. *Review of Economics and Statistics, 90*(2), 347–368.
2. Amiti, M., McGuire, P., & Weinstein, D. E. (2019). International bank flows and the global financial cycle. *IMF Economic Review, 67,* 61–108.
3. Bank for International Settlement. (BIS). (2011). Global liquidity—concept, measurement and policy implications. CGFS Papers, No.45.
4. Barth, J. R., Capri, G., & Levine, R. (2013). Bank regulation and supervision in 180 countries from 1999 to 2011. *Journal of Financial Economic Policy, 5*(2), 111–219. https://doi.org/10.1108/17576381311329661
5. Bremus, F., & Fratzscher, M. (2015). Drivers of structural change in cross-border banking since the global financial crisis. *Journal of International Money and Finance, 52,* 32–59.
6. Bruno, V., & Shin, H. S. (2015). Cross-border banking and global liquidity. *Review of Economic Studies, 82,* 535–564.

2 Destination of Global Liquidity Before the Global Financial Crisis …

7. Cerutti, E. (2015). Drivers of cross-border banking exposures during the crisis. *Journal of Banking & Finance, 55*, 340–357.
8. Cerutti, E., Hale, G., & Minoiu, C. (2015). Financial crises and the composition of cross-border lending. *Journal of International Money and Finance, 52*, 60–81.
9. Cerutti, E., Claessens, S., & Ratnovski, L. (2017). Global liquidity and cross-border bank flows. *Economic Policy*, 81–125.
10. Cerutti, E., & Claessens, S. (2016). The great cross-border bank deleveraging: Supply constraints and intra-group frictions. *Review of Finance*, 201–236.
11. Cetorelli, N., & Goldberg, L. S. (2011). Global Banks and international shock transmission: Evidence from the crisis. *IMF Economic Review, 59*(1), 41–76.
12. Cetorelli, N., & Goldberg, L. S. (2012). Banking globalization and monetary transmission. *Journal of Finance, 111*(5), 1811–1843.
13. Cetorelli, N., & Goldberg, L. S. (2012). Follow the money: Quantifying domestic effects of foreign bank shocks in the great recessions. *American Economic Review Paper and Proceedings, 102*(3), 213–218.
14. Cetorelli, N., & Goldberg, L. S. (2012). Liquidity management of U.S. global banks: Internal capital markets in the great recession. *Journal of International Economics, 88*, 299–311.
15. Chinn, M. D., & Ito, H. (2008). A new measure of financial openness. *Journal of Comparative Policy Analysis, 10*(3), 309–322.
16. Claessens, S., & Van Horen, N. (2014). Foreign banks: Trends and impact. *Journal of Money, Credit, and Banking, 46*(1), 295–326.
17. Claessens, S., & Van Horen, N. (2015). The Impact of the global financial crisis on banking globalization. *IMF Economic Review, 63*(4), 868–918.
18. Claessens, S., Van Horen, N., Gurcanlar, T., & Mercado, J. (2008). Foreign bank presence in developing countries 1995–2006: Data and trends. mimeo.
19. Cull, R., & Pería, M. S. (2013). Bank ownership and lending patterns during the 2008–2009 financial crisis: Evidence from Latin America and Eastern Europe. *Journal of Banking and Finance, 37*(12), 4861–4878.
20. Emter, L., Schmitz, M., & Tirpak, M. (2018). Cross-border banking in the EU since the crisis: What is driving the great retrenchment?. *ECB Working Paper Series*, No. 2130.
21. Forbes, K. J., & Warnock, F. E. (2012). Capital flow waves: Surges, stops, flight, and retrenchment. *Journal of International Economics, 88*, 235–251.
22. Giannetti, M., & Laeven, L. (2012). The flight home effect: Evidence from the syndicated loan market during financial cries. *Journal of Financial Economics, 104*, 23–43.
23. Giannetti, M., & Laeven, L. (2012). The flight abroad effect. *American Economic Review Paper and Proceedings, 102*(3), 219–224.
24. Gourinchas, P.-O., & Jeane, O. (2013). Capital flows to developing countries: The allocation puzzle. *Review of Economics Studies, 80*, 1484–1515.
25. Hahm, J.-H., Shin, H.-S., & Shin, K. (2013). Non-core bank liabilities and financial vulnerabilities. *Journal of Money, Credit, and Banking, 45*(S-1), 3–36.
26. Hale, G., & Obstfeld, M. (2016). The euro and the geography of international debt flows. *Journal of the European Economic Association, 14*(1), 115–144.
27. Hoffmann, A. (2016). The collateral effects of political integration on credit growth in the new member states of the EU. *Economic Systems, 40*, 658–669.
28. Houston, J. F., Lin, C., & Ma, Y. (2012). Regulatory arbitrage and international bank flows. *Journal of Finance, 161*(5), 1845–1895.
29. Judit, T., & Banai, A. (2017). The drivers of foreign bank lending in central and Eastern Europe: The role of parent, subsidiary and host market traits. *Journal of International Money and Finance, 79*, 157–173.
30. Kapan, T., & Minoiu, C. (2014). Liquidity shocks and the supply of credit after the 2007–2008 crisis. *International Journal of Finance and Economics, 19*, 12–23.
31. Kapan, T., & Minoiu, C (2013). Balance sheet strength and bank lending during the global financial crisis. *IMF Working Paper*.

32. Lane, P. R., & McQuade, P. (2014). Domestic credit growth and international capital flows. *The Scandinavian Journal of Economics, 116*(1), 218–252.
33. McGuire, P., & von Peter, G. (2009). The US dollar shortage in the global banking and the international policy response. *BIS Working Paper*, No. 291, October.
34. McGuire, P., & von Peter, G. (March 2016). The resilience of bank's international operations. *BIS Quarterly Review*, 65–78.
35. Okada, K. (2013). The interaction effects of financial openness and institutions on international capital flows. *Journal of Macroeconomics, 35*, 131–143.
36. Papaioanou, E. (2009). What drives international financial flows? Politics, institutions and other determinants. *Journal of Development Economics, 88*, 269–281.
37. Reinhardt, D., & Riddiough, S. J. (2015). The two faces of cross-border banking flows. *IMF Economic Review, 63*(4), 751–791.
38. Shin, H.-S. (2012). Global banking glut and loan risk premium. *IMF Economic Review, 60*, 155–192.
39. Snyder, T. J. (2013). Increasing returns, institutions, and capital flows. *Eastern Economic Journal, 39*, 285–308.

Shingo Iokibe is an associate professor of economics at Doshisha University in Japan. He received his Ph.D. from Kobe University, and his main research interest is international macroeconomics.

Chapter 3
Global Liquidity and Reallocation of Domestic Credit

Kimiko Sugimoto and Masahiro Enya

Abstract This study examines whether receiving sectors and types of capital inflows cause a change in domestic bank credit allocation, between households and nonfinancial corporations (business) using a panel data on quarterly data for 27 economies over 2000–2016. Total capital inflows are classified into four types: portfolio equity investment, portfolio bond investment, bank loans, and foreign direct investment. They proceed to three receiving sectors: public, private banking, and private non-banking business sectors. First, foreign capital flows into the banking sector in advanced economies increase domestic bank credit to business more than to households, but not in emerging economies. Rather, these flows into banks in emerging economies, especially in European countries, increase their credit to households more than to business. Second, for foreign capital flows into the corporate sector in the form of direct investments, the presence of recipient corporations with low demand for funds leads to a decrease in borrowing from domestic banks as alternative investors. Consequently, domestic banks increase their credit to households as alternative borrowers. As global liquidity increases because of quantitative easing measures by major advanced economies during the post-crisis period, capital inflows to the business sector crowd out domestic bank lending to business. Thus, domestic bank credit is reallocated away from lending to business toward lending to households. Meanwhile, it should be noted that credit to households (share of gross domestic product [GDP])

An earlier version of this paper was presented at the workshops of "Risk Management of Global Liquidity" at Kobe University on September 8, 2017, and August 4, 2018. The authors would like to thank Shigeto Kitano, Akira Kohsaka, participants of these workshops, and a discussant Mikhail Klimenko, Yushi Yoshida, Takashi Matsuki, participants of the first International Conference on Risk in Economics and Society at Shiga University on November 18, 2017, and participants of the 16th EAEA International Convention at National Taiwan University in Taipei, and the Singapore Economic Review Conference 2019 on 5–7 August 2019.

K. Sugimoto (✉)
Hirao School of Management, Konan University, Nishinomiya, Japan
e-mail: kimiko@konan-u.ac.jp

M. Enya
Faculty of Economics and Management, Kanazawa University, Kanazawa, Japan
e-mail: enya@staff.kanazawa-u.ac.jp

© The Author(s), under exclusive license to Springer Nature Singapore Pte Ltd. 2022
Y. Matsubayashi and S. Kitano (eds.), *Global Financial Flows in the Pre- and Post-global Crisis Periods*, Kobe University Monograph Series in Social Science Research,
https://doi.org/10.1007/978-981-19-3613-5_3

does not increase provided the GDP grows at the same speed as these credits do. This chain reaction can be observed in both advanced and emerging Asian economies. Third, for foreign capital flows into the corporate sector other than direct investment, recipient corporations increase borrowings from domestic banks, indicating buoyant fund demand. Accordingly, domestic banks do not increase their credit to their households. If any, its credit growth is the same as or less than the GDP growth. Thus, credits to households (share of GDP) are not significantly positive. The positive impact of inflows into the business sector on household credit share reflects the substitution effects between capital inflows into the business sector and bank credit to business. The cross-border effect of global liquidity increased and diversified the fundraising route after the global financial crisis. Therefore, recipient countries have to pay attention to this unintended side effect, that is, domestic credit reallocation.

Keywords Capital inflow · Global liquidity · Domestic credit allocation · Macro-prudential policy · Dynamic panel

3.1 Introduction

This study examines whether foreign capital inflows affect the allocation of domestic bank credit to households and nonfinancial corporations (business). Foreign capital inflows can be the main financial resource for firms in bank loans, portfolio equity, bond investments, and foreign direct investments (FDIs). Global liquidity (i.e., ease of financing in international financial markets) expanded rapidly during the post-Global Financial Crisis period, particularly in emerging countries (Cohen et al. [15], Aldasoro and Ehlers [2]). This trend has allowed firms to use various fundraising methods in addition to borrowing funds from domestic banks or raising funds from domestic equity and bond markets. If foreign capital inflows go to economies with many investment opportunities, more capital inflows can contribute to their economic growth. Kaminsky et al. [21] state that "external borrowing increases in good times and falls in bad times."

However, capital inflows are not always procyclical in the post-crisis period. Blanchard et al. [11] suggest that bond inflows can lead to currency appreciation and contractionary effects on credit. Moreover, foreign capital inflows may substitute for domestic bank lending to business when foreign capital flows into economies with few investment opportunities. In the latter, global liquidity can reallocate domestic bank credit away from lending to business towards households.

Thus, our research questions are as follows: (1) What kind of effect does capital inflow have on households credit (and its share)?; (2) What type of capital inflow affects household credit?; and (3) What are the differences in these effects between developed and emerging Asia, emerging Europe, and Latin America? This study distinguishes between three destinations (capital inflows to the public sector, banks, and corporate sector) and four capital inflow types (FDI, portfolio equity, portfolio bonds, and bank loans). This study hypothesizes capital inflows into the corporate sector positively affect HH (household) credit share as domestic banks may lend more to HHs when corporations finance from abroad than domestically.

Figure 3.1 shows the average credit-to-gross domestic product (GDP) ratios of the advanced 20 countries (see Fig. 3.1a) and nine emerging countries (see Fig. 3.1b). Domestic credits are divided by types of borrowers into three sectors: credits to the government, households, and nonfinancial firms. Both the advanced and emerging groups experienced common structural changes before and after the global financial crisis. As shown by Avdjiev et al. [5], during the post-crisis period, a shift occurred in the composition and drivers of global liquidity, and more globally integrated borrower countries in both advanced and emerging market economies are more easily exposed to financial vulnerabilities. Bezemer and Zhang [9] point that the balance between the growth in mortgage credit and business credit can be a main factor of post-crisis macroeconomic vulnerability.

Figure 3.1a indicates that credits to both firms and households grew in advanced economies until just before the global financial crisis and maintained this level during the post-crisis period. Credit to the government increased substantially in the post-crisis period. These movements suggest that domestic banks' lending attitudes in advanced economies have been becoming negative after the global financial crisis. In emerging countries, Figure 3.1b shows that credit to firms decreased during the pre-crisis period but increased during the post-crisis period. Moreover, emerging countries consistently increased credit to households, irrespective of the crisis. By contrast, advanced economies could not raise bank credit to households in the post-crisis period. Accordingly, this study examines whether domestic bank credit, affected by foreign capital inflows, could be reallocated away from lending to business and toward lending to households.

Beck et al. [7], Mian et al. [22], and Bezemer et al. [8] conclude that a change in domestic credit allocation (i.e., lending less to business and more to households) causes slower economic growth. Jorda et al. [20] find more than two thirds of the increase in credit-to-GDP for 17 advanced countries over 1960–2010 is caused by the increase in lending to households. Moreover, Barba and Pivetti [6], Büyükkarabacak and Valev [12], and Jappelli et al. [19] indicate that an increase in bank lending to households leads to an increase in probability of crises and longer recessions. Existing research warns about the negative macroeconomic impact driven by the reallocation of domestic bank credits. Other studies examined the factors of foreign capital inflows causing an increase in credit to households. Beck et al. [7], Igan and Tan [18], and Enya and Shinkai [16] suggested that the financial structure of the economy, capital type, and borrower type are key factors. Igan and Tan [18] insist that bank loan inflows are positively linked with household credit regardless of financial structure, whereas FDI and portfolio inflows are positively associated with credit to the corporate sector only in a bank-based economy.

Samarina and Bezemer [24] find a change in the allocation of domestic bank credit since the 1990s using dynamic panel data.[1] They recognize the importance

---

[1] Their definition of non-banking sector includes nonfinancial business firms, non-bank (non-deposit-taking corporations) financial firms and households.

(a) Advanced 20 countries

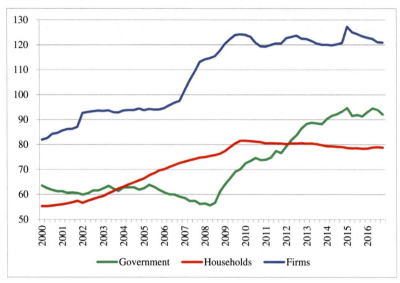

(b) Emerging 9 countries

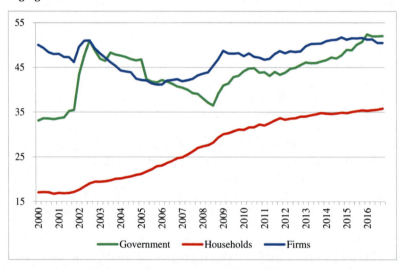

Fig. 3.1 Total credit to government, households, and firms (average credit to GDP (%)). *Note* Advanced 20 economies include, Austria, Australia, Belgium, Canada, Switzerland, Germany, Denmark, Spain, Finland, France, United Kingdom, Greece, Ireland, Italy, Japan, Luxembourg, Netherlands, Norway, Portugal and Sweden. Emerging 9 economies include Korea, Thailand, Argentina, Brazil, Colombia, Mexico, Czech Republic, Hungary and Poland. Total credit is provided by domestic bank, all other sectors of the economy and non-residents. Credit covers loans and debt securities. *Source* BIS long series on total credit updated 6 June 2017

3 Global Liquidity and Reallocation of Domestic Credit   71

of sectoral destinations—banking and non-banking sectors (e.g., firms, households, and the government)—in determining the effects of foreign capital flows on domestic credit allocation. Thus, they use the share of credit to nonfinancial business in all bank credit as a dependent variable, and bank inflows, non-bank inflows, and FDI as independent variables. They revealed that foreign capital inflows into the non-banking sector led to a lower share of lending to the business sector in domestic bank credit. They also suggest that capital inflows into the non-banking sector have a side effect on the credit allocation of domestic banks by crowding out domestic bank loans and call this effect the substitution effect between domestic bank loans and foreign capital. However, they do not have special interest in types of foreign capital. Cerutti and Hong [13] found that capital inflows disaggregated by both types of instrument and borrower are heterogeneity. This study focuses on capital types in addition to sectoral destination of foreign capital.

Figure 3.2a shows the capital flows to the nine emerging countries, divided into three types of capital: portfolio equity investments, portfolio bond investments, and bank loans. Fluctuations in capital inflows differ with the type of capital. Figure 3.2b shows the same flows but divided into three sectoral destinations: public sector, private nonfinancial business sector (firms), and banking sector. Fluctuations in capital inflow to the three sectors remain similar. However, the degree of their decrease directly to the business sector is smaller than that to the banking sector during the post-crisis period. Figure 3.2c shows the composition of the same flows, showing the importance of capital inflows to the business sector as forms of equity investment and foreign bank loans and those to the public sector in the form of bonds. The sudden stop in capital flows during the COVID-19 crisis was faster and more incisive than the Global Financial crisis. Because of the global dollar liquidity shortage, OECD [23] confirmed unprecedented capital outflows from emerging economies during the COVID-19 turmoil, about four times larger than during GFC. We must ensure whether these capital market dynamics are driven by global push factors or domestic pull factors.

Finally, this study considers four types of capital: (1) portfolio equity investments (EI), (2) portfolio bond investments (BI), (3) bank loans (OI), and (4) direct investments (DI). Furthermore, we examine three sectoral directions. (1) banking (Bank), (2) non-financing business (Corp), and (3) public (Public). The remainder of this paper is organized as follows. Section 3.2 introduces the data and analytical framework. Section 3.3 presents the empirical results of the study. Finally, Sect. 3.4 concludes the paper with a discussion of the policy implications.

(a) Types of international capital

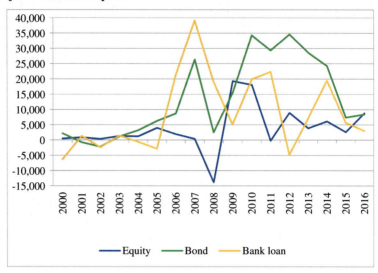

(b) Sectoral destinations of international capital inflows

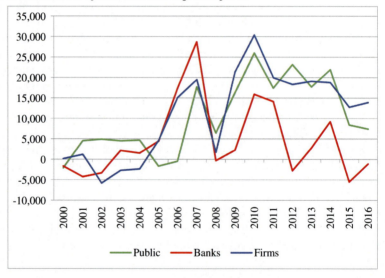

Fig. 3.2 Types and compositions of capital flows to emerging 9 economies in U.S. dollars. *Note* Emerging 9 economies include Korea, Thailand, Argentina, Brazil, Colombia, Mexico, Czech Republic, Hungary and Poland. The annual data is obtained by the annual average of quarterly data. Case 3 is the average value of three periods like before, during and after the global financial crisis. *Source* Balance of Payments statistics by IMF 2017

(c) Composition of international capital inflows

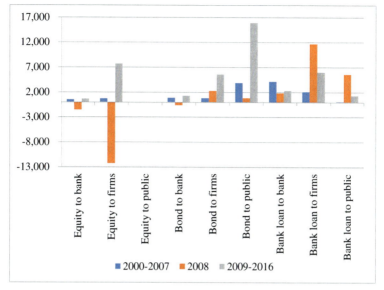

Fig. 3.2 (continued)

3.2 Data and Methodology

3.2.1 Data

This study examines a 2001–2016 quarterly dataset covering 27 countries, which were divided into two groups: 17 advanced and 15 emerging economies (Table 3.5). The selection of sample countries depends on data availability. The important variables in this study are (1) domestic credit to households and (2) foreign capital inflows, classified by capital type and borrower type.

First, data for domestic credits to households were derived from the BIS database. "Total credit to households" and "Bank credit to the private non-financial sector" are available in the BIS database. Total credit is provided not only by domestic banks but also by all other sectors of the economy and non-residents. Credit covers loans and debt securities. Therefore, identifying bank credit to households from credit data in this database is difficult. However, if credit to households provided by all sectors other than domestic banks is negligible, total credit to households can be considered as that provided by domestic banks. Thus, total household credit is assigned to bank credit to households.

While Samarina and Bezemer [24] focus on the share of credit to nonfinancial businesses in total bank credit using data provided by each central bank, this study focuses on the share of credit to households in total bank credit by using total credit to households derived from the BIS data. "Bank credit to the private non-financial sector" in BIS data includes domestic banks' lending to both non-financial corporations and households. Thus, this study focuses on the share of credit to households in the bank credit to the private non-financial sector (*ShareCR_HH*). Table 3.6 gives the names of each variable, details, and sources for all data.

Second, capital inflows classified by capital and borrower type are derived from the IMF balance of payment (BOP) database. The BOP database is first broken down by type of capital inflow and then by type of borrower. While each type of capital inflow can theoretically be disaggregated by borrower type, in practice, sectoral data are sometimes missing. Therefore, this study proceeded with the internal filling exercises by Avdjiev et al. [4]. More concretely, this study fills the missing data for the fourth sector with the value by subtracting three reported sectors from the total when the BOP database reports the total for the category and data for three of the four sectors.

This study focuses on four types of capital inflow and three types of borrowers. Types of capital inflows include direct investment (*DI*), portfolio equity investment (*EI*), portfolio debt investment (bonds, *BI*), and other investment debt (loans, *OI*), and the borrowers consist of the public sector (central bank and general government, *public*), deposit-taking corporations except for the central bank (*bank*), and other sectors (mainly corporations, *Corp*). Moreover, gross total inflows (*TI*) by sector are constructed as the sum of *EI*, *BI*, and *OI* in each sector. Only direct investment data are not available separately by destination type in the BOP database. However, if direct investment flows from nonfinancial firms to financial firms are negligible, all direct investments can be treated as flows to nonfinancial firms (*Corp*). We assume that direct investment inflows are assigned to the FDI inflows to the corporate sector.

This study does not focus on "net" inflows (i.e., the differences between gross inflows and gross outflows) but focuses on "gross" inflows. Data for gross inflows are derived from the gross liability flows in the BOP database. Gross liability flows are interpreted as net inflows from foreign investors; conversely, gross asset flows are interpreted as net outflows from domestic investors.

Bezemer et al. [10] examine the driver of the phenomenon of "debt shift" (i.e., lowering the share of lending to the business sector in domestic bank credits) using the new dataset of four types of bank credits: home mortgages, consumer credits, bank loans to non-bank financials, and loans to nonfinancial business. They show that the debt shift is larger in advanced economies with a stronger foreign bank presence and much more promoted financial deregulation. This study uses the same variables as foreign bank presence, leverage, bank deposits, and so on as the drivers of debt shift.

Finally, data for macro-prudential measures were derived from Akinci and Olmstead-Rumsey [1]. Macro-prudential policy was used to stabilize financial conditions, which can affect domestic credit volume or credit allocation. Some studies have constructed an index of macro-prudential policies. Both Akinci and Olmstead-Rumsey [1] and Cerutti et al. [14] recorded change in a policy instrument with a positive or negative value $(1, -1)$, depending on whether the policy tool was tightened or loosened in a given quarter. When the policy tool remains unchanged, the

3 Global Liquidity and Reallocation of Domestic Credit 75

index equals zero (0). The cumulative indicator for each tool in each quarter has been defined as the sum of the tightening or easing since 2000.

Akinci and Olmstead-Rumsey [1] focus on seven categories of macro-prudential tools in 57 economies from 2000Q1 to 2013Q4. Of these tools, three are targeted at the housing market: cap on loan to value (LTV) ratio for a mortgage loan, cap on the debt service to income (DSTI) ratio of the borrower, and other housing measures. The other four tools target banks' balance sheets: capital requirements (CR), loan loss provisioning requirements, consumer loan limits, and ceilings on credit growth. They report the macro-prudential policy housing index (the sum of the cumulative variables for the LTV, DSTI, and other housing measures) and the macro-prudential policy non-housing index (the sum of the cumulative variables for the other four measures of the non-housing market).[2] This study uses the macro-prudential policy housing index and non-housing index by Akinci and Olmstead-Rumsey [1] (*MP_C_H* and *MP_C_NH*, respectively). Indexes by Akinci and Olmstead-Rumsey [1] examine the impact of housing tools and non-housing tools on credits.

3.2.2 Methodology

This study uses panel regression to investigate the effects of capital inflows on the share of household credit in total bank credit. The basic regression model is as follows:

$$ShareCR\_HH_{it} = \alpha + \beta_1\ GINF_{it-1} + \gamma X_{it} + u_i + \varepsilon_{it}.$$

Here, *ShareCR_HH*$_{it}$ is the share of credit to households in the bank credit to the private non-financial sector of country I in period t. *GINF*$_{it-1}$ is a matrix of explanatory variables of gross capital inflows, as described above. Inflow variables are ratios of seasonally adjusted GDP.

The positive (negative) significance of β_1 means that capital inflows contribute to the increase (decrease) in the share of bank credit to households. X is a matrix of control variables: (1) three macroeconomic conditions—(*g_domestic*) real GDP growth rate forecast in country *i*, (*inflation*) quarterly annualized-inflation-rate, and (*houseprice*) real residential housing price index; (2) monetary market condition—(*i_domestic*) real interest rate in country *i*; (3) financial depth—(*CR_PS*) total credit to the private sector by the depository money bank; (4) bank characteristics—(*Foreign-bankpresence*) the ratio of the number of foreign owned banks, (*leverage*) the ratio

---

[2] Cerutti et al. [14] focus on nine categories of tools in 64 countries during the period from 2000Q1 to 2014Q4. These cover general capital requirements, three sectoral specific capital buffers (on real estate credit, consumer credit, and other sectors), reserve requirements, concentration limits, interbank exposure limits, loan to value ratio, and two reserve requirements (on foreign currency-denominated accounts and local currency-denominated accounts). Overall macro-prudential policy index is defined as the sum of the cumulative measures of these nine instruments and reported by country *i* and time *t*.

of bank credit to bank deposit, and (*deposit*) the ratio of Bank Credit to Deposit, and (5) macro-prudential policy indexes—(*MP_C_H* and *MP_C_NH*) (see Table 3.6). u_i is a country fixed term and ε_{it} is an error term.

This study examines changes in both bank credit allocation and the level of bank credit to households. Thus, the regression model was as follows:

$$CR\_HH_{it} = \alpha + \beta_2\, GINF_{it-1} + \gamma X_{it} + u_i + \varepsilon_{it}.$$

Here, CR_HH_{it} is the bank credit to households to the GDP of country i in period t (*CR_HH*). The positive (negative) significance of β_2 means that capital inflows contribute to the increase (decrease) in bank credit to households. Accordingly, we can expect the following results under the four combinations of the signs of β_1 and β_2:

(i) $\beta_1 > 0$ and $\beta_2 > 0$: domestic banks lend to households more than to business.
(ii) $\beta_1 > 0$ and $\beta_2 < 0$: Domestic banks are less reluctant to lend to households than to business.
(iii) $\beta_1 < 0$ and $\beta_2 > 0$: Domestic banks lend to households less than to business.
(iv) $\beta_1 < 0$ and $\beta_2 < 0$: Domestic banks are more reluctant to lend to households than to business.

GMM estimation is used as total bank credit and share of bank credit to households are likely to be jointly determined. To check the differences between advanced and emerging economies and between regional groups, as the control variables of the extended model, we include dummies (emerging, regional, and period dummies after the global financial crisis) and a lagged dependent variable in the case of the dynamic panel model. To test for consistency of estimates and validity of instruments, we conduct Arellano-Bond tests for first- and second-order autocorrelation of the residuals.

We checked the correlation matrix among dependent and explanatory variables for use in regressions (not shown to save space). Among capital inflow types, only gross bond investment inflows to the business sectors (*BI_Corp*) show a positive correlation with gross equity investment inflows to banks (*EI_Bank*). Moreover, among domestic factors, only leverage (*leverage*) and bank deposits to GDP (*deposit*) are positively correlated with bank credit to the private sector. Almost none of the variables showed high correlations, which allowed us to include them as dependent or explanatory variables.

3.3 Empirical Results

3.3.1 Credit Allocation and Sectoral Destination of Capital Inflows

Table 3.1 shows the estimated results on the effect of total capital inflows classified by type of borrower on the share of bank credit to households in the nonfinancial private sector. Columns (1) and (2) of Table 3.1 demonstrate the effect of total capital inflows to each sector on the share of household credit. Conversely, columns (3) and (4) show the effect of capital inflows on each sector for each type of capital. The difference between columns (1) and (2) is whether the macroprudential policy variables are included. First, the coefficient estimates of capital inflows to the banking sector (TI_Bank) are negative and significant with or without macroprudential policy variables. Domestic banks lend more to business and less to households as their rate of return on credit to business is normally higher than that to households. Consequently, the share of credit to households decreases.

Second, coefficient estimates of capital inflows to the corporate sector in the form of direct investment (DI_Corp) are positive and significant in columns (1) and (2). Banks seem to have reduced lending to business as corporations have raised funds in the form of alternatives to bank borrowing. Because of corporate lending decline, the share of household lending increases. Increase in capital inflow into the corporate sector in the form of FDI decreases borrowing from domestic banks, who have no choice but to lend to households. As Samarina and Bezemer [24] highlight, this finding is consistent with the substitution effects between domestic bank loans and capital inflows. Third, the coefficient estimates of capital flowing into the corporate sector in forms other than direct investment ($DI\_Corp\_excl.DI$) are negative and significant in both columns (1) and (2). Corporations that have raised funds from overseas have also increased their borrowing from domestic banks. This result may reflect a strong demand for corporate funds. Fourth, as shown in Columns (1) and (2), increase in total inflows into the public sector (TI_Public) significantly decreases share of household credit. Previous studies have highlighted that capital inflows into the public sector tend to increase when capital inflows into the private sector decrease and that capital inflows into the public sector are counter-cyclical (see Avdjiev et al. [3]). This may reflect capital inflows into the public sector during the downturn in the business cycle, driven by bank lending to households like subprime mortgages.

Next, we refer to the effects of the control variables on credit allocation in Columns (1) and (2) of Table 3.1. First, the effect of the one-year-ahead forecast of GDP growth is not robust. Anticipation of economic boom increases demand for both investment and housing, which accelerates domestic bank credit to both households and business. However, the increase in credit for households seems smaller than that for business. Second, real interest rate is statistically significant, with a negative sign in columns (1) and (2) of Table 3.1. An increase in the real interest rate decreases demand for borrowing. Households' sensitivity to changes in the interest rate seems stronger than that of business sector. Third, both columns (1) and (2) of Table 3.1

78   K. Sugimoto and M. Enya

Table 3.1 The effect of capital inflows classified by sectoral destination on the share of household credit

Dependent variable: household credit share	(1)	(2)	(3)	(4)
$CR\_PS\,(-1)$	0.081*** (0.014)	0.099*** (0.016)	0.093*** (0.014)	0.161*** (0.022)
$TI\_Bank\,(-1)$	−0.040*** (0.007)	−0.053*** (0.007)		
$EI\_Bank\,(-1)$			0.015 (0.025)	−0.116*** (0.029)
$BI\_Bank\,(-1)$			0.128*** (0.023)	0.023 (0.029)
$OI\_Bank\,(-1)$			−0.081*** (0.011)	−0.072*** (0.014)
$DI\_Corp\,(-1)$	0.231*** (0.012)	0.167*** (0.013)	0.208*** (0.013)	0.169*** (0.018)
$TI\_Corp\_excl.DI\,(-1)$	−0.042*** (0.014)	−0.094*** (0.014)		
$EI\_Corp\,(-1)$			−0.028 (0.023)	−0.009 (0.029)
$BI\_Corp\,(-1)$			−0.212*** (0.050)	−0.325*** (0.064)
$OI\_Corp\,(-1)$			−0.094*** (0.028)	0.226*** (0.037)
$TI\_Public\,(-1)$	−0.076*** (0.010)	−0.047*** (0.010)		
$BI\_Public\,(-1)$			0.052** (0.027)	0.126*** (0.035)
$OI\_Public\,(-1)$			−0.071*** (0.011)	0.012 (0.014)
$g\_domestic$	0.015 (0.122)	1.442*** (0.128)	0.040 (0.126)	1.789*** (0.165)
$i\_domestic$	−2.082*** (0.078)	−2.173*** (0.079)	−2.066*** (0.081)	−2.127*** (0.110)
$ForeignBankPresence$	0.001*** (0.000)	-0.000 (0.000)	0.001*** (0.000)	−0.000*** (0.000)
$Leverage$	0.058*** (0.009)	0.001 (0.011)	0.056*** (0.010)	−0.036** (0.014)
$Deposit$	0.000*** (0.000)	0.001*** (0.000)	0.001*** (0.000)	0.000 (0.000)
$Houseprice$	−0.003*** (0.000)	−0.002*** (0.000)	−0.003*** (0.000)	−0.003*** (0.000)
$Inflation$	−0.027 (0.050)	0.067 (0.049)	0.001 (0.052)	0.117* (0.065)

(continued)

3 Global Liquidity and Reallocation of Domestic Credit

Table 3.1 (continued)

Dependent variable: household credit share	(1)	(2)	(3)	(4)
MP_H (−1)		0.010*** (0.001)		0.010*** (0.001)
MP_NH (−1)		−0.091*** (0.002)		−0.100*** (0.004)
Q1	−0.005* (0.003)	−0.011*** (0.003)	−0.005* (0.003)	−0.005 (0.003)
Q2	−0.001 (0.003)	−0.004 (0.003)	−0.002 (0.003)	−0.006* (0.003)
Q3	0.001 (0.003)	0.001 (0.003)	0.001 (0.003)	0.003 (0.003)
GFC	−0.035*** (0.006)	−0.015*** (0.006)	−0.030*** (0.006)	−0.017** (0.007)
Constant	0.739*** (0.015)	0.778*** (0.018)	0.719*** (0.016)	0.846*** (0.024)
AR(1)	0.000	0.000	0.000	0.000
AR(2)	0.390	0.943	0.614	0.956
Observations	1,161	934	1,161	934
Countries	27	27	27	27

Note Dependent Variable is the *ShareCR_HH*. Standard errors are reported in parentheses
***, ** and *indicate statistical significance at the 1, 5 and 10% levels, respectively. AR(1) and AR(2) are the Arellano-Bond tests for first and second order serial correlation of residuals, respectively

obtain robust results concerning the ratio of bank deposits to GDP. An increase in bank deposits, as an index of lending capacity, generally promotes bank lending to households relative to lending to business. Fourth, housing prices are statistically significant with negative signs in columns (1) and (2) of Table 3.1. Growing demand for housing business, accompanied by an increase in housing prices, contributes to an increase in credit to business, which decreases the share of credit to households. Fifth, the effects of foreign bank presence, leverage (i.e., the ratio of bank credit to bank deposit), and inflation are not robust. These factors may not determine the lending direction to business or households.

As most household lending is mortgage lending, tightening macroprudential policies for housing is expected to reduce the share of household lending. However, the opposite result was achieved: tightening macro-prudential measures for housing significantly increases households' share of credit. This result may be because of the fact that causality goes in the opposite direction (i.e., higher share of credit to households requires tighter macro-prudential measures for housing). The Global Financial Crisis dummy is statistically significant with a negative sign. During the global financial crisis, banks seemed to reduce lending to households more than they did to business.

Table 3.2 The effect of capital inflows classified by sectoral destination on the ratio of household credit to GDP

Dependent variable: household credit/GDP	(1)	(2)	(3)	(4)
CR_HH (−1)	0.827***	0.840***	0.829***	0.842***
	(0.027)	(0.031)	(0.027)	(0.031)
TI_Bank (−1)	−0.114*	−0.097		
	(0.069)	(0.093)		
EI_Bank (−1)			0.887**	0.949**
			(0.394)	(0.452)
BI_Bank (−1)			−0.177	−0.202
			(0.534)	(0.542)
OI_Bank (−1)			−0.149	−0.127
			(0.134)	(0.155)
DI_Corp (−1)	0.227	0.319	0.293	0.393
	(0.303)	(0.369)	(0.254)	(0.314)
TI_Corp_excl.DI (−1)	0.384	0.367		
	(0.412)	(0.507)		
EI_Corp (−1)			1.498*	1.516
			(0.900)	(1.106)
BI_Corp (−1)			−0.524	−0.759
			(0.674)	(0.905)
OI_Corp (−1)			−0.517*	−0.547
			(0.314)	(0.413)
TI_Public (−1)	−0.357*	−0.356*		
	(0.187)	(0.184)		
BI_Public (−1)			−0.061	−0.093
			(0.396)	(0.532)
OI_Public (−1)			−0.369*	−0.362*
			(0.205)	(0.210)
g_domestic	−12.766	−11.357	−14.338	−12.902
	(9.446)	(9.355)	(9.726)	(9.611)
i_domestic	−9.763**	−11.596**	−8.807**	−10.666**
	(4.336)	(4.818)	(4.421)	(5.009)
ForeignBankPresence	−0.035**	−0.040*	−0.040**	−0.046**
	(0.018)	(0.021)	(0.016)	(0.020)
Leverage	5.580***	4.955***	5.334***	4.685***
	(1.328)	(1.419)	(1.330)	(1.420)
Deposit	0.106***	0.111***	0.099***	0.104***
	(0.029)	(0.034)	(0.029)	(0.033)
Houseprice	0.039***	0.038**	0.039***	0.039***
	(0.014)	(0.015)	(0.014)	(0.014)
Inflation	−2.416***	−2.585***	−2.220***	−2.319***
	(0.902)	(0.980)	(0.833)	(0.883)

(continued)

3 Global Liquidity and Reallocation of Domestic Credit

Table 3.2 (continued)

Dependent variable: household credit/GDP	(1)	(2)	(3)	(4)
MP_H (−1)		−0.218 (0.134)		−0.218 (0.145)
MP_NH (−1)		−0.238 (0.198)		−0.252 (0.203)
Q1	−0.259*** (0.062)	−0.321*** (0.054)	−0.263*** (0.065)	−0.325*** (0.057)
Q2	0.037 (0.065)	0.002 (0.070)	0.046 (0.065)	0.013 (0.072)
Q3	−0.087 (0.067)	−0.104 (0.081)	−0.081 (0.067)	−0.090 (0.079)
GFC	−0.112 (0.224)	−0.096 (0.232)	−0.040 (0.219)	−0.020 (0.228)
Constant	−6.979** (2.757)	−6.530** (2.870)	−6.162** (2.864)	−5.666* (3.031)
AR(1)	0.009	0.016	0.010	0.019
AR(2)	0.765	0.818	0.653	0.882
Observations	1,126	899	1,126	899
Countries	27	27	27	27

Note Dependent Variable is the *CR_HH*. Standard errors are reported in parentheses
***, ** and *indicate statistical significance at the 1, 5 and 10% levels, respectively. AR(1) and AR(2) are the Arellano-Bond tests for first and second order serial correlation of residuals, respectively

We classify capital inflows into each sector and capital types and investigate how capital inflows deconstructed into both sectoral destination and capital type affect the share of household lending. Columns (3) and (4) of Table 3.1 show the effects of any type of capital inflow into each borrowing sector on the share of household lending, and we present the following results. First, the other investment inflows (i.e., bank loan inflows) into the banking sector (*OI_Bank*) have a negative and significant effect on household lending share. Second, regarding capital inflows into the corporate sector, as the inflows in the form of debt (e.g., bonds and bank loans (*BI_Corp* and *OI_Corp*)) increase, bank lending to business also increases, and ratio of lending to households decreases. Third, interestingly, capital inflows in the form of FDI (*DI_Corp*) and equities (*EI_Corp*) significantly increase share of household credit, although not significantly for equity inflows. The difference between the inflow effects of debt and equity may be attributable to the difference in the priority of financing for corporations. Owing to the low transaction costs, corporations tend to prefer both internal and domestic financing over both external and foreign financing, respectively. Internal financing such as direct investment and equities can be a substitute for borrowing from domestic banks, but cross-border external financing such as foreign borrowing will not be a substitute for borrowing from domestic banks.

3.3.2 Credit Allocation, Credit to Households and Sectoral Destination of Capital Inflows

Table 3.2 shows the estimated results of examining whether banks have increased their lending to households as a percentage of GDP due to capital inflows. Columns (1) and (2) of Table 3.2 show the effect of total capital inflows to each sector on the ratio of household credit to GDP. Columns (3) and (4) show the effect of capital inflows distinguished by both destination sector and capital type on the ratio. The difference between columns (1) and (2) and the difference between columns (3) and (4) indicate whether macroprudential policy variables are included.

First, the capital inflows into the banking sector (*TI_Bank*, *BI_Bank*, and *OI_Bank*) have significant and negative effects on the household lending share (Table 3.1) but have no significant effects on its lending ratio to GDP (Table 3.2). Banks seem to increase lending to business more than to households when debt inflows into the banking sector increase. Second, FDI inflows into the corporate sector (*DI_Corp*) have a positive significant effect on the household lending share (Table 3.1); however, they have no significant positive effect on its ratio to GDP (Table 3.2). As capital inflows into the corporate sector in the form of internal capital, such as FDIs and equities (*DI_Corp* and *EI_Corp*), banks reduce corporate lending, while banks instead increase household lending. However, increase in household lending by banks does not seem to be large enough to increase its ratio to GDP. Third, the effect of capital inflows into the public sector (*TI_Public* and *OI_Public*) on the household credit-to-GDP ratio is significantly negative. Capital inflows into the public sector increased during the recession when lending to households declined.

Results of the control variables are also interesting. First, impact of growth expectations (*g_domestic*) on household lending is positive for its share in Table 3.1 and negative for its ratio to GDP in Table 3.2; however, neither is significant. High growth expectations increase bank lending but do not have significant impact on credit allocation; an increase in household lending is not enough to raise its ratio to GDP. Second, the impact of the real interest rate (*i_domestic*) on household lending is significantly negative for both cases of its share and its ratio to GDP in Tables 3.1 and 3.2, respectively. An increase in the real interest rate decreases demand for borrowing. Households' sensitivity to changes in the interest rate seems stronger than that of firms.

Third, impact of foreign bank presence (*ForeignBankPresence*) on household lending is not robust for its share in Table 3.1 and is significantly negative for its ratio to GDP in Table 3.2. Countries with a high presence of foreign banks may have a small ratio of household lending to GDP owing to their large GDP. Fourth, impact of leverage (*leverage*) and of lending capacity (*deposit*) are not robust for household lending share in Table 3.1, but they are significant with a positive sign for and its household credit to GDP ratio in Table 3.2. The active stance of lending does not turn out to be limited only to households but tends to increase ratio of credit to households to GDP. Fifth, housing price (*houseprice*) is significant with a negative sign for household credit share in Table 3.1, but significant with a positive sign for the household credit to GDP ratio in Table 3.2. The booming housing price market is expected to increase banks' business lending to housing and related industries and mortgage lending to households. As banks increased business lending to the housing and related industries more than they did to households, proportion of lending to households may have declined as a result. Sixth, macro-prudential policy tightening is not significant but is a negative sign in Table 3.2.

3.3.3 Differences Between Advanced and Emerging Economies and Between Regional Groups

Next, we discuss differences between advanced and emerging economies and those between regional groups such as East Asia, Central and Eastern Europe, and Latin America in the relationship between capital inflows and lending to households. Tables 3.3 and 3.4 show the estimated results of effects of capital inflows on the share of credit to households in total bank credit and on bank credit to households as a % of GDP, respectively. To check for differences between country groups, we use interaction terms of each capital inflow and country group dummy (i.e., emerging dummy (*emerging*) for emerging economies) the East Asia dummy (*EA*) for emerging Asian economies, the Central and Eastern Europe dummy (*CEE*) for emerging European economies, and the Latin America dummy (*LA*) for emerging Latin American economies.

The effects identified appear to be dominated by those of advanced economies (Tables 3.1 and 3.2). The effects of emerging economies differ from those of advanced economies and vary widely across regions of emerging economies. The following results were quite interesting. First, in emerging European economies, the increase in capital inflows into the banking sector increases both the share of household lending and its ratio to GDP (Columns (3), (4), (7), and (8) of Tables 3.3 and 3.4). Banks in emerging European economies appear more likely to lend to households than business than in advanced and other emerging economies.

Second, in emerging Asian economies, increase in inflows of direct investment into the corporate sector increases the share of household lending significantly more than in advanced economies (Columns (5) and (6) of Tables 3.3 and 3.4). However, in emerging European and Latin American economies, this has little effect on the increase in the share of household loans. This result may reflect that corporations in advanced and emerging Asian economies can raise funds from abroad and reduce borrowing from domestic banks owing to weak demand for funds or stable FDI financing against the backdrop of a solid supply chain. This result may reflect that corporations in emerging European economies, even if they can raise funds from abroad, do not reduce their borrowing from domestic banks owing to strong demand for funds or unstable foreign financing.

Third, in advanced economies, when non-direct investment inflows into the corporate sector, corporations increase domestic banks borrowing. However, in emerging

Table 3.3 Regional differences in the effect of capital inflows classified by sectoral destination on the share of household credit

Dependent variable: household credit share	(1)	(2)	(3)	(4)	(5)	(6)	(7)	(8)	(9)	(10)
CR_PS (−1)	0.081*** (0.014)	0.099*** (0.016)	−0.007 (0.019)	−0.054*** (0.020)	0.188*** (0.017)	0.151*** (0.018)	0.071*** (0.014)	0.188*** (0.037)	−0.043* (0.024)	0.117*** (0.028)
TI_Bank (−1)	−0.040*** (0.007)	−0.053*** (0.007)	−0.097*** (0.010)	−0.055*** (0.009)	−0.083*** (0.009)	−0.034*** (0.008)	−0.015* (0.008)	−0.006 (0.016)	−0.108*** (0.012)	−0.095*** (0.012)
TI_Bank (−1) × EMEs			1.136*** (0.138)	0.867*** (0.121)						
TI_Bank (−1) × EA					0.185 (0.145)	0.449*** (0.120)				
TI_Bank (−1) × CEE							1.170*** (0.130)	2.521*** (0.380)		
TI_Bank (−1) × LA									−0.918 (0.633)	−1.253* (0.676)
DI_Corp (−1)	0.231*** (0.012)	0.167*** (0.013)	0.119*** (0.022)	0.101*** (0.020)	0.223*** (0.016)	0.161*** (0.014)	0.170*** (0.013)	0.239*** (0.034)	0.227*** (0.022)	0.165*** (0.023)
DI_Corp (−1) × EMEs			−0.172*** (0.048)	−0.093** (0.042)						
DI_Corp (−1) × EA					1.015*** (0.267)	0.520** (0.222)				
DI_Corp (−1) × CEE							−0.153*** (0.034)	−0.385*** (0.100)		
DI_Corp (−1) × LA									−0.858** (0.364)	−1.100** (0.443)
TI_Corp_excl.DI (−1)	−0.042*** (0.014)	−0.094*** (0.014)	−0.171*** (0.021)	−0.091*** (0.019)	−0.030* (0.018)	−0.102*** (0.015)	−0.126*** (0.014)	−0.039 (0.034)	0.017 (0.024)	0.005 (0.026)

(continued)

Table 3.3 (continued)

Dependent variable: household credit share	(1)	(2)	(3)	(4)	(5)	(6)	(7)	(8)	(9)	(10)
TI_Corp_excl.DI (−1) × EMEs			−0.376** (0.148)	0.072 (0.132)						
TI_Corp_excl.DI (−1) × EA					0.051 (0.171)	0.498*** (0.136)				
TI_Corp_excl.DI (−1) × CEE							2.348*** (0.244)	−1.289* (0.774)		
TI_Corp_excl.DI (−1) × LA									−1.272** (0.522)	1.074 (0.655)
TI_Public (−1)	−0.076*** (0.010)	−0.047*** (0.010)	−0.096*** (0.013)	−0.066*** (0.012)	−0.059*** (0.012)	−0.068*** (0.011)	−0.067*** (0.010)	0.027 (0.022)	−0.050*** (0.016)	0.005 (0.016)
TI_Public (−1) × EMEs			0.546*** (0.126)	0.729*** (0.111)						
TI_Public (−1) × EA					0.242 (0.175)	0.183 (0.122)				
TI_Public (−1) × CEE							−0.050 (0.112)	0.057 (0.277)		
TI_Public (−1) × LA									4.529*** (0.708)	4.083*** (0.786)
g_domestic	0.015 (0.122)	1.442*** (0.128)	1.560*** (0.180)	1.663*** (0.161)	2.501*** (0.168)	2.651*** (0.154)	−1.106*** (0.119)	0.642** (0.277)	0.661*** (0.199)	1.968*** (0.213)
i_domestic	−2.082*** (0.078)	−2.173*** (0.079−	−1.825*** (0.110)	−1.187*** (0.105)	−1.892*** (0.100)	−2.059*** (0.088)	−2.731*** (0.080)	−2.056*** (0.183)	−1.698*** (0.151)	−1.974*** (0.169)
ForeignBankPresence	0.001*** (0.000)	−0.000 (0.000)	0.002*** (0.000)	0.002*** (0.000)	−0.000 (0.000)	−0.000 (0.000)	0.002*** (0.000)	−0.000 (0.000)	0.000* (0.000)	−0.001*** (0.000)

(continued)

Table 3.3 (continued)

Dependent variable: household credit share	(1)	(2)	(3)	(4)	(5)	(6)	(7)	(8)	(9)	(10)
Leverage	0.058*** (0.009)	0.001 (0.011)	0.038*** (0.013)	0.022* (0.013)	0.005 (0.012)	−0.013 (0.011)	0.058*** (0.009)	−0.081*** (0.024)	0.080*** (0.016)	−0.038** (0.018)
Deposit	0.000*** (0.000)	0.001*** (0.000)	0.000 (0.000)	0.001*** (0.000)	0.000* (0.000)	0.001*** (0.000)	0.000 (0.000)	−0.000 (0.000)	0.001*** (0.000)	0.000 (0.000)
Houseprice	−0.003*** (0.000)	−0.002*** (0.000)	−0.001*** (0.000)	−0.003*** (0.000)	−0.002*** (0.000)	−0.002*** (0.000)	−0.002*** (0.000)	−0.003*** (0.000)	−0.002*** (0.000)	−0.002*** (0.000)
Inflation	−0.027 (0.050)	0.067 (0.049)	0.414*** (0.068)	0.196*** (0.059)	0.047 (0.064)	−0.094* (0.056)	0.026 (0.051)	0.133 (0.118)	0.155* (0.083)	0.217*** (0.083)
MP_H (−1)		0.010*** (0.001)		0.023*** (0.001)		0.018*** (0.001)		0.015*** (0.002)		0.008*** (0.002)
MP_NH (−1)		−0.091*** (0.002)		0.014*** (0.005)		−0.050*** (0.003)		−0.091*** (0.007)		−0.090*** (0.005)
Q1	−0.005* (0.003)	−0.011*** (0.003)	−0.005 (0.003)	−0.006** (0.003)	−0.009*** (0.003)	−0.011*** (0.003)	−0.000 (0.003)	−0.006 (0.005)	−0.005 (0.004)	−0.007 (0.004)
Q2	−0.001 (0.003)	−0.004 (0.003)	0.003 (0.003)	−0.003 (0.003)	0.001 (0.003)	−0.004 (0.003)	−0.003 (0.003)	−0.011** (0.005)	-0.000 (0.004)	−0.000 (0.004)
Q3	0.001 (0.003)	0.001 (0.003)	0.002 (0.003)	0.005 (0.003)	0.006* (0.003)	0.005* (0.003)	−0.003 (0.003)	−0.002 (0.005)	0.002 (0.004)	0.003 (0.004)
GFC	−0.035*** (0.006)	−0.015*** (0.006)	0.020** (0.008)	0.037*** (0.007)	0.013* (0.008)	0.032*** (0.007)	−0.052*** (0.006)	0.002 (0.011)	−0.047*** (0.009)	−0.016* (0.009)
EMEs			−0.269*** (0.008)	−0.348*** (0.010)						
EA					−0.314*** (0.011)	−0.249*** (0.012)				

(continued)

Table 3.3 (continued)

Dependent variable: household credit share	(1)	(2)	(3)	(4)	(5)	(6)	(7)	(8)	(9)	(10)
CEE							−0.162*** (0.010)	−0.133*** (0.035)		
LA									−0.199*** (0.025)	−0.102*** (0.027)
Constant	0.739*** (0.015)	0.778*** (0.018)	0.779*** (0.021)	0.920*** (0.022)	0.625*** (0.019)	0.722*** (0.020)	0.753*** (0.015)	0.986*** (0.039)	0.745*** (0.026)	0.882*** (0.031)
AR(1)	0.000	0.000	0.000	0.000	0.000	0.000	0.000	0.000	0.000	0.000
AR(2)	0.390	0.943	0.561	0.411	0.156	0.191	0.158	0.947	0.980	0.968
Observations	1161	934	1161	934	1161	934	1161	934	1161	934
Countries	27	27	27	27	27	27	27	27	27	27

Note Dependent Variable is the *ShareCR_HH*. Standard errors are reported in parentheses

***, ** and *indicate statistical significance at the 1, 5 and 10% levels, respectively. AR(1) and AR(2) are the Arellano-Bond tests for first and second order serial correlation of residuals, respectively

Table 3.4 Regional differences in the effect of capital inflows classified by sectoral destination on the ratio of household credit to GDP

Dependent variable: household credit / GDP	(1)	(2)	(3)	(4)	(5)	(6)	(7)	(8)	(9)	(10)
CR_HH (−1)	0.827*** (0.027)	0.840*** (0.031)	0.827*** (0.027)	0.841*** (0.030)	0.824*** (0.028)	0.837*** (0.032)	0.831*** (0.026)	0.845*** (0.028)	0.826*** (0.027)	0.839*** (0.031)
TI_Bank (−1)	−0.114* (0.069)	−0.097 (0.093)	−0.145** (0.070)	−0.138 (0.088)	−0.107 (0.070)	−0.094 (0.094)	−0.135** (0.068)	−0.118 (0.088)	−0.122* (0.069)	−0.103 (0.092)
TI_Bank (−1) × EMEs			2.936** (1.219)	3.548*** (1.187)						
TI_Bank (−1) × EA					1.835 (1.831)	2.405 (1.913)				
TI_Bank (−1) × CEE							3.995** (1.903)	5.341*** (1.606)		
TI_Bank (−1) × LA									2.450 (1.605)	2.105 (1.328)
DI_Corp (−1)	0.227 (0.303)	0.319 (0.369)	−0.095 (0.162)	−0.111 (0.242)	0.234 (0.306)	0.327 (0.372)	−0.101 (0.162)	−0.114 (0.244)	0.234 (0.307)	0.322 (0.373)
DI_Corp (−1) × EMEs			1.079*** (0.341)	1.165*** (0.402)						
DI_Corp (−1) × EA					−3.304 (3.480)	−4.168 (3.808)				
DI_Corp (−1) × CEE							1.120*** (0.394)	1.181*** (0.414)		
DI_Corp (−1) × LA									0.522 (1.298)	0.441 (1.146)
TI_Corp_excl.DI (−1)	0.384 (0.412)	0.367 (0.507)	0.487 (0.387)	0.514 (0.476)	0.354 (0.426)	0.356 (0.521)	0.477 (0.377)	0.495 (0.461)	0.424 (0.410)	0.398 (0.510)

(continued)

Table 3.4 (continued)

Dependent variable: household credit / GDP	(1)	(2)	(3)	(4)	(5)	(6)	(7)	(8)	(9)	(10)
$TI\_Corp\_excl.DI\,(-1)$ × EMEs			−1.829* (0.968)	−2.626*** (0.934)						
$TI\_Corp\_excl.DI\,(-1)$ × EA					1.823 (2.176)	0.721 (1.918)				
$TI\_Corp\_excl.DI\,(-1)$ × CEE							−5.143*** (1.817)	−6.783*** (2.312)		
$TI\_Corp\_excl.DI\,(-1)$ × LA									−4.848*** (1.646)	−4.802*** (1.769)
$TI\_Public\,(-1)$	−0.357* (0.187)	−0.356* (0.184)	−0.379* (0.215)	−0.374* (0.218)	−0.368* (0.191)	−0.368* (0.192)	−0.365* (0.209)	−0.362* (0.209)	−0.355* (0.190)	−0.353* (0.187)
$TI\_Public\,(-1)$ × EMEs			1.617** (0.776)	1.562* (0.891)						
$TI\_Public\,(-1)$ × EA					1.090 (1.320)	1.341 (1.412)				
$TI\_Public\,(-1)$ × CEE							2.058* (1.067)	1.939 (1.389)		
$TI\_Public\,(-1)$ × LA									1.335 (1.938)	1.380 (1.760)
g_domestic	−12.766 (9.446)	−11.357 (9.355)	−13.785 (9.396)	−12.651 (9.352)	−13.256 (9.532)	−11.882 (9.556)	−13.732 (9.073)	−12.712 (8.828)	−12.984 (9.543)	−11.655 (9.403)
i_domestic	−9.763** (4.336)	−11.596** (4.818)	−10.775** (4.643)	−12.524** (4.947)	−10.228** (4.506)	−12.304** (4.985)	−10.027** (4.348)	−11.483** (4.641)	−10.200** (4.280)	−12.065*** (4.681)
ForeignBankPresence	−0.035** (0.018)	−0.040* (0.021)	−0.034** (0.017)	−0.039* (0.020)	−0.035** (0.017)	−0.041** (0.021)	−0.030* (0.017)	−0.034* (0.019)	−0.035** (0.018)	−0.040* (0.021)

(continued)

Table 3.4 (continued)

Dependent variable: household credit / GDP	(1)	(2)	(3)	(4)	(5)	(6)	(7)	(8)	(9)	(10)
Leverage	5.580*** (1.328)	4.955*** (1.419)	5.525*** (1.292)	4.896*** (1.372)	5.629*** (1.349)	4.986*** (1.439)	5.412*** (1.230)	4.751*** (1.305)	5.620*** (1.332)	4.989*** (1.421)
Deposit	0.106*** (0.029)	0.111*** (0.034)	0.105*** (0.028)	0.110*** (0.033)	0.108*** (0.029)	0.113*** (0.034)	0.102*** (0.027)	0.106*** (0.031)	0.106*** (0.029)	0.111*** (0.034)
Houseprice	0.039*** (0.014)	0.038** (0.015)	0.038*** (0.014)	0.038** (0.015)	0.039*** (0.014)	0.039** (0.015)	0.038*** (0.014)	0.036** (0.014)	0.039*** (0.014)	0.039*** (0.015)
Inflation	−2.416*** (0.902)	−2.585*** (0.980)	−2.081** (0.853)	−2.136** (0.904)	−2.299** (0.911)	−2.377** (1.044)	−2.094*** (0.777)	−2.175*** (0.807)	−2.398*** (0.892)	−2.564*** (0.972)
MP_H (−1)		−0.218 (0.134)		−0.235* (0.127)		−0.224* (0.135)		−0.220* (0.128)		−0.217 (0.134)
MP_NH (−1)		−0.238 (0.198)		−0.195 (0.196)		−0.225 (0.194)		−0.244 (0.193)		−0.224 (0.195)
Q1	−0.259*** (0.062)	−0.321*** (0.054)	−0.262*** (0.060)	−0.323*** (0.054)	−0.253*** (0.061)	−0.318*** (0.055)	−0.262*** (0.062)	−0.324*** (0.054)	−0.264*** (0.061)	−0.323*** (0.053)
Q2	0.037 (0.065)	0.002 (0.070)	0.028 (0.067)	−0.008 (0.074)	0.037 (0.065)	−0.001 (0.071)	0.031 (0.066)	−0.005 (0.072)	0.035 (0.065)	0.001 (0.071)
Q3	−0.087 (0.067)	−0.104 (0.081)	−0.098 (0.067)	−0.119 (0.082)	−0.086 (0.067)	−0.103 (0.080)	−0.091 (0.068)	−0.109 (0.082)	−0.091 (0.068)	−0.109 (0.083)
GFC	−0.112 (0.224)	−0.096 (0.232)	−0.108 (0.222)	−0.095 (0.236)	−0.077 (0.226)	−0.059 (0.238)	−0.128 (0.225)	−0.109 (0.236)	−0.117 (0.226)	−0.103 (0.236)
Constant	−6.979** (2.757)	−6.530** (2.870)	−6.795** (2.734)	−6.366** (2.817)	−7.007** (2.805)	−6.555** (2.930)	−6.674*** (2.569)	−6.138** (2.612)	−7.027** (2.779)	−6.585** (2.886)
AR(1)	0.009	0.016	0.009	0.018	0.009	0.016	0.008	0.015	0.009	0.017

(continued)

3 Global Liquidity and Reallocation of Domestic Credit

Table 3.4 (continued)

Dependent variable: household credit / GDP	(1)	(2)	(3)	(4)	(5)	(6)	(7)	(8)	(9)	(10)
AR(2)	0.765	0.818	0.568	0.803	0.731	0.896	0.507	0.657	0.755	0.871
Observations	1126	899	1126	899	1126	899	1126	899	1126	899
Countries	27	27	27	27	27	27	27	27	27	27

Note Dependent Variable is the *CR_HH*. Standard errors are reported in parentheses
***, ** and *indicate statistical significance at the 1, 5 and 10% levels, respectively. AR(1) and AR(2) are the Arellano-Bond tests for first and second order serial correlation of residuals, respectively

Table 3.5 List of countries included in estimation

17 advanced countries:
(1) Europe: Austria (2002–16), Belgium (2005–16), Denmark (2001–16), Finland (2001–16), France (2001–16), Germany (2001–16), Greece (2001–16), Ireland (2005–13), Italy (2001–16), Netherlands (2004–16), Norway (2001–16), Portugal (2013–16), Spain (2008–16), Sweden (2001–12)
(2) Other regions: Australia (2001–16), Canada (2001–16), Japan (2001–16)

10 Emerging Economies:
(1) East Asia (EA): Korea (2006–16), Malaysia (2006–09), Thailand (2001–16)
(2) Central and Eastern Europe (CEE): Czech Republic (2001–16), Hungary (2001–16), Poland (2001–16)
(3) Latin America (LA): Brazil (2001–16), Chile (2002–16), Colombia (2001–16), Mexico (2001–16)

Note The BIS database on credit to the non-financial sector covers 44 economies, both advanced and emerging economies, such as Argentina, Australia, Austria, Belgium, Brazil, Canada, Chile, China, Colombia, Czech Republic, Denmark, Euro area, Finland, France, Germany, Greece, (Hong Kong SAR), Hungary, India, Indonesia, Ireland, Israel, Italy, Japan, Korea, (Luxembourg), Malaysia, Mexico, Netherlands, New Zealand, Norway, Poland, Portugal, Russia, Saudi Arabia, (Singapore,) South Africa, Spain, Sweden, (Switzerland,) Thailand, Turkey, (United Kingdom) , United States. The data for the macro-prudential policy measure is available only for 38 economies. 5 international financial centers economies in parentheses are excluded. Since data is not available, some other economies are excluded, and unbalanced panel dataset is used

economies, these effects do not seem robust (Tables 3.3 and 3.4). For corporations, internal financing, such as direct investment and equity financing, is generally considered to have higher priority than borrowing from domestic banks. Conversely, borrowing from abroad has a lower priority than from domestic banks. Generally, corporations do not reduce borrowing from domestic banks even if borrowing from abroad increases. However, if domestic finance is fragile, corporations may reduce domestic borrowing by increasing foreign borrowing. Samarina and Bezemer [24] conclude that capital inflows into banks do not correlate with domestic credit allocations. Contrary to their conclusion, this study confirms this correlation by dividing countries into regional groups.

3.4 Conclusion

This study focuses on the destination and type of capital flows to examine whether the directions and types of cross-border capital flows caused a change in domestic bank credit allocation for 27 economies over 2001–2016. The main findings are as follows. First, capital inflows into the banking sector negatively affect household lending shares. Banks seem to increase lending to business more than to households when debt inflows into the banking sector increase. This negative impact on the household lending ratio can be seen in advanced economies; conversely, positive impacts can be confirmed in emerging European economies. Banks' real estate lending to households

3 Global Liquidity and Reallocation of Domestic Credit

Table 3.6 Variable definitions and data sources

Variable	Definition	Data sources
Bank credits		
ShareCR_HH	Total credit to households/bank credit to the private non-financial sector	BIS
CR_HH	Total credit to households/GDP	BIS
CR_PS	Credit to private sector by depository money bank, as a % of GDP	IFS, IMF
Gross capital inflows (% of GDP)		
By sectoral destination (to Bank, Corporate, Public sectors)		
TI_Bank	Gross total inflows to bank sector, % of GDP	Balance of Payment, IMF
DI_Corp	Gross direct investment inflows, % of GDP	Balance of Payment, IMF
TI_Corp_excl.DI	Gross total inflows to other sectors minus *DI_CORP*, % of GDP	Balance of Payment, IMF
TI_Public	Gross total inflows to central bank and general government sectors, % of GDP	Balance of Payment, IMF
By capital type and sectoral destination (Types: Portfolio Equity, Bond, Other Investment, Destinations: to Bank, Corporate, Government sectors)		
EI_Bank	Gross portfolio equity investment inflows to bank sector, % of GDP	Balance of Payment, IMF
BI_Bank	Gross portfolio debt (bond) investment inflows to bank sector, % of GDP	Balance of Payment, IMF
OI_Bank	Gross other investment inflows to bank sector, % of GDP	Balance of Payment, IMF
EI_Corp	Gross portfolio equity investment inflows to other sectors, % of GDP	Balance of Payment, IMF
BI_Corp	Gross portfolio debt (bond) investment inflows to other sectors, % of GDP	Balance of Payment, IMF
OI_Corp	Gross other investment inflows to other sectors, % of GDP	Balance of Payment, IMF
BI_Public	Gross portfolio debt (bond) investment inflows to Government sectors, % of GDP	Balance of Payment, IMF
OI_Public	Gross other investment inflows to central bank and general government sectors, % of GDP	Balance of Payment, IMF

(continued)

Table 3.6 (continued)

Variable	Definition	Data sources
Other variables		
g_domestic	real GDP growth rate forecast in country i (one-year ahead) (spring → Q1, Q2, fall → Q3,Q4), semiannual frequency	WEO, IMF
i_domestic	real interest rate in country i (policy rate, deflated by forecast inflation(one-year ahead), semiannual frequency)	IFS, IMF; WEO, IMF
ForeignBankPresence	Foreign bank presence, The ratio of the number of foreign owned banks (>50% of its share are owned by foreigners) to the number of the total banks	GFDD
Leverage	The ratio of Bank credits to Bank deposits	IFS, IMF
Deposit	Bank Deposits, % of GDP	IFS, IMF
Houseprice	Real residential housing price index	BIS
Inflation	CPI growth rate, yoy	IFS, IMF
MP_C_H	Changes (relative to 2000q1) in Macroprudential policies: Related to housing (Loan-to-Value Cap, Debt-to-Income Cap, and Other measures)	Akinci and Olmstead-Rumsey (2017)
MP_C_NH	Changes (relative to 2000q1) in Macroprudential policies: Related to non-housing Countercyclical capital requirements, Loan-loss provisioning, and Consumer loan measures	Akinci and Olmstead-Rumsey (2017)
GFC	Global Financial Crisis Period Dummy (1 for 4th quarter of 2008 and the 1st quarter of 2009)	

has become more cautious after collapse of subprime loans in advanced economies. However, banks in emerging European economies, which have been more affected by the banking business model of advanced economies, still tend to increase household lending.

Second, capital inflows in the form of FDI into the corporate sector have a positive effect on the household lending share. This positive impact on the household lending ratio can be seen in advanced economies and emerging Asian economies. Conversely, nonsignificant impacts can be seen in emerging economies other than East Asia. Generally, corporations prefer internal financing, such as direct investment and equity financing, to external financing, such as debt financing, because of the transaction costs of financing. Hence, banks reduce corporate lending, while banks increase household lending as capital inflows into the corporate sector in the form of internal capital. However, the increase in household lending by banks does not seem to be large enough to increase its ratio to GDP. Substitution effect between domestic bank loans and capital inflows works in advanced and emerging Asian economies; however, why does it not work in emerging economies other than East Asia? The inflow of direct investment into emerging Asia has been solid and stable against the backdrop of a solid supply chain but not in emerging European and Latin American economies (Enya et al. [17]). Unsolid and unstable capital inflows may weaken the substitution effect.

Third, as capital inflows in the form of capital other than direct investment in the corporate sector increase, corporations increase borrowing from domestic banks in advanced economies but not in emerging economies. Why does the substitution effect not work in advanced economies? Corporations generally prefer borrowing from domestic banks over borrowing from abroad because of home bias or the various risks associated with foreign borrowing (e.g., foreign exchange risk). Generally, corporations do not reduce borrowing from domestic banks, even if they increase their borrowing from abroad. However, if the home bias is small or the domestic financial system is fragile, as is often the case in emerging markets, corporations may reduce domestic borrowing instead of increasing foreign borrowing.

Samarina and Bezemer [24] suggest that capital inflows into the non-banking sector have a side effect on the credit allocation of domestic banks by crowding out domestic bank loans and call this effect the substitution effect. However, this study confirms this correlation by dividing countries into regional groups. Our results demonstrate the circumstances under which the substitution effect is easy and difficult to work. We find that the substitution effect works well in economies where direct investment inflows are stable and solid. This applies to advanced and emerging Asian economies, where home bias is small, or the domestic financial system is fragile like emerging economies, and where the demand for funds or investment opportunities is weak.

The expansion of global liquidity could strengthen the substitution effect and increase household lending accompanied by a significant reduction in foreign funding costs. This could increase the volatility of the macroeconomy. There is no "one size fits all" prescription to capital flow management. Therefore, focusing on the relationship between capital inflows and credit allocation is necessary.

References

1. Akinci, O., & Olmstead-Rumsey, J. (2018). How effective are macroprudential policies? An empirical investigation. *Journal of Financial Intermediation*, 33, 33–57.
2. Aldasoro, I., & Ehlers, T. (2018). Global liquidity: Changing instrument and currency patterns. BIS Quarterly Review, 17–27.
3. Avdjiev, S., Gambacorta, L., Goldberg, L., & Schiaffi, S. (2020a). The shifting drivers of global liquidity. *Journal of International Economics*, 125, 1–17.

4. Avdjiev, S., Hardy, B., Kalemli-Ozcan, S., & Servén, L. (2018b). Gross capital inflows to banks, corporates, and sovereigns. BIS Working Papers, 760.
5. Avdjiev, S., Binder, S., & Sousa, R. (2021). External debt composition and domestic credit cycles. *Journal of International Money and Finance*, 115, 1–19.
6. Barba, A., & Pivetti, M. (2009). Rising household debt: Its causes and macroeconomic implications-A long-period analysis. *Cambridge Journal of Economics*, 33, 113–137.
7. Beck, T., Büyükkarabacak, B., Rioja, F. K., & Valev, N. (2012). "Who gets the credit? And does it matter? Household vs. firm lending across countries. *B.E. Journal of Macroeconomics*, 12(1), 1–46.
8. Bezemer, D., Grydaki, M., & Zhang, L. (2016). More mortgages, lower growth? *Economic Inquiry*, 54(1), 652–674.
9. Bezemer, D., & Zhang, L. (2019). Credit composition and the severity of post-crisis recessions. *Journal of Financial Stability*, 42, 52–66.
10. Bezemer, D., Samarina, A., & Zhang, L. (2017). The shift in bank credit allocation: New data and new findings. De Nederlandsche Bank Working Paper, 559.
11. Blanchard, O., Ostry, J.D., Ghosh, A.R., & Chamon, M. (2015). Are capital inflows expansionary or contractionary? Theory, policy implications, and some evidence. *American Economic Review*, 106(5), 565–69.
12. Büyükkarabacak, B., & Valev, N. T. (2010). The role of household and business credit in banking crises. *Journal of Banking & Finance*, 34(6), 1247–1256.
13. Cerutti, E., & Hong, G. H. (2018). Portfolio inflows eclipsing banking inflows: Alternative facts? IMF Working Paper, WP/18/29.
14. Cerutti, E., Correa, R., Fiorentino, E., & Segalla, E. (2017). Changes in prudential policy instruments-A new cross-country database. *International Journal of Central Banking*, 477–03.
15. Cohen, B. H., Domanski, D., Fender, I., & Shin, H. S. (2017). Global liquidity: A selective review. *Annual Review of Economics*, 9(1), 587–612.
16. Enya, M., & Shinkai, J. (2016). Capital inflows, asset prices, financial systems in East Asia. Paper presented at the 15th International Convention of the East Asian Economic Association, 5–6 November 2016, Bandung, Indonesia.
17. Enya, M., Kohsaka, A., & Sugimoto, K. (2019). Capital flow dynamics in emerging market economies. OSIPP Discussion Paper, 19E011, Osaka University.
18. Igan, D., & Tan, Z. (2017). Capital inflows, credit growth, and financial systems. *Emerging Markets Finance and Trade*, 53(12), 2649–2671.
19. Jappelli, T., Pagano, M., & di Maggio, M. (2013). Households' indebtedness and financial fragility. *Journal of Financial Management, Markets and Institutions*, 1, 26–35.
20. Jordà, Ò., Schularick, M., & Taylor, A. M. (2016). The great mortgaging: housing finance, crises, and business cycles. *Economic Policy*, 31(85), 107–152.
21. Kaminsky, G. L., Reinhart, C. M. & Vegh, C. A. (2004). When it rains, it pours: Procyclical capital flows and macroeconomic policies, NBER Working paper, 10780.
22. Mian, A. R., Sufi, A., & Verner, E. (2017). Household debt and business cycles worldwide. *The Quarterly Journal of Economics*, 132(4), 1755–1817.
23. OECD. (2020). COVID-19 and global capital flows, *OECD Policy Responses to Coronavirus (COVID-19)*, 1–11.
24. Samarina, A., & Bezemer, D. (2016). Do capital flows change domestic credit allocation? *Journal of International Money and Finance*, 62, 98–121.

Kimiko Sugimoto is a professor at the Hirao School of Management at Konan University in Japan. She received her Ph.D. from Osaka University, and her main research interests include monetary integration, international financial transmission and financial development in Africa.

Masahiro Enya is an associate professor of economics at Kanazawa University in Japan. He received his Ph.D. from Osaka University, also in Japan, and his main research interest is international finance.

Chapter 4
Global Financial Crisis and Demand for the US Dollar as an International Currency

Takeshi Hoshikawa and Kazuyuki Inagaki

Abstract In the late 2000s, demand deposits from foreign countries increased rapidly in the United States. Why did amounts of US demand deposits from abroad increase so rapidly? What is the relation between the global financial crisis and the rapid increase in demand deposits from foreign countries? Few studies have emphasized studies of demand deposits from abroad. Therefore we specifically examine the US dollar holdings of foreign financial institutions. This study was conducted to respond to the following questions: how US dollar holdings are determined by foreign financial institutions and why they have risen so rapidly. The analysis identified the following factors. (1) When financial markets tighten because of some crisis, demand for the US dollar as an international currency increases. (2) An increase in global trade volumes will raise demand for the US dollar. (3) If interest rates in the USrise, demand for US dollars from foreign countries can be expected to decrease. (4) A stronger US dollar will increase demand for the US dollar. (5) Foreign commercial banks and foreign official institutions have different effects on US demand deposits from foreign countries. As discussed above, US demand deposits from foreign countries increase because of multiple factors such as high global trade volume, low interest rates, a strong US dollar, and the financial crisis.

Keywords Cointegration · Demand deposits · Demand for the dollar · Global financial crisis · International currency

---

T. Hoshikawa (✉)
Faculty of Economics, Kindai University, 3-4-1, Kowakae, Higashi-Osaka 577-8502, Japan
e-mail: hoshikawa@kindai.ac.jp

K. Inagaki
Department of Economics, Nanzan University, 18 Yamazato-cho, Showa-ku, Nagoya 466-8673, Japan
e-mail: inagaki@nanzan-u.ac.jp

© The Author(s), under exclusive license to Springer Nature Singapore Pte Ltd. 2022
Y. Matsubayashi and S. Kitano (eds.), *Global Financial Flows in the Pre- and Post-global Crisis Periods*, Kobe University Monograph Series in Social Science Research,
https://doi.org/10.1007/978-981-19-3613-5_4

4.1 Money Demand Function of the US Dollar as an International Currency

Since 2008, demand deposits from foreign commercial banks and foreign official institutions have been increasing rapidly in the United States. Figures 4.1 and 4.2 respectively present Demand Deposits Due to Foreign Commercial Banks and Demand Deposits Due to Foreign Official Institutions. What has caused the sharp rise in foreign holdings of US demand deposits? Is there any connection between the increase in demand deposits from foreign countries and the global financial crisis? One underlying reason for this phenomenon might be a shift to safe assets during global financial crises: the US dollar is a high-liquidity asset. The dollar is also important from the perspective of global liquidity. This report of our study explains how foreign financial institutions choose to hold demand deposits in the US. Furthermore, we examine the question of why demand deposits from abroad have increased.

The US dollar serves two important roles as a domestic currency and as an international currency. The Bank of International Settlements [1] stated that "The US dollar remained the dominant vehicle currency, being on one side of 88% of all trades in April 2016." The importance of the US dollar as an international currency has remained consistently high since WWII. Indeed, demand for the US dollar as an international currency differs from demand for other currencies. Put most simply, the US dollar is demanded not only in the USbut also in other countries. Many earlier studies have examined the money demand function in the United States, but they do not consider demand from outside the country. A few studies have elucidated demand from outside the US. Bergstrand and Bundt [2] assessed demand of other

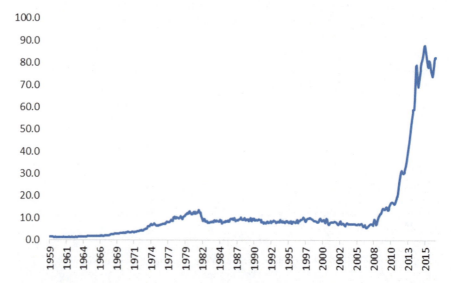

Fig. 4.1 Demand deposits due to Foreign Commercial Banks. *Source* Federal Reserve Bank of St. Louis. Billions of dollars, monthly, not seasonally adjusted

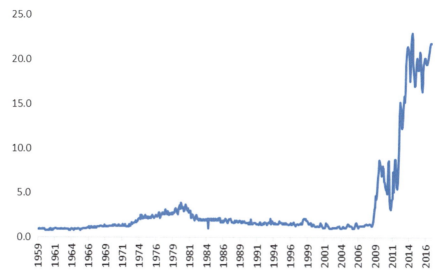

Fig. 4.2 Demand deposits due to Foreign Official Institutions. *Source* Federal Reserve Bank of St. Louis. Billions of dollars, monthly, not seasonally adjusted

countries for the US dollar. They used cointegration analysis to account for currency substitutes and estimated demand for the currency. As important variables affecting demand for the international currency, Bergstrand and Bundt [2] listed the US interest rate, interest rates in other countries, the US income level, income levels in other countries, and exchange rates. The sample period used by Bergstrand and Bundt [2] was 1978–1988. This study is an extension of that work, including some analysis of the global financial crisis in 2008. This study includes the period during which foreign demand for US demand deposits increased rapidly.

Key variables are income and interest rates in the money demand function as a domestic currency. Demand for transactions is one factor affecting demand for money. Increased income or consumption can be expected to increase transactions, which can then be expected to result in stronger demand for money, thereby providing a liquidity benefit of holding money for expenditure. However, neither cash nor bank deposits can earn interest. The interest rate is also important because it represents the opportunity cost of holding money. Numerous studies have particularly addressed the demand function in the US. Such studies were well summarized by Walsh [13]. For example, Nakashima and Saito [9] and Dreger and Wolters [3] estimated the money demand function for the Euro area and Japan. In fact, many studies ignore demand from outside a country when estimating the money demand functions countries. Studies of currency substitution incorporate demand for money from abroad. Felices and Tuesta [4] and Kumamotoand Kumamoto [6] respectively explain money demand functions including foreign demand. When considering money demand from foreign countries, variables such as exchange rates, foreign income, and interest rates are expected to play an important role. Studies of currency substitution that examine demand for foreign money specifically elucidate findings for economically developing countries or emphasize the dollarization of small countries. Few specifically examine demand for money in the United States. This paper presents consideration of money demand from foreign countries, with particular examination of the United States. Another feature of this study is that it particularly elucidates the relation between the global financial crisis and foreign holdings as demand deposits. The degree of financial market tightness is applied as a variable.

The period of a sharp rise in demand deposits around 2008 coincided with implementation of a quantitative easing policy and interest rates at a zero lower bound. The quantitative easing policy effects must therefore be considered when examining the rapid increase in demand deposits. During this period, analysis of the quantity of money and the interest rate becomes important as a policy tool. Moreover, very few studies have used data of Demand Deposits Due to Foreign Commercial Banks. Following are the salient contributions of these analyses.

Results of this study indicate the following conclusions: (1) demand for the US dollar as an international currency increases when financial markets are tight; (2) an increase in global trade volume stimulates demand for the US dollar as an international currency; (3) an increase in the US interest rate reduces US dollar demand deposits from foreign countries; (4) appreciation of the US dollar encourages demand for the US dollar as an international currency; and (5) foreign commercial banks and foreign public institutions have different effects on demand for the US dollar.

This paper is organized as follows. Section 4.2 explains what variables are important for assessing and quantifying international currency demand. Section 4.3 presents the estimation model and results. Section 4.4 is the conclusion.

4.2 Important Variables as an International Currency

Using the data of Demand Deposits Due to Foreign Commercial Banks, one can analyze demand for the dollar as an international currency. The definition of M1 for money supply includes demand deposits at commercial banks, but excludes amounts held by foreign banks and official institutions. Therefore, demand for M1 is regarded as representing domestic demand from the US. Demand deposits held by foreign commercial banks and foreign official institutions are regarded as international demand for the dollar as an international currency. Using these data, one can analyze demand for money from domestic and foreign sources separately. As described in this paper, we analyze changes in Demand Deposits Due to Foreign Commercial Banks and Demand Deposits Due to Foreign Official Institutions as shown in Figs. 4.1 and 4.2.

Figures 4.1 and 4.2 show that demand deposits held by foreign commercial banks and foreign official institutions tended to increase in the 1970s, around the time of the first oil crisis in 1973 and the second oil crisis in 1979. The holdings are stable from the mid-1980s to the early 2000s. Subsequently, a sharp increase occurred during the global financial crisis in 2008. This finding suggests that a relation might

Fig. 4.3 World trade volume

exist between the financial crisis and demand deposits held by foreign countries. The key explanatory variables in the analysis of this paper are the world trade volume, the USinterest rate, the exchange rate, and tightness of financial markets. First, an increase in world trade volumes is expected to increase demand for the dollar as an international currency. Figure 4.3 presents trends in world trade volumes since 1992. The graph presents an upward trend, indicating that the world trade volume has been increasing throughout the period. However, a temporary decrease occurred in 2008 during the global financial crisis.

Figure 4.4 portrays the trend of interest rates in the United States. The US interest rate is the yield on 10-year government bonds in this figure. In considering demand for money, the interest rate is the opportunity cost of holding money. When the interest rate reaches the zero lower bound, the opportunity cost of holding money is zero. If interest rates in the US rise, then demand will shift from money to bonds in the US. Consequently, the demand for money to hold US currency can be expected to decrease. Compared to earlier periods when interest rates were higher, a strong incentive to hold money prevailed because US interest rates were low in the 2000s.

The exchange rate is an important variable for transactions and asset holdings between the US and foreign countries. Figure 4.5 presents changes that have occurred in the effective exchange rate of the US dollar. The dollar increased in value until around 2002 and decreased in value for several years thereafter. In 2008, when the global financial crisis occurred, the dollar appreciated temporarily, although the crisis originated in the US. The value of the dollar decreased again around 2010; it has continued to increase since 2015. For foreign financial institutions, a strong dollar has the effect of increasing the value of their dollar deposits. Therefore, exchange rate trends affect dollar demand.

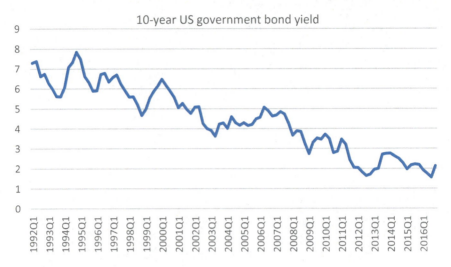

Fig. 4.4 US interest rates

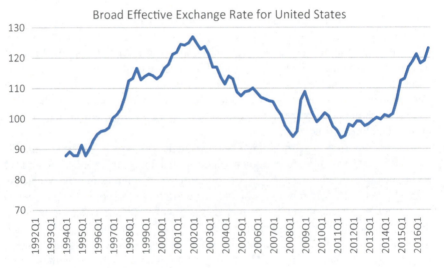

Fig. 4.5 Effective US dollar exchange rate

Because the sample period includes the global financial crisis, financial market tightness is an important variable. During a crisis, a flight to safer cash will occur. During an international financial crisis, the possibility exists that a phenomenon such as dollar buying for a safe haven might occur. Figure 4.6 shows the variable of the degree of financial market tightness as the degree of financial crisis. This financial market stress variable is called the St. Louis Fed Financial Stress Index, which was created from 18 different weekly datasets. A value of zero represents

Fig. 4.6 Tightness of financial markets

normal conditions. When it is positive, financial markets are tight. A negative value indicates that financial stress is lower than normal. During the global financial crisis in 2008, the degree of financial market tightness immediately shifted to a positive value (Fig. 4.6).

4.3 Models and Results of Estimation

4.3.1 Estimation Models and Data

The analyses presented in this paper specifically examine demand deposits held abroad, as shown in Figs. 4.1 and 4.2, which increased sharply during the global financial crisis of 2008. This surge apparently illustrates the dollar-holding behavior of foreign financial institutions when a crisis occurs. The US monetary base shown in Fig. 4.7, however, also increased rapidly during that period. This increase might reflect the quantitative easing policy as a shock on the money supply side. Therefore, to remove effects of the quantitative easing policy shock, we use dollar demand deposits held by foreign countries divided by the US monetary base. In Fig. 4.8, BANK/MB represents dollar demand deposits held by foreign banks divided by the US monetary base. Also, OFFICIAL/MB represents dollar demand deposits held by foreign official institutions divided by the USmonetary base. Furthermore, TOTAL/MB is the sum of dollar demand deposits held by foreign banks and foreign official institutions divided by the monetary base. Since approximately 2006, dollar demand deposits held by foreign countries have increased compared to the US monetary base. In other words, the dollar demand deposits of foreign banks and official

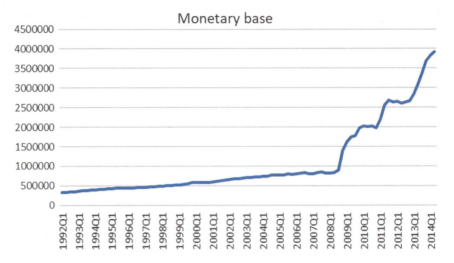

Fig. 4.7 US monetary base

institutions have increased even after consideration of quantitative easing policy effects.

The estimation equation is presented below.

$$Y_t = X'_t \beta + \sum_{j=-k}^{k} \Delta X'_{t-j} \gamma_j + u_t$$

Explained variable Y_t represents the US dollar demand deposits of foreign banks and official institutions such as TOTAL/MB, BANK/MB, and OFFICIAL/MB in Fig. 4.8. Variable Y_t is dividing US dollar demand deposits held in foreign countries by the monetary base.

TOTAL/MB = US dollar demand deposits held in foreign countries (total) ÷ US monetary base
BANK/MB = US dollar demand deposits held in foreign countries (banks) ÷ US monetary base
OFFICIAL/MB = US dollar demand deposits held in foreign countries (official institutions) ÷ US monetary base

The explanatory variables are $X_t = [WT_t, IR_t, ER_t, ES_t]'$, where WT_t, IR_t, ER_t, and FS_t respectively represent the world trade volume, the interest rate, the effective exchange rate, and variables of financial stress index. The estimation method is based on the Dynamic OLS (DOLS) method. We add the leads and lags of differences of the explanatory variables as $\Delta X'_{t-j} = X'_{t-j} - X'_{t-j-1}$.[1]

---

[1] This study's analysis assumed $k = 1$.

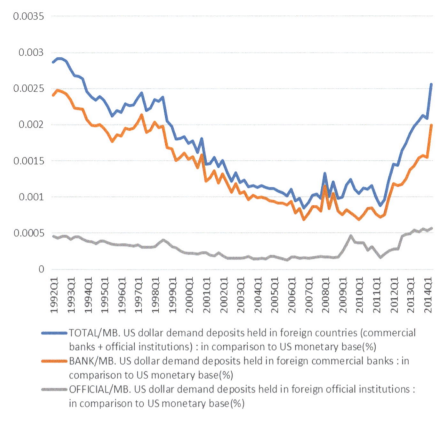

Fig. 4.8 US dollar deposits-to-monetary base ratio held by foreign banks and foreign official institutions. Percentage in US monetary base (unit: %)

The explanatory variables are the logarithmic value of the world trade volume WT_t, 10-year US government bond yield IR_t, the logarithmic value of effective US dollar exchange rate[2] ER_t, and the index of financial market tightness FS_t. These are presented in Figs. 4.3, 4.4, 4.5 and 4.6.

The expected signs of parameters must be explained next. The sign assumed for the coefficient of the world trade volume WT_t is positive because an increase in the world trade volume increases as the volume of international transactions grows and induces growth in demand for international currencies. Although data such as GDP are often used when assessing domestic demand for money, trade volume is more appropriate when analyzing demand for an international currency.

The expected sign of the coefficient of 10-year USgovernment bond yield IR_t is negative. When considering ordinary demand for money, an interest rate represents the opportunity cost of holding money that does not earn interest. Because US dollar demand deposits do not earn interest, an interest rate affects the selection between

---

[2] Extensive data that include China are used.

holding US dollar deposits and holding US dollar bonds. An increase in the interest rate is likely to reduce demand for US dollar demand deposits that earn no interest. The interest rate variable is not logarithmic, but is used in the level data.

The expected sign of the coefficient of effective US dollar exchange rate ER_t cannot be ascertained. From a foreign country's perspective, if the asset is held in dollars, then there will be earnings from interest rates and earnings or losses from changes in exchange rates. The demand for dollars might increase because of depreciation of the dollar. Alternatively, the demand for dollars might increase because of appreciation of the dollar.

As for the coefficient of the financial stress index FS_t, the assumed sign is ambiguous. If a financial crisis occurs in the USand financial markets become tight, then a possibility exists that US dollar demand will decrease. In response to a crisis in the United States, foreign financial institutions might reduce their dollar holdings. By contrast, if a phenomenon such as dollar buying as a safe haven occurs, then demand for the dollar as an international currency will increase as a safe asset because of tight financial markets. If the coefficient of the estimated financial stress index is negative, then the demand for dollars will decrease because of the tightness of the financial market. If the coefficient is positive, then demand for dollars can be expected to increase.

As depicted in Fig. 4.1 and 4.2, changes in US dollar demand deposits held in foreign countries changed considerably from the time before to the time after the global financial crisis. Therefore, dividing the period into those before and after the crisis, this study specifically examines the time after the crisis. Consequently, the period between the first quarter of 2006 and the second quarter of 2014[3] was used for estimation. Figure 4.8 depicting US dollar deposits divided by the monetary base began rising in 2006. That period is used for analyses hereinafter.

Each of these variables might have a unit root. Because spurious regression occurs when the dependent and explanatory variables have a unit root, a unit root test was conducted for each variable as a pretest. Table 4.1 presents results of unit root tests obtained using the method described by Ng and Perron [10]. The null hypothesis is that the variable has a unit root. Data presented in Table 4.1 suggest that no variable can reject the null hypothesis based on the level. Therefore, they presumably have unit roots. When the first difference was taken, all variables rejected the null hypothesis and were I(1) variables.

Table 4.2 presents results of cointegration tests using the method presented by Shin [12]. The null hypothesis is that cointegration exists, that the 5% critical value is 0.121, and that the 10% critical value is 0.094.

When BANK/MB is used as the dependent variable, which is the case of foreign commercial banks, the statistic of cointegration test is 0.093, which does not reject the null hypothesis that cointegration exists. When OFFICIAL/MB is used as the dependent variable, which is the case of foreign official institutions, the statistic is 0.099, which is rejected at the 10% level, but not at the 5% level. The statistic applied

---

[3] Data until the second quarter of 2014 are used because it is a period for which world trade volume data are available.

4 Global Financial Crisis and Demand for the US Dollar … 109

Table 4.1 Unit root test

Variable	Level	First difference
US dollar demand deposits (foreign, total)	–0.539	–9.661*
US dollar demand deposits (foreign banks)	0.174	–8.240*
US dollar demand deposits (foreign official institutions)	–1.157	–20.830**
Financial stress index	–5.341	–20.714**
Effective US dollar exchange rate	–5.343	–17.531**
World trade volume	–4.679	–23.374**
10-year US government bond yield	–0.504	–15.747**

Note MZ_{α} test, Ng and Perron [10]: The null hypothesis is that a unit root exists
*5% significance level; **1% significance level. Spectral estimation method: GLS-detrended AR based on SBIC

Table 4.2 Cointegration test

	Foreign holders of US dollar demand deposits		
	Banks	Official Institutions	Total
Statistics	0.093	0.099	0.061

Note Shin [12]: The null hypothesis is that cointegration exists. The 10% critical value is 0.094. Therefore, there is no cointegration at the 10% significance level in the case of official institutions. Spectral estimation method: GLS-detrended AR based on SBIC

when using TOTAL/MB, which aggregates the holdings of foreign banks and official institutions, is 0.061. The null hypothesis is not rejected. Therefore, a cointegration relation can be inferred between these variables.

4.3.2 Results of Estimation

Table 4.3 through Table 4.5 present cointegration estimation results. Table 4.3 presents results obtained when the left-hand side dependent variable is the sum of

Table 4.3 Estimation results

Explained variable: TOTAL/MB (total)		
Variable	Coefficient	Standard error
World trade volume	5.954**	0.792
US interest rate	–0.175**	0.057
Effective US dollar exchange rate	8.898**	1.463
Financial stress index	0.269**	0.045

**1% significance level. Estimated using DOLS. Leads and lags and constant terms are omitted

Table 4.4 Estimation results

Explained variable: BANK/MB (foreign commercial banks)		
Variable	Coefficient	Standard Error
World trade volume	6.403**	1.263
US interest rate	−0.076	0.090
Effective US dollar exchange rate	8.991**	2.333
Financial stress index	0.223**	0.072

**1% significance level. Estimated using DOLS. Leads and lags and constant terms are omitted

Table 4.5 Estimation results

Explained variable: OFFICIAL/MB (foreign official institutions)		
Variable	Coefficient	Standard Error
World trade volume	5.726**	1.760
US interest rate	−0.398**	0.126
Effective US dollar exchange rate	9.896**	3.251
Financial stress index	0.404**	0.101

**1% significance level. Estimated using DOLS. Leads and lags and constant terms are omitted

dollar demand deposits (TOTAL/MB) held by banks and official institutions. Table 4.4 presents results obtained when the dependent variable is BANK/MB, the demand deposits held by foreign commercial banks. Table 4.5 presents results for the case in which the dependent variable is OFFICIAL/MB, which are demand deposits held by foreign official institutions. The lead, lag, and constant terms are not shown.

First, one must address how the volume of worldwide trade affects demand for the dollar as an international currency. Table 4.3 shows that the coefficient of world trade volume is 5.954 and that it is significantly positive. In Tables 4.4 and 4.5, the respective coefficients of world trade volume are 6.403 and 5.726, which are notably both positive and which represent similar results. Because the coefficient of foreign commercial banks is larger than that of official institutions, foreign commercial banks are presumably more affected by the volume of world trade. Therefore, when the world trade volume increases, demand for the dollar as an international currency increases. Because the coefficient is positive and significant, probably demand exists for the dollar as an international currency for trade.

How does the yield on 10-year US government bonds affect demand for the dollar as an international currency? In Table 4.3, the coefficient of the US interest rate is −0.175, which is significant and negative. It shows that an increase in the US interest rate decreases the variable TOTAL/MB of total dollar demand deposits held by foreign banks and official institutions.

How does the 10-year US government bond yield affect demand for the dollar as an international currency? As presented in Table 4.3, the coefficient of the US interest rate is −0.175, which is significant and negative. That finding shows that an increase in the US interest rate has the effect of decreasing the variable TOTAL/MB of the total dollar demand deposits held by foreign banks and official institutions. The coefficient of the US interest rate in Table 4.4 is also negative but not significant: −0.076. Because the US interest rate on the variable BANK/MB for foreign commercial banks is not significant, the US interest rate is unimportant for foreign commercial banks. After 2006, the effect of interest rates as an opportunity cost might be small because the US interest rate is low. However, Table 4.5 shows that the US interest rate is significant and negative at −0.398 for foreign official institutions. Also, official institutions are more likely to be affected by the US interest rate.

Specifically, the effects of the exchange rate, as represented by the coefficients of the dollar effective exchange rate in Tables 4.3, 4.4, and 4.5 are, respectively, 8.898, 8.991, and 9.896: all are significant and positive. It is apparent that a strong dollar increases demand for the dollar as an international currency. When the currency value is high, demand for the dollar as an international currency is expected to increase.

Finally, on must address the relation between the degree of financial market tightness and demand for the dollar as an international currency. As shown in Table 4.3, the coefficient of the financial stress index is 0.269, which is significant and positive. The coefficients of the financial stress index in Tables 4.4 and 4.5 are, respectively, 0.223 and 0.404. Both are significant and positive and similar, which indicates that when financial markets are tight because of a crisis, demand for the dollar as an international currency increases.

In summary, increases in dollar demand deposits held by foreign countries might have been caused by an increase in the volume of world trade and a decline in US interest rates. Furthermore, the results suggest that demand for the dollar as an international currency increased because of actions to ensure liquidity during the global financial crisis. The combination of these factors has led to a sharp increase in dollar demand deposits held abroad since 2008.

4.4 Conclusion

As described in this paper, we analyzed demand for the US dollar as an international currency using data for demand deposits held by foreign commercial banks and foreign official institutions. From our analysis, it is apparent that demand for the dollar as an international currency depends on the following factors. First, as the world trade volume increases, demand for the dollar as an international currency increases. Particularly, foreign commercial banks are more affected by world trade volumes than foreign official institutions are. Second, higher US interest rates can be expected to reduce foreign holdings of dollar demand deposits. Results of this study also show that foreign commercial banks are unaffected by interest rates, whereas public institutions are affected by interest rates. Third, a strong dollar increases demand for the dollar as an international currency, which indicates a stronger incentive to hold international currencies during periods of high currency value. Finally, demand for the dollar as an international currency increases when financial markets are tight. An issue to be addressed in future studies is analysis of international demand for the dollar, including structural changes. Furthermore, other variables and other factors must be added to consider demand for the dollar as an international currency.

It will be interesting to elucidate how foreign dollar holdings will be affected when interest rates in the US rise in the future.

Acknowledgements This work was supported by KAKENHI (20K01760, 21K01592).

References

1. Bank for International Settlements. (2016). Triennial Central Bank Survey of foreign exchange, OTC derivatives markets in 2016.
2. Bergstrand, J. H., & Bundt, T. P. (1990). Currency substitution and monetary autonomy: The foreign demand for US demand deposits. *Journal of International Money and Finance, 9*(3), 325–334.
3. Dreger, C., & Wolters, J. (2010). Investigating M3 money demand in the euro area. *Journal of International Money and Finance*, 29(1), 111–122.
4. Felices, G., & Tuesta, V. (2013). Monetary policy in a dual currency environment. *Applied Economics, 45*(34), 4739–4753.
5. Inagaki, K. (2009). Estimating the interest rate semi-elasticity of the demand for money in low interest rate environments. *Economic Modelling, 26*(1), 147–154.
6. Kumamoto, H., & Kumamoto, M. (2014). A panel time series approach to currency substitution. *Economics and Finance Review, 3*, 1–12.
7. McKinnon, R. I. (1982). Currency substitution and instability in the world dollar standard. *The American Economic Review, 72*(3), 320–333.
8. Miyao, R. (1996). Does a cointegrating M2 demand relation really exist in the United States? *Journal of Money, Credit and Banking, 28*(3), 365–380.
9. Nakashima, K., & Saito, M. (2012). On the comparison of alternative specifications for money demand: The case of extremely low interest rate regimes in Japan. *Journal of the Japanese and International Economies*, 26(3), 454–471.
10. Ng, S., & Perron, P. (2001). Lag length selection and the construction of unit root tests with good size and power. *Econometrica, 69*, 1519–1554.
11. Obstfeld, M., & Rogoff, K. (1996). *Foundations of international macroeconomics*. Cambridge, MA: MIT Press.
12. Shin, Y. (1994). A residual-based test of the null of cointegration against the alternative of no cointegration. *Econometric Theory, 10*(1), 91–115.
13. Walsh, C. (2017). Monetary Theory and Policy, 4th. ed., The MIT Press.

Takeshi Hoshikawa is a professor of economics at Kindai University in Japan. He received his Ph.D. from Kobe University, and his main research interest is international finance.

Kazuyuki Inagaki is a professor of economics at Nanzan University in Japan. He received his Ph.D. from Kobe University, and his main research interest is international macroeconomics.

Chapter 5
Sovereign Credit Default Swaps and U.S. Economic Policy Uncertainty After the Global Financial Crisis

Masahiro Inoguchi

Abstract This paper empirically investigates factors for sovereign credit default swap (CDS) spreads as a proxy for sovereign credit risk. We focus on U.S. economic policy uncertainty as a global factor and employ weekly data following the global financial crisis. In addition, we highlight the difference between advanced and emerging economies. The results show that U.S. economic policy uncertainty index changes influenced sovereign CDS spreads during quantitative easing (QE) 1 in emerging economies and during QE2 and QE3 in advanced economies. The U.S. stock index and the VIX affected the sovereign CDS spreads for all subsample periods in emerging economies, except QE2. This suggests that U.S. financial market factors are more important than economic policy uncertainty for the sovereign credit risk in emerging economies.

Keywords Sovereign CDS spreads · U.S. economic policy uncertainty · Global risk · Large-scale asset purchases · Emerging economies

5.1 Introduction

An assessment of sovereign credit risk may help reduce the likelihood of sovereign default. In particular, investigating the factors driving sovereign credit risk is essential for both governments and investors, especially if the risk is relatively high, as in emerging economies. Therefore, this study empirically explores factors of sovereign credit risk and primarily focuses on the influence of U.S. economic policy uncertainty as a global factor.

Various metrics are monitored to measure sovereign credit risk, including sovereign credit default swap (CDS) spreads and government bond yields. While

---

This research was supported in part by the Japanese MEXT KAKENHI (Grant No. 16K03759).

M. Inoguchi (✉)
College of Business Administration, Ritsumeikan University, 2-150, Iwakura-cho, Ibaraki, Osaka, Japan
e-mail: inoguchi@fc.ritsumei.ac.jp

© The Author(s), under exclusive license to Springer Nature Singapore Pte Ltd. 2022
Y. Matsubayashi and S. Kitano (eds.), *Global Financial Flows in the Pre- and Post-global Crisis Periods*, Kobe University Monograph Series in Social Science Research,
https://doi.org/10.1007/978-981-19-3613-5_5

we can gauge the sovereign credit risk by the difference between the government bond yield of a specified country and that of a benchmark country, the sovereign CDS spread of a country by itself reflects its sovereign credit risk. The sovereign CDS spread is useful in directly measuring sovereign credit risk; thus, we use it to explore factors that affect sovereign credit risk. We utilize weekly sovereign CDS spread data for 33 sample countries from February 25, 2008–March 25, 2016.

Sovereign credit risk is affected not only by fiscal conditions but also by other domestic economic conditions and global factors. As Table 5.1 shows, previous studies argue an influence of foreign shocks on sovereign credit risk, and some explore the global correlations of sovereign CDS markets to discuss the international transmission of sovereign debt shocks [4, 8, 10–13, 18]. Additionally, some studies use daily or weekly sovereign CDS data to focus on specific shocks and investigate their influence on sovereign CDS markets [1, 7, 9, 14, 16]. Many studies examine the effect of domestic factors driving sovereign credit risk on the monthly, quarterly, and yearly statistics of the sovereign CDS spreads [2, 3, 6, 17].

Fewer studies have analyzed both global and domestic factors driving sovereign CDS spreads. Among previous articles, Longstaff et al. [17] and Kim et al. [16] investigated the impacts of both domestic and global factors on sovereign CDS spreads. Longstaff et al. [17] tested monthly data of emerging economies from October 2000 to January 2010, demonstrating that sovereign CDS spreads relate to global factors more than local factors.[1] Kim et al. [16] used daily data of 19 emerging and advanced economies and studied the impact of macroeconomic news on sovereign CDS spreads and spread volatility from November 2007 to March 2012. They found that sovereign CDS spreads and volatility respond to both foreign and domestic news. Though the two studies use different sample data, their results suggest the critical role of foreign factors.[2]

This paper focuses on the influence of U.S. economic policy uncertainty as a global factor, which previous studies did not investigate. Following the global financial crisis (GFC), monetary policy in the U.S. went through a transition from a period of the U.S. large-scale asset purchases (LSAPs), including three phases of quantitative easing (QE) and tapering of QE, to a period of rising interest rates after the LSAPs. Uncertainty in the U.S. economic policy, including changes in the monetary policy, is likely to influence investor attitudes to credit risk because the LSAPs and tapering of QE are unprecedented for investors worldwide. We employ the U.S. economic policy uncertainty index provided by Baker et al. [5]. In addition, we explore the different factors for sovereign CDS spreads between advanced and emerging economies because financial markets and the governments in emerging economies are generally smaller, and the influence of global shocks on the sovereign credit risk of emerging markets may be more significant than that of advanced markets.

---

[1] Longstaff et al. [17] also decomposed the sovereign credit spreads into their risk premium and default risk components and explored global factors driving those components.

[2] With respect to domestic factors, Kim et al. [16] implied the influence of both domestic and foreign factors on the sovereign credit risk, which is different from that by Longstaff et al. [17].

5 Sovereign Credit Default Swaps and U.S. Economic Policy ... 115

Table 5.1 Related studies

Paper	Main target	Sample countries	Period	Data frequency
International transmission of sovereign debt shocks				
Ang and Longstaff [4]	Correlation between sovereign credit risk in US states and that in European countries	10 US states and 11 eurozone countries	May 14, 2008–January 5, 2011	Daily
Calice et al. [8]	Liquidity and credit interactions for sovereign bond and CDS spreads in Europe	10 eurozone countries	January 1, 2007–October 1, 2010	Daily
Delatte et al. [10]	Transmission of shock in sovereign debt market during the European sovereign crisis	11 European countries	January 1, 2008–July 27, 2010	Daily
Grammatikos and Vermeulen [11]	Transmission of shock in financial market from the US to Europe	15 EMU countries	January 2003–August 2010	Daily
Gunduz and Kaya [12]	Co-movements of sovereign CDS spreads with the financial crisis	10 eurozone countries	January 2006–November 2013	Daily
Hui and Chung [13]	Correlation between the dollar-euro currency option prices and the sovereign CDS spreads	11 eurozone countries	January 2, 2006–April 30, 2010	Daily
Kalbaska and Gatkowski [15]	Correlation of sovereign credit risk among European countries and the US	9 countries	August 2005–September 2010	Daily
Wang and Moore [18]	Influence of the sovereign CDS spreads in the US on other countries and the correlation's driver	38 advanced and emerging countries	January 2007–December 2009	Daily

(continued)

Table 5.1 (continued)

Paper	Main target	Sample countries	Period	Data frequency
Influence of specific shocks on sovereign CDS markets				
Afonso et al. [1]	Effect of sovereign credit rating change announcements on sovereign yield and CDS spreads in EU countries	24 EU countries	January 1995–October 2010	Daily
Blau and Roseman [7]	Effect of sovereign credit rating downgrade of the US on the CDS spreads in Europe	31 European countries	21-day period surrounding the August 5th, 2011	Daily
Calice et al. [9]	Dynamic behavior of the sovereign CDS term premium	10 European countries	September 2007–February 2012	Daily
Ismailescu and Kazemi [14]	Effect of sovereign credit rating change announcements on the CDS spreads	22 emerging countries	January 2, 2001 –April 22, 2009	Daily
Kim et al. [16]	Impact of macroeconomic news on the sovereign CDS spreads	19 countries	14 November 2007–31 March 2012	Daily
Domestic and global factors for sovereign credit risk				
Ahmed et al. [2]	Role of economic fundamentals in the transmission of international shocks	64 emerging countries	1990–2016	Monthly
Aizenman et al. [3]	Effect of sovereign credit rating changes on CDS spreads in EU countries	26 EU countries	January 2005–August 2012	Monthly
Beirne and Fratzscher [6]	Drivers of sovereign credit risk during the European sovereign debt crisis	31 advanced and emerging countries	1999–2011	Monthly
Longstaff et al. [17]	Factors for sovereign credit risk	26 advanced and emerging countries	October 2000–January 2010	Monthly

5 Sovereign Credit Default Swaps and U.S. Economic Policy ...

The regression result shows that the U.S. economic policy uncertainty influenced sovereign CDS spreads in emerging economies for QE1 and advanced economies for the periods of QE2 and QE3. By contrast, the U.S. stock market price and the VIX affected sovereign CDS spreads of emerging economies in every subsample period except QE2. This suggests that, as a global factor, U.S. financial market factors are more important than the U.S. economic policy uncertainty for sovereign credit risk in emerging economies. Furthermore, this propensity is more evident in emerging economies than in advanced economies.

The remainder of the paper is structured as follows. Section 5.2 graphically illustrates the fluctuation of sovereign CDS spreads and the global variables. Section 5.3 discusses the methods used to estimate the influence on sovereign CDS spreads, and Sect. 5.4 provides some concluding remarks.

5.2 An Overview of Sovereign CDS Spreads and the U.S. Financial Markets

This section graphically illustrates the fluctuations in sovereign CDS spreads with the following global variables: the S&P 500 index, the 5-year U.S. Treasury yield, the VIX index, and the U.S. economic policy uncertainty index. All data are monthly averages of daily statistics from December 2008 to March 2016. Figures 5.1, 5.2, 5.3 and 5.4 depict the rates of change in sovereign CDS spreads in each sample country. Figures 5.1, 5.2 and 5.3 illustrate the rates of change in emerging economies' sovereign CDS spreads according to the region (Europe and Africa, Asia and the Middle East, and Latin America), and Fig. 5.4 shows the advanced economies' CDS spreads. Figures 5.5, 5.6, 5.7 and 5.8 present the average rates of change in sovereign CDS spreads of our sample countries and the fluctuations of the U.S. indices.

Figure 5.1 shows that the rates of change in sovereign CDS spreads for Europe and Africa are similar. Most emerging countries' sovereign CDS spreads rose primarily in February 2009, May and June 2010, September 2011, and June 2013. Thus, the sovereign credit risk for emerging economies in Europe and Africa significantly increased in those periods. The sovereign CDS spreads of Slovenia and Russia fluctuated most from December 2008 to September 2014 and March 2014 to March 2016, respectively. Figure 5.2 presents the rates of change in sovereign CDS spreads in Asian and Middle Eastern emerging economies. While their fluctuations are similar, the change in the sovereign spreads of Kazakhstan is more prominent than other emerging economies in this group. Figure 5.3 shows that the rates of change in sovereign CDS spreads are similar among Latin American emerging countries. Figures 5.4 depicts the rates of change in sovereign CDS spreads in advanced economies. The fluctuation was significant from the end of 2008 to the middle of 2011, which includes the GFC and the sovereign debt crisis in the Euro area. From Figs. 5.1, 5.2, 5.3 and 5.4, most countries' sovereign CDS spreads rise and fall in similar periods, and most sample countries' change rates are not significantly

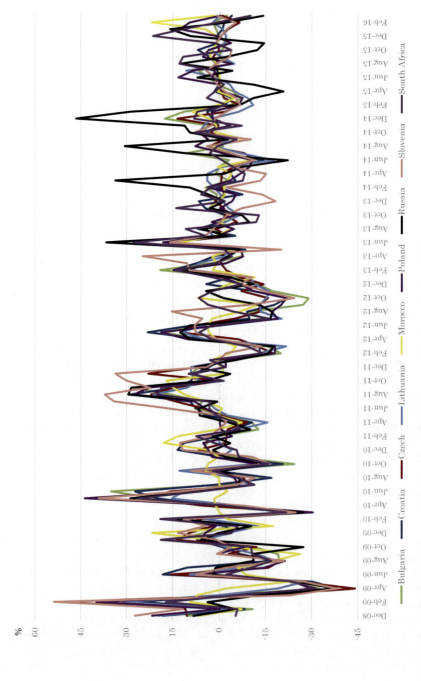

Fig. 5.1 Rate of change in CDS spreads in European and African emerging economies (monthly)

5 Sovereign Credit Default Swaps and U.S. Economic Policy ...

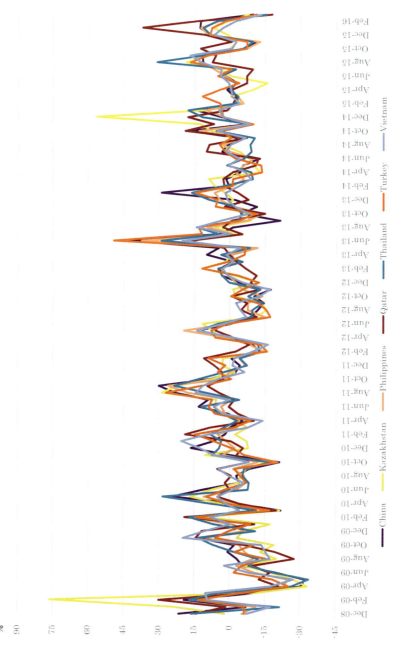

Fig. 5.2 Rate of change in CDS spreads in Asian and Middle-Eastern emerging economies (monthly)

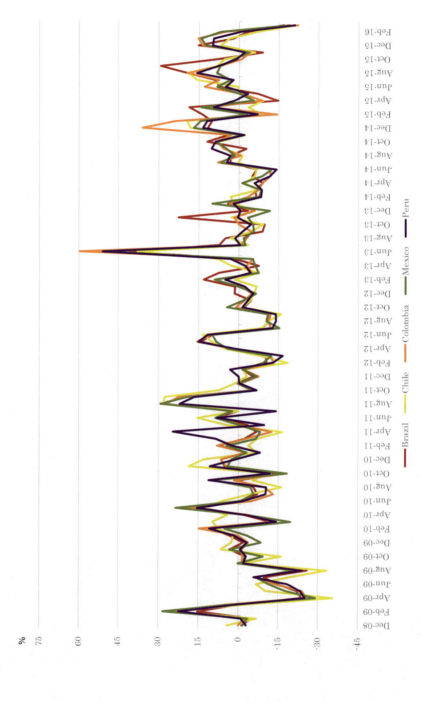

Fig. 5.3 Rate of change in CDS spreads in Latin-American emerging economies (monthly)

5 Sovereign Credit Default Swaps and U.S. Economic Policy …   121

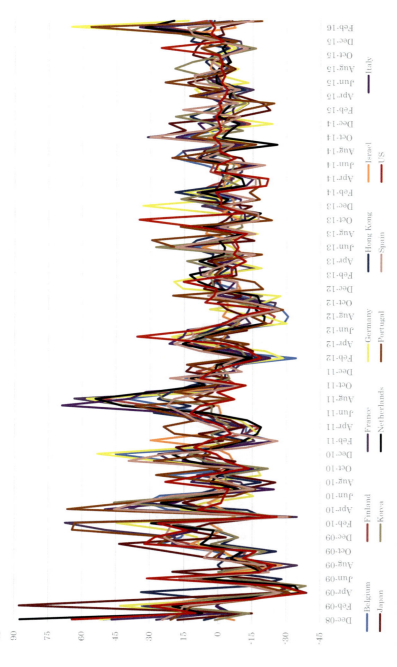

Fig. 5.4 Rate of change in CDS spreads in advanced economies (monthly)

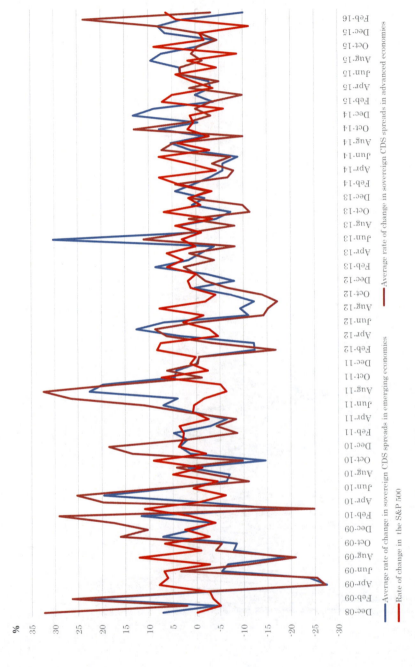

Fig. 5.5 Rates of change in sovereign CDS spreads and the U.S. stock index

5 Sovereign Credit Default Swaps and U.S. Economic Policy ...

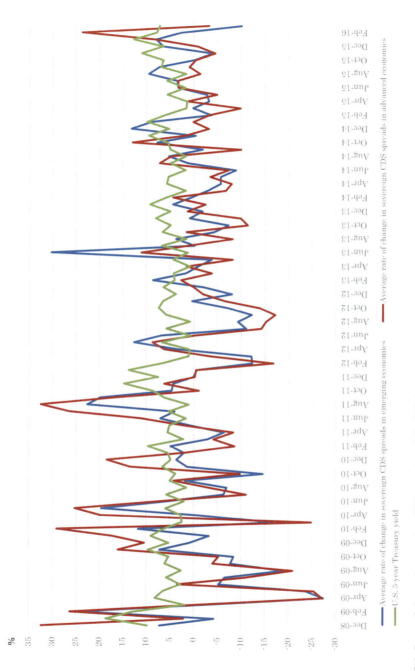

Fig. 5.6 Rates of change in sovereign CDS spreads and the U.S. interest rate

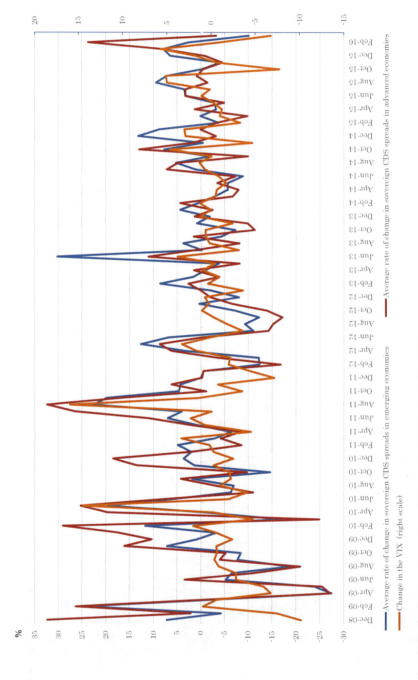

Fig. 5.7 Rates of change in sovereign CDS spreads and changes in the VIX

5 Sovereign Credit Default Swaps and U.S. Economic Policy ... 125

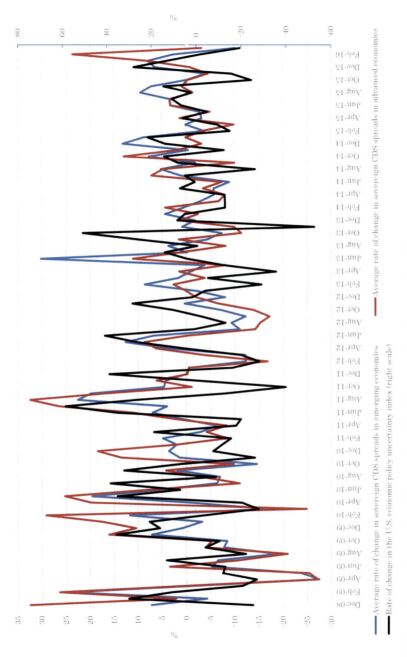

Fig. 5.8 Rates of change in sovereign CDS spreads and the U.S. economic policy uncertainty index

different. This implies that each country's sovereign CDS spread is affected by global shocks because it is part of an integrated market.

Figure 5.5 presents the average rates of change in sovereign CDS spreads for the sample countries in advanced and emerging economies and the rate of change in the U.S. S&P 500 index. The similar fluctuations between sovereign CDS spreads in advanced and emerging economies are consistent with the fluctuations among each country's sovereign CDS spreads, as illustrated in Figs. 5.1, 5.2, 5.3 and 5.4. Figure 5.5 also shows that sovereign CDS spreads tend to rise (fall) in the period of the fall (rise) in the S&P 500. Since a high CDS spread means a surge in credit risk, this shows that sovereign credit risk increases when the U.S. stock market is bearish. Figure 5.6 illustrates the average rates of change in sovereign CDS spreads and the U.S. 5-year Treasury yield fluctuation. Sovereign CDS spreads decline (increase) when the U.S. Treasury yield falls (rises), implying that sovereign CDS spreads rose during the period of monetary restraint in the United States. Figure 5.7 shows the co-movement between average rates of change in sovereign CDS spreads (left scale) and the change in the VIX (right scale). This implies that sovereign credit risk would be high when volatility in the U.S. stock market rises. Figure 5.8 also shows similar fluctuations between average sovereign CDS spreads (left scale) and the U.S. economic policy uncertainty index (right scale) in most periods. Figures 5.5, 5.6, 5.7 and 5.8 suggest that U.S. financial market conditions and economic policy uncertainty correlate with sovereign CDS markets.

5.3 Empirical Analysis

This paper analytically explores how domestic and foreign factors affect the sovereign CDS spreads in emerging and advanced economies in the period after the GFC. The regression data are of weekly frequency, and we employ panel data for financial markets. Our analysis utilizes the domestic stock index and foreign exchange rate (to the U.S. dollar) as domestic factors and the U.S. economic policy uncertainty index, the U.S. stock index, the U.S. interest rate, and the VIX as foreign factors. In addition, we regress subsample periods for QE1, QE2, QE3, and the period after the LSAPs, to analyze changes in the relationship between sovereign CDS spreads and factors.

5.3.1 Data

Following the previous studies regarding sovereign credit risk, we assume that the 5-year sovereign CDS spread represents sovereign credit risk. The regression employs the U.S. economic policy uncertainty index developed by Baker et al. [5] to measure U.S. economic policy uncertainty. This index is based on newspaper articles in the U.S. that include policy-related economic uncertainty. We also use the U.S. financial indices for global factors driving the fluctuation in sovereign credit risk: the S&P 500 index, the 5-year U.S. Treasury yield, and the VIX index. In addition to global variables, our regression utilizes two domestic explanatory variables: domestic stock price index and foreign exchange rate. The U.S. economic policy uncertainty index is obtained from Baker et al.'s [5] website, and the sovereign CDS data come from the Datastream database. All other data are obtained from the Datastream and CEIC database.

According to data availability of sovereign CDS spreads, the regression period is from February 25, 2008 to March 25, 2016. To compare the effects on sovereign CDS spreads during the U.S. LSAPs, our analysis focuses on four subsample periods: QE1 (December 5, 2008–March 3, 2010), QE2 (November 12, 2010–June 30, 2011), QE3 and the tapering of QE (September 14, 2012–October 31, 2014), and the period following the end of QE (November 1, 2014–March 25, 2016). All weekly data used for the regression analysis are for the last trading day of the week.

The countries in our sample are as follows: Belgium, Brazil, Bulgaria, Chile, China, Colombia, Croatia, Czech Republic, Finland, France, Germany, Hong Kong, Israel, Italy, Japan, Kazakhstan, Korea, Lithuania, Mexico, Morocco, Netherlands, Peru, the Philippines, Poland, Portugal, Qatar, Russia, Slovenia, South Africa, Spain, Thailand, Turkey, and Vietnam. The sample countries do not include the U.S. because the U.S. financial market indices, used as global factors, are domestic factors for the U.S. regression. To analyze how the influence of domestic and foreign factors on sovereign CDS spreads differs between advanced and emerging economies, we divide our sample into emerging countries and advanced countries. We follow the IMF's definition when classifying countries as advanced or emerging. Our advanced sample economies are Belgium, Finland, France, Germany, Hong Kong, Israel, Italy, Japan, Korea, Netherlands, Portugal, and Spain. The emerging economies are Brazil, Bulgaria, Chile, China, Colombia, Croatia, Czech Republic, Kazakhstan, Lithuania, Mexico, Morocco, Peru, the Philippines, Poland, Qatar, Russia, Slovenia, South Africa, Thailand, Turkey, and Vietnam.[3]

5.3.2 Regression Analysis

We use rates of change in the 5-year sovereign CDS spreads for the dependent variable representing credit risk. The explanatory variables consist of each country's rates of change in domestic stock price indexes and foreign exchange rates, the rate of change in the U.S. economic policy uncertainty index, the rate of change in the S&P 500 index, change in the 5-year U.S. Treasury yields, and change in the VIX index. The regression equation is as follows:

---

[3] The Czech Republic is defined as an advanced economy for 2009–2013 and an emerging economy for 2014–2016 by the IMF's definition, and we added the Czech Republic to the subsamples of emerging economies.

$$CDS_{i,t} = \alpha + \beta_1 DST_{i,t} + \beta_2 FX_{i,t} + \beta_3 UNC_t + \beta_4 USST_t$$
$$+ \beta_5 USTR_t + \beta_6 VIX_t + \varepsilon_{i,t}, \tag{5.1}$$

where

$CDS_{i,t}$: the rate of change in the sovereign CDS spread in country i and period t,

$DST_{i,t}$: the rate of change in the domestic stock index in country i and period t,

$FX_{i,t}$: the rate of change in the foreign exchange rates (to the U.S. dollar) in country i and period t,

UNC_t: the rate of change in the U.S. economic policy uncertainty index in period t,

$USST_t$: the rate of change in the S&P 500 in period t,

$USTR_t$: change in the 5-year U.S. Treasury yield in period t,

VIX_t: change in the VIX in period t,

$\varepsilon_{i,t}$: residual errors.

The analysis employs a generalized method of moments (GMM) estimation method, using panel data from February 25, 2008 to March 25, 2016. A GMM estimator is used to alleviate endogeneity problems between sovereign CDS spreads and domestic explanatory variables. In the regression, we treat global factors as exogenous variables and domestic factors as endogenous.[4]

The expected sign of the coefficient for the domestic stock index (DST) is negative because a rise in the domestic stock price responds to a favorable economic condition, which reduces sovereign credit risk, thus reducing the sovereign CDS spreads by increasing tax revenues. The sovereign CDS spreads can rise when a large net capital outflow causes domestic currency depreciation. The coefficient of the variable for the foreign exchange rate (FX) would then be positive. When a rise in U.S. economic policy uncertainty increases the sovereign credit risk, the U.S. economic policy uncertainty index (UNC) coefficient is positive. The expected signs of the coefficients for the rates of change in the S&P 500 ($USST$) are negative, and the VIX (VIX) are positive. This is because a positive global financial market condition causes a rise in the global stock price and a fall in the VIX, reducing the sovereign CDS spreads. When monetary policy is tight and interest rates are high, the capital inflows to the U.S. are larger, and the sovereign credit risk in another country can rise because of capital outflows. Therefore, it is expected that the coefficient for the 5-year U.S. Treasury yields ($USTR$) will be positive.

5.3.3 Regression Results

Tables 5.2, 5.3, 5.4, 5.5 and 5.6 show the regression results for the determinants of the sovereign CDS spreads. Table 5.2 reports the results for the full sample

---

[4] In the GMM regression, we use the second and the third lagged level variables as instruments for the explanatory variables of domestic factors.

Table 5.2 Determinants of sovereign CDS spread: full sample period

		All sample countries				Advanced economies			
Domestic stock index	Std. err	−6.10456 (4.21502)	−4.46447 (2.86118)	0.09220 (2.94778)	−4.35901** (1.88428)	−6.31017 (4.78106)	−4.41316 (5.40446)	3.70632 (2.88467)	−8.15781 (6.68665)
Foreign exchange rate	Std. err	−0.43223 (7.85010)	1.83961 (5.37884)	10.17032 (7.07776)	2.08729 (4.37607)	12.13573* (7.11341)	12.00270** (4.98713)	15.77878*** (6.07504)	5.30130 (8.74704)
Economic policy uncertainty	Std. err	−0.02648** (0.01123)	−0.02256** (0.01003)	−0.01048 (0.00975)	−0.01997*** (0.00665)	−0.02717* (0.01519)	−0.01881 (0.01416)	−0.01313 (0.01614)	−0.00590 (0.01446)
US stock index	Std. err	2.06343* (1.17315)	1.35860 (1.19613)			5.94659** (2.99989)	4.02854 (4.58914)		
US Treasury	Std. err	0.04277 (0.09562)		−0.09835 (0.13431)		−0.20432 (0.14092)		−0.50059** (0.21965)	
VIX	Std. err	0.00027 (0.00369)			−0.00743 (0.00491)	−0.00166 (0.00778)			−0.04047 (0.03394)
Constant	Std. err	0.00577 (0.00791)	0.00396 (0.00502)	−0.00382 (0.00780)	0.00544 (0.00480)	−0.00742 (0.00599)	−0.00488 (0.00483)	−0.00618 (0.00581)	0.00553 (0.00782)
Hansen's J-statistics (p-value)		0.1221	0.1132	0.2110	0.3016	0.6720	0.6070	0.6468	0.8816
Number of observations		13,814	13,814	13,814	13,814	5033	5033	5033	5033

(continued)

Table 5.2 (continued)

		Emerging economies			
Domestic stock index	Std. err	−7.48393*** (2.57201)	−7.64204** (3.03317)	−7.05764*** (2.50404)	−7.86054*** (3.00657)
Foreign exchange rate	Std. err	−8.51312 (6.86031)	−9.79595 (8.30678)	−7.82478 (6.28499)	−10.19747 (8.61159)
Economic policy uncertainty	Std. err	-0.04495*** (0.01613)	−0.04698** (0.01927)	−0.04131*** (0.01539)	−0.04859** (0.01954)
US stock index	Std. err	0.53676 (0.84257)	0.04846 (1.09276)		
US Treasury	Std. err	0.14679* (0.07545)		0.12667* (0.07254)	
VIX	Std. err	0.00513* (0.00277)			0.00100 (0.00634)
Constant	Std. err	0.01762* (0.00930)	0.01924* (0.01088)	0.01727** (0.00831)	0.01988* (0.01085)
Hansen's J-statistics (p-value)		0.9512	0.9296	0.9766	0.9038
Number of observations		8812	8812	8812	8812

Notes *, **, and ***indicate that the statistics are significant at the 10, 5, and 1% level, respectively. Hansen's J test is the test for null hypothesis that the overidentifying restriction is satisfied. Full sample period covers weeks from February 25, 2008 to March 25, 2016. The dependent variable is the rate of change in sovereign 5-year CDS spread. The independent variables are as follows: *Domestic stock index* is the rate of change in domestic stock index, *Foreign exchange rate* is the rate of change in exchange rate to the U.S. dollar, *Economic policy uncertainty* is the rate of change in the U.S. economic policy uncertainty index, *US stock index* is the rate of change in S&P 500 index, *US Treasury* is change in 5-year US Treasury yield, and *VIX* is change in VIX index

Table 5.3 Determinants of sovereign CDS spread: subsample period of QE1

		All sample countries				Advanced economies			
Domestic stock index	Std. err	1.26095 (0.91597)	1.04525 (0.90593)	−1.75226 (3.32690)	−1.09689 (2.65946)	−3.41323** (1.35831)	−3.10610** (1.38975)	−2.58845** (1.11694)	−2.48289*** (0.91794)
Foreign exchange rate	Std. err	0.98143 (2.93901)	−0.56257 (3.35809)	16.97532 (14.76456)	21.24876 (22.15029)	3.11965 (2.12876)	4.04064* (2.38420)	5.15865* (2.67881)	5.33315** (2.68209)
Economic policy uncertainty	Std. err	0.02339 (0.02090)	0.03594* (0.01990)	−0.05282 (0.06031)	−0.07359 (0.10128)	−0.04194** (0.01776)	−0.03827** (0.01603)	−0.02767 (0.02254)	−0.03296* (0.01827)
US stock index	Std. err	−1.80790** (0.78068)	−2.17106*** (0.83571)			1.84944** (0.88283)	1.72844* (1.02898)		
US Treasury	Std. err	−0.06214 (0.04959)		0.08311 (0.31680)		−0.05113 (0.06908)		0.06327 (0.11900)	
VIX	Std. err	0.00156 (0.00116)			−0.02290 (0.03426)	−0.00143 (0.00273)			−0.01013* (0.00590)
Constant	Std.err	−0.00623 (0.00483)	−0.00480 (0.00515)	0.00776 (0.02030)	−0.00295 0.01666)	0.01249** (0.00540)	0.01068* (0.00585)	0.01418** (0.00643)	0.01095* (0.00594)
Hansen's J-statistics (p-value)		0.0019	0.0013	0.6351	0.7563	0.1389	0.2279	0.7510	0.7950
Number of observations		2244	2244	2244	2244	792	792	792	792

(continued)

Table 5.3 (continued)

		Emerging economies			
Domestic stock index	Std. err	−0.67844 (0.50826)	−0.47685 (0.51400)	−1.24394*** (0.44174)	−1.26438*** (0.44849)
Foreign exchange rate	Std. err	−1.50738 (2.05183)	−1.41420 (1.99665)	1.03207 (1.78331)	0.71644 (1.69326)
Economic policy uncertainty	Std. err	0.05660*** (0.01749)	0.06091*** (0.01612)	0.02831** (0.01184)	0.03575*** (0.01172)
US stock index	Std. err	−1.06775** (0.46274)	−1.32323*** (0.46124)		
US Treasury	Std. err	−0.02209 (0.02763)		−0.07175** (0.03142)	
VIX	Std. err	0.00181 (0.00122)			0.00417* (0.00226)
Constant	Std. err	−0.00082 (0.00400)	−0.00245 (0.00413)	0.00008 (0.00356)	0.00030 (0.00384)
Hansen's J-statistics (p-value)		0.0531	0.1189	0.0070	0.0102
Number of observations		1474	1474	1474	1474

Notes *, **, and *** indicate that the statistics are significant at the 10, 5, and 1% level, respectively. Hansen's J test is the test for null hypothesis that the overidentifying restriction is satisfied. The sample period covers the weeks of quantitative easing 1 (December 5, 2008–March 31, 2010). The dependent variable is the rate of change in sovereign 5-year CDS spread. The independent variables are as follows: *Domestic stock index* is the rate of change in domestic stock index, *Foreign exchange rate* is the rate of change in exchange rate to the U.S. dollar, *Economic policy uncertainty* is the rate of change in the U.S. economic policy uncertainty index, *US stock index* is the rate of change in S&P 500 index, *US Treasury* is change in 5-year US Treasury yield, and *VIX* is change in VIX index

Table 5.4 Determinants of sovereign CDS spread: subsample period of QE2

		All sample countries				Advanced economies			
Domestic stock index	Std. err	−4.60056** (2.15574)	−3.69424* (2.02238)	−3.51490*** (1.14098)	−4.62183* (2.56019)	2.31438 (2.30719)	3.30114 (2.40334)	−3.51101 (2.62564)	3.07013 (2.69943)
Foreign exchange rate	Std. err	1.03523 (2.67041)	0.82954 (2.22864)	−0.74204 (2.02432)	1.23358 (2.67675)	-0.75508 (4.44581)	1.24372 (4.99125)	−3.60891 (4.55389)	1.29576 (5.19859)
Economic policy uncertainty	Std. err	0.04109* (0.02324)	0.04118** (0.01848)	0.03467** (0.01624)	0.04531** (0.02097)	0.07633*** (0.02894)	0.10775*** (0.02830)	0.09303*** (0.03229)	0.11502*** (0.02881)
US stock index	Std. err	1.85066 (1.38056)	1.25583 (1.42639)			−3.35441** (1.52104)	−4.07184** (1.67682)		
US Treasury	Std. err	−0.04236 (0.03503)		0.06166 (0.07685)		−0.16449 (0.11280)		0.11233 (0.25013)	
VIX	Std. err	−0.00128 (0.00250)			−0.01184 (0.01127)	−0.00165 (0.00292)			0.02274** (0.01124)
Constant	Std. err	0.00023 (0.00677)	0.00328 (0.00670)	0.00642** (0.00299)	0.00535 (0.00447)	0.02420** (0.00957)	0.03053*** (0.01102)	0.00618 (0.00879)	0.02140** (0.00915)
Hansen's J-statistics (p-value)		0.5263	0.4941	0.6604	0.8808	0.2035	0.5879	0.0535	0.2600
Number of observations		1666	1666	1666	1666	576	576	576	576

(continued)

Table 5.4 (continued)

		Emerging economies			
Domestic stock index	Std. err	−3.47105** (1.54962)	−2.94622* (1.53066)	−3.22873*** (1.21583)	−3.05952** (1.34752)
Foreign exchange rate	Std. err	−1.50480 (3.11593)	−1.32297 (2.71445)	−1.64990 (2.66123)	−1.38454 (2.90318)
Economic policy uncertainty	Std. err	−0.00551 (0.02305)	−0.00342 (0.02075)	−0.00825 (0.01852)	−0.00343 (0.01873)
US stock index	Std. err	0.45410 (0.67800)	−0.13152 (0.90771)		
US Treasury	Std. err	−0.04526 (0.02826)		−0.03790 (0.06879)	
VIX	Std. err	0.00156 (0.00305)			0.00089 (0.00518)
Constant	Std. err	0.00438 (0.00395)	0.00679 (0.00431)	0.00586** (0.00276)	0.00631** (0.00276)
Hansen's J-statistics (p-value)		0.9658	0.9671	0.9644	0.9527
Number of observations		1078	1078	1078	1078

Notes *, **, and ***indicate that the statistics are significant at the 10%, 5%, and 1% level, respectively. Hansen's J test is the test for null hypothesis that the overidentifying restriction is satisfied. The sample period covers weeks of quantitative easing 2 (November 12, 2010–June 30, 2011). The dependent variable is rate of change in of sovereign 5-year CDS spread. The independent variables are as follows: *Domestic stock index* is the rate of change in of domestic stock index, *Foreign exchange rate* is the rate of change in exchange rate to the U.S. dollar, *Economic policy uncertainty* is the rate of change in the U.S. economic policy uncertainty index, *US stock index* is the rate of change in S&P 500 index, *US Treasury* is change in 5-year US Treasury yield, and *VIX* is change in VIX index

Table 5.5 Determinants of sovereign CDS spread: subsample period of QE3

		All sample countries				Advanced economies			
Domestic stock index	Std. err	−15.80148 (47.44357)	−2.72564 (3.32186)	−1.63231 (1.46152)	−2.63490 (1.89073)	2.21550 (2.76774)	0.71336 (1.67554)	0.31560 (0.90161)	−0.37047 (1.04506)
Foreign exchange rate	Std. err	26.07787 (107.96022)	−4.40227 (7.47487)	−7.02288 5.81182)	−4.75420 (4.53759)	−11.21998* (6.05504)	−6.37927** (3.09275)	−8.02757** (3.53884)	−5.04439** (2.28613)
Economic policy uncertainty std.err	Std. err	−0.03620 (0.19507)	0.02355 (0.02103)	0.03155 (0.02283)	0.02538* (0.01308)	0.04988* (0.02864)	0.02975* (0.01587)	0.04418* (0.02023)	0.02496* (0.01311)
US stock index	Std. err	8.19842 (29.34438)	0.08408 (2.38825)			−3.92105 (2.86042)	−1.66962 (1.56382)		
US Treasury	Std. err	−0.51667 (2.46048)		0.20595* (0.11733)		0.17873 (0.11717)		0.12776* (0.07756)	
VIX	Std. err	−0.01669 (0.06608)			−0.00066 (0.00876)	−0.00580 (0.00564)			0.00316 (0.00641)
Constant	Std. err	−0.02762 (0.12046)	0.00766 (0.01100)	0.00718* (0.00383)	0.00814** (0.00347)	0.01086 (0.00815)	0.00440 (0.00433)	−0.00066 (0.00341)	−0.00003 (0.00307)
Hansen's J-statistics (p-value)		0.9783	0.6095	0.5034	0.6615	0.8531	0.2312	0.7796	0.1161
Number of observations		3135	3135	3135	3135	1140	1140	1140	1140

(continued)

Table 5.5 (continued)

		Emerging economies			
Domestic stock index	Std. err	0.62595 (1.40165)	0.89041 (1.91855)	1.42700 (1.78651)	0.80313 (1.88269)
Foreign exchange rate	Std. err	5.32387 (3.72410)	6.31842 (5.47098)	5.83941 (4.33386)	6.60468 (5.58528)
Economic policy uncertainty std.err	Std. err	−0.01018 (0.01103)	−0.01098 (0.01826)	−0.00344 (0.01247)	−0.01354 (0.01929)
US stock index	Std. err	−0.83669** (0.37695)	−1.29114** (0.50565)		
US Treasury	Std. err	0.04141 (0.08012)		−0.00282 (0.09210)	
VIX	Std. err	0.00367* (0.00202)			0.00820** (0.00330)
Constant	Std. err	−0.00140 (0.00498)	−0.00109 (0.00758)	−0.00652 (0.00615)	−0.00560 (0.00836)
Hansen's J-statistics (p-value)		0.2702	0.3375	0.6140	0.3728
Number of observations		2016	2016	2016	2016

Notes *, **, and ***indicate that the statistics are significant at the 10, 5, and 1% level, respectively. Hansen's J test is the test for null hypothesis that the overidentifying restriction is satisfied. The sample period covers weeks of quantitative easing 3 and the tapering of QE (September 14, 2012–October 31, 2014). The dependent variable is the rate of change in sovereign 5-year CDS spread. The independent variables are as follows: *Domestic stock index* is the rate of change in domestic stock index, *Foreign exchange rate* is the rate of change in exchange rate to the U.S. dollar, *Economic policy uncertainty* is the rate of change in the U.S. economic policy uncertainty index, *US stock index* is the rate of change in S&P 500 index, *US Treasury* is change in 5-year US Treasury yield, and *VIX* is change in VIX index

Table 5.6 Determinants of sovereign CDS spread: subsample period after the U.S. LSAPs

		All sample countries				Advanced economies			
Domestic stock index	Std. err	−3.46925* (1.81271)	−3.31519* (1.72831)	−2.73277 (2.43889)	−3.07804* (1.64906)	−3.71655** (1.60901)	−3.18488* (1.63860)	−1.44165 (0.90649)	−4.72109** (2.17015)
Foreign exchange rate	Std. err	2.56894 (1.69847)	2.62787 (1.66353)	2.44205 (2.26043)	1.82549 (1.29516)	3.09203 (2.41392)	4.12130* (2.45543)	2.57546 (1.81615)	−0.19714 (3.53604)
Economic policy uncertainty	Std. err	0.00454 (0.01803)	0.00360 (0.01741)	−0.00426 (0.01475)	−0.00608 (0.01234)	−0.00900 (0.01245)	−0.00819 (0.01253)	−0.00952 (0.01031)	−0.02852 (0.01762)
US stock index	Std. err	1.72187 (1.25976)	1.38248 (1.33289)			2.39269* (1.28566)	1.65896 (1.42877)		
US Treasury	Std. err	−0.06849* (0.03783)		0.00659 (0.12390)		−0.13404** (0.06147)		−0.10931 (0.06691)	
VIX	Std. err	0.00040 (0.00194)			−0.00553 (0.00636)	−0.00136 (0.00330)			−0.01904 (0.01217)
Constant	Std. err	−0.00180 (0.00477)	−0.00153 (0.00463)	−0.00045 (0.00541)	0.00089 (0.00334)	−0.00108 (0.00473)	−0.00220 (0.00480)	−0.00067 (0.00372)	0.00565 (0.00668)
Hansen's J-statistics (p-value)		0.5982	0.6428	0.2323	0.4484	0.5778	0.2920	0.0807	0.9270
Number of observations		2335	2335	2335	2335	852	852	852	852

(continued)

Table 5.6 (continued)

		Emerging economies			
Domestic stock index	Std. err	−0.17796 (0.91868)	−0.33563 (0.91023)	−0.07370 (0.95823)	0.07854 (1.15166)
Foreign exchange rate	Std. err	−0.32880 (1.03881)	−0.47895 (1.03568)	−0.13884 (1.02278)	0.19958 (0.93862)
Economic policy uncertainty	Std. err	−0.03194** (0.01476)	−0.03449** (0.01438)	−0.01842 (0.01193)	−0.02123* (0.01163)
US stock index	Std. err	−0.98113 (0.61673)	−1.36944** (0.61155)		
US Treasury	Std. err	0.01080 (0.02462)		−0.10303** (0.04492)	
VIX	Std. err	0.00293** (0.00148)			0.00799** (0.00371)
Constant	Std. err	0.00834** (0.00341)	0.00873*** (0.00331)	0.00721** (0.00312)	0.00691** (0.00298)
Hansen's J-statistics (p-value)		0.1691	0.2173	0.5068	0.1423
Number of observations		1462	1462	1462	1462

Notes *, **, and ***indicate that the statistics are significant at the 10, 5, and 1 level, respectively. Hansen's J test is the test for null hypothesis that the overidentifying restriction is satisfied. The sample period covers weeks after the end of QE by the U.S. (November 1, 2014–March 25, 2016). The dependent variable is the rate of change in sovereign 5-year CDS spread. The independent variables are as follows: *Domestic stock index* is the rate of change in domestic stock index, *Foreign exchange rate* is the rate of change in exchange rate to the U.S. dollar, *Economic policy uncertainty* is the rate of change in the U.S. economic policy uncertainty index, *US stock index* is the rate of change in of S&P 500 index, *US Treasury* is change in 5-year US Treasury yield, and *VIX* is change in VIX index

period. The results for subsamples of advanced and emerging economies are not similar; the coefficient for foreign exchange rate is significantly positive in advanced economies, whereas the coefficient for the domestic stock index is significantly negative in emerging economies. The coefficients for global factor variables are mostly insignificant or have unexpected signs. The difference among subsample period results reflects this result for the full sample period.

Tables 5.3, 5.4, 5.5 and 5.6 suggest that important factors for sovereign CDS spreads vary between emerging and advanced economies for subsample periods. Table 5.3 indicates the results for the subsample period during QE1. In emerging economies, the coefficient for the U.S. economic policy uncertainty index is significantly positive. The coefficients for the U.S. stock index and the VIX index also have an expected sign.[5] In advanced economies, the coefficients for domestic factors are significant and have an expected sign. Table 5.4 shows the results for QE2. The coefficients for the U.S. economic policy uncertainty, the U.S. stock index, and the VIX are significant in advanced economies; however, the coefficient for the domestic stock index is significantly negative in emerging economies.[6] Table 5.5 reports the results for the period of QE3. In the advanced economies, the coefficients for the U.S. economic policy uncertainty and the U.S. Treasury yields are significant and have an expected sign. By contrast, the coefficients for the U.S. stock index and the VIX are significant in emerging economies. Table 5.6 indicates that the coefficients for the U.S. stock index and the VIX have the expected sign and are significant in emerging economies after the LSAPs period. In advanced economies, the coefficient for the domestic stock index is significantly negative.[7]

The regression results show that a rise in the U.S. economic policy uncertainty increases sovereign CDS spreads in emerging economies for QE1 and advanced economies for QE2 and QE3. However, other global factors (the U.S. stock market index and the VIX) affect sovereign CDS spreads of emerging economies in every subsample period, except QE2. In advanced economies, global financial factors are also significant during QE2 and QE3. This suggests that U.S. financial market conditions play a more important role as a global factor in emerging economies' sovereign CDS spreads than U.S. economic policy uncertainty. This propensity is more evident in emerging economies than in advanced economies.

---

[5] The overidentifying restriction of the GMM estimation is not satisfied in the test for emerging economies during QE1, except for the model using the U.S. economic policy uncertainty index and the U.S. stock price as global factors.

[6] The overidentifying condition of the GMM estimation is not satisfied in the test for the period of QE2 using the U.S. economic policy uncertainty index and the U.S. Treasury yields as global factors in advanced economies.

[7] The overidentifying condition of the GMM estimation is not satisfied in the test after the LSAPs using the U.S. economic policy uncertainty index and the U.S. Treasury yields as global factors in advanced economies.

5.4 Conclusion

Given that a country's sovereign default delivers a sizable adverse shock to its economy, it is beneficial for policymakers to understand key factors that influence sovereign credit risk and the economic reforms that may mitigate such risk. This paper empirically explored how domestic and global factors affect sovereign CDS spreads, concentrating on the effect of U.S. economic policy uncertainty and the difference between advanced and emerging economies in the period after the GFC.

We find that the U.S. economic policy uncertainty only influenced the sovereign CDS spreads of emerging economies in QE1. In contrast, the impacts of the U.S. stock price and the VIX were significant in every subsample period, except QE2. This suggests that the fluctuation in the U.S. financial market is more important than that in the U.S. economic policy uncertainty as a global factor for the sovereign credit risk of emerging economies. In advanced economies, global factors, including the U.S. economic policy uncertainty, affected the sovereign CDS spreads in QE2 and QE3. Therefore, global factors, except U.S. economic policy uncertainty, played a more crucial role in the sovereign credit risk of emerging economies than that of advanced economies.

In addition, the result for the influence of U.S. financial market factors supports the argument that increasing capital flows from and to the U.S. can influence the sovereign credit risk in emerging economies. If changes in U.S. financial market conditions caused significant capital flows in emerging economies after the GFC, they may have enhanced the impact of U.S. financial market factors on the sovereign credit risk of emerging economies.

References

1. Afonso, A., Furceri, D., Gomes, P. (2012). Sovereign credit ratings, financial markets linkages: Application to European data. *Journal of International Money, Finance, 31*(3), 606–638.
2. Ahmed, S., Coulibaly, B., & Zlate, A. (2017). International financial spillovers to emerging market economies: How important are economic fundamentals? *Journal of International Money and Finance, 76*, 133–152.
3. Aizenman, J., Hutchison, M., & Jinjarak, Y. (2013). What is the risk of European sovereign debt defaults? Fiscal space, CDS spreads and market pricing of risk. *Journal of International Money and Finance, 34*, 37–59.
4. Ang, A., & Longstaff, F. A. (2013). Systemic sovereign credit risk: Lessons from the US and Europe. *Journal of Monetary Economics, 60*(5), 493–510.
5. Baker, S. R., Bloom, N., & Davis, S. J. (2016). Measuring economic policy uncertainty. *The Quarterly Journal of Economics, 131*(4), 1593–1636.
6. Beirne, J., & Fratzscher, M. (2013). The pricing of sovereign risk and contagion during the European sovereign debt crisis. *Journal of International Money and Finance, 34*, 60–82.
7. Blau, B. M., & Roseman, B. S. (2014). The reaction of European credit default swap spreads to the US credit rating downgrade. *International Review of Economics & Finance, 34*, 131–141.
8. Calice, G., Chen, J., & Williams, J. (2013). Liquidity spillovers in sovereign bond and CDS markets: An analysis of the Eurozone sovereign debt crisis. *Journal of Economic Behavior & Organization, 85*, 122–143.

9. Calice, G., Mio, R., Štěrba, F., & Vašíček, B. (2015). Short-term determinants of the idiosyncratic sovereign risk premium: A regime-dependent analysis for European credit default swaps. *Journal of Empirical Finance, 33*, 174–189.
10. Delatte, A.-L., Gex, M., & López-Villavicencio, A. (2012). Has the CDS market influenced the borrowing cost of European countries during the sovereign crisis? *Journal of International Money and Finance, 31*(3), 481–497.
11. Grammatikos, T., & Vermeulen, R. (2012). Transmission of the financial and sovereign debt crises to the EMU: Stock prices, CDS spreads and exchange rates. *Journal of International Money and Finance, 31*(3), 517–533.
12. Gündüz, Y., & Kaya, O. (2014). Impacts of the financial crisis on eurozone sovereign CDS spreads. *Journal of International Money and Finance, 49*, 425–442.
13. Hui, C.-H., & Chung, T.-K. (2011). Crash risk of the euro in the sovereign debt crisis of 2009–2010. *Journal of Banking & Finance, 35*(11), 2945–2955.
14. Ismailescu, I., & Kazemi, H. (2010). The reaction of emerging market credit default swap spreads to sovereign credit rating changes. *Journal of Banking & Finance, 34*(12), 2861–2873.
15. Kalbaska, A., & Gątkowski, M. (2012). Eurozone sovereign contagion: Evidence from the CDS market (2005–2010). *Journal of Economic Behavior & Organization, 83*(3), 657–673.
16. Kim, S.-J., Salem, L., & Wu, E. (2015). The role of macroeconomic news in sovereign CDS markets: Domestic and spillover news effects from the US, the Eurozone and China. *Journal of Financial Stability, 18*, 208–224.
17. Longstaff, F. A., Pan, J., Pedersen, L. H., & Singleton, K. J. (2011). How Sovereign Is Sovereign Credit Risk? *American Economic Journal: Macroeconomics, 3*(2), 75–103. https://doi.org/10.1257/mac.3.2.75
18. Wang, P., & Moore, T. (2012). The integration of the credit default swap markets during the US subprime crisis: Dynamic correlation analysis. *Journal of International Financial Markets, Institutions and Money, 22*(1), 1–15.

Masahiro Inoguchi is a Professor at Ritsumeikan University in Japan. He received his Ph.D. from Hitotsubashi University in Tokyo, and his main research interests include international finance and development finance.

Chapter 6
Global Liquidity and Uncovered Interest Rate Parity Puzzle

Yukio Fukumoto

Abstract The purpose of this study is to explore the relationship between global liquidity and the Uncovered Interest rate Parity (UIP) puzzle. As indicators of global liquidity, we use international claims expressed by the growth rate. We find that the correlation between the expected rate of change in the exchange rate and bilateral interest rate differentials is small when global liquidity and deviation from the UIP are highly correlated. This indicates that global liquidity and the UIP puzzle are related. We also find that this relationship is stronger: (i) in developed countries than in developing ones; (ii) in periods when global liquidity is high rather than low; and (iii) in the non-banking sector rather than in the banking sector when global liquidity is low.

Keywords Global liquidity · UIP puzzle · Correlation coefficients

6.1 Introduction

The term "global liquidity," used by the Committee on the Global Financial System [6], refers to the ease of financing in global financial markets. Global liquidity increased until just before the global financial crisis triggered by the Lehman Brothers investment bank collapse in September 2008 and dropped suddenly just after the crisis. Around the time of the Lehman shock, exchange rates and interest rates fluctuated wildly; thus, it is reasonable to consider that global liquidity and financial markets are strongly related.

We focus on global liquidity as a factor in the UIP puzzle. UIP means that the same revenue is obtained regardless of whether a safe asset is operated in the currency of country A or B. For example, if the interest rate in country A is 5% higher than that in country B annually, the currency in country A will depreciate 5% annually relative to that in country B. In this situation, the expected rate of change in the exchange

---

Y. Fukumoto (✉)
Department of Economics, Osaka University of Economics, 2-2-8 Osumi Higashiyodogawa-ku, Osaka 533-8533, Japan
e-mail: fukumoto@osaka-ue.ac.jp

© The Author(s), under exclusive license to Springer Nature Singapore Pte Ltd. 2022
Y. Matsubayashi and S. Kitano (eds.), *Global Financial Flows in the Pre- and Post-global Crisis Periods*, Kobe University Monograph Series in Social Science Research,
https://doi.org/10.1007/978-981-19-3613-5_6

144 Y. Fukumoto

rate is equal to the bilateral interest rate differentials. Interestingly, several previous studies have presented empirical findings that are skeptical about the validity of the UIP, and the UIP puzzle has been researched for decades (e.g., 2, 4, 7, 9, 10, 12). However, the relationship between global liquidity and the UIP puzzle has not yet been investigated.

The remainder of this study is organized as follows. In Sect. 6.2, we discuss the possibility that global liquidity influences the UIP puzzle. In Sect. 6.3, we explain our methods and data, and in Sect. 6.4, we discuss the empirical results. Finally, Sect. 6.5 concludes the study.

6.2 Previous Studies About the UIP Puzzle

The basic UIP equation used in empirical analyses is as follows.

$$s_{t+1} - s_t = \alpha + \beta \left(i_t - i_t^* \right) + e_t$$

s_{t+1} and s_t are the logged exchange rates (domestic currency units per foreign currency unit) at time $t + 1$ and t, respectively; i_t and i^*_t are domestic and foreign interest rates at time t, respectively; e_t is the disturbance term at time t. If the UIP holds, then $\alpha = 0$ and $\beta = 1$ is expected.[1] However, many previous empirical studies show that they do not hold, as is explained by the UIP puzzle.

Frankel and Poonawala [8] draw attention to the effects of sample countries. They insist that the UIP puzzle is more likely to occur for the currencies of developed countries than those of developing countries. Lothian and Wu [11] focus on the effects of the sample period. They highlight that the UIP puzzle was observed after the 1970s, based on an analysis of historical time series data from 1800 to 1999. the UIP requires an efficient foreign exchange rate market. Subrahmanyam [13] insists that market liquidity affects price efficiency. If fluctuating global liquidity momentarily influences countries asymmetrically, it is possible that the UIP puzzle appears for a specific sample country or during a specific period. Therefore, fluctuations in global liquidity can be a driving force of the empirical results of Frankel and Poonawala [8] and Lothian and Wu [11].

---

[1] In empirical analysis, the *expected* exchange rate of the next period, s^e_{t+1} is usually specified as $s_{t+1} = s^e_{t+1} + u_t$, and the *realized* exchange rate of the next period is used. Here, it is assumed that the mean of u_t is zero and its variance is constant.

6 Global Liquidity and Uncovered Interest Rate Parity Puzzle

6.3 Method and Data

Previous studies find that various factors are involved in the UIP puzzle.[2] If the UIP holds, the expected rate of change in the exchange rate and bilateral interest rate differentials will react not only to global liquidity but also similarly to any economic shock. That is, if global liquidity and deviation from the UIP are not related, their relationship will not influence the expected rate of change in the exchange rate and bilateral interest rate differentials.[3] We focus on the correlation coefficient between global liquidity and deviation from the UIP and between the expected rate of change in the exchange rate and bilateral interest rate differentials. Specifically, we examine whether the correlation between global liquidity and deviation from the UIP can explain the correlation between the expected rate of change in the exchange rate and bilateral interest rate differentials based on regression analysis.

In this study, global liquidity denotes international claims expressed by growth rate. Deviation from the UIP, the expected rate of change in the exchange rate, and bilateral interest rate differentials are expressed as $s_{t+1} - s_t - i_t - i^*_t$, $s_{t+1} - s_t$, and $i_t - i^*_t$, respectively. We set the United States (US) as the foreign country and selected sample countries, excluding the US, as domestic countries.

According to Frankel and Poonawala [8] and Lothian and Wu [11], the relationship between the two correlation coefficients may change depending on sample countries and periods. Therefore, we divide the sample countries into two groups: developed countries and developing countries, and two sample periods: the former and latter periods.

We use quarterly data as an indicator of global liquidity, the expected rate of change in the exchange rate, and bilateral interest rate differentials from the 1st quarter (1Q) of 2000 to the 4th quarter (4Q) of 2015. The expected rate of change in the exchange rate includes not only the current but also the exchange rate of the next quarter, therefore we use exchange rate data from the 1Q of 2000 to the 1Q of 2016. Indicators of global liquidity and interest rate data covered the 1Q of 2000 to the 4Q of 2015. The exchange rate and interest rate data were obtained from the International Financial Statistics published by the International Monetary Fund. We use the exchange rate at the end of period and the interest rate of the money market rate.[4] Interest rate data is annual; hence we suppose the interest rate of one-quarter to be one-fourth of the annual interest rate. We consider representative indicators for global liquidity, such as international claims in the banking and non-banking sectors,

---

[2] For example, some studies deny the UIP puzzle using very short-horizon and very long-horizon data. See Bekaert, Wei and Xing [1], Chaboud and Wright [3], and Chinn and Meredith [5].

[3] Deviation from the UIP is not always zero; thus, the correlation between global liquidity and deviation from the UIP will become high or low in the immediate term even if they are not related.

[4] The exchange rate data code following the country code is AE.ZF..., AG.ZF..., or WE.ZF..., for example, the yen–dollar exchange rate is 158..AE.ZF.... Similarly, the interest rate data code is 60B..ZF...., for example, Australian interest rate is 19360B..ZF.... International Financial Statistics has the data of interest rate other than 60B..ZF...; however, we do not use it because available countries are less than the case of 60B..ZF....

Table 6.1 Sample countries

Developed countries	Developing countries
Australia	Armenia
Canada	Brazil
Chile	Bulgaria
Czech Republic	Colombia
Euro Area	Dominican Republic
Iceland	Indonesia
Japan	Jamaica
New Zealand	Mauritius
Poland	Mexico
Republic of Korea	Morocco
Sweden	Mozambique
Switzerland	Pakistan
United Kingdom	Papua New Guinea
Uruguay	Paraguay
	Peru
	Philippines
	Romania
	Russian Federation
	South Africa
	Thailand
	Vanuatu

Note Developed countries are those categorized as high-income economies according to the World Bank's country classification. See the following website: https://datahelpdesk.worldbank.org/knowledgebase/articles/906519-world-bank-count

expressed by growth rate.[5] Global liquidity data are available from the website of the Bank for International Settlements (http://www.bis.org/statistics/gli.htm) and were downloaded in July 2017.[6]

Table 6.1 presents the sample countries, excluding the US. We include 36 countries whose data are available for all periods from the International Financial Statistics.[7] The sample countries are classified based on their income in Table 6.1.

---

[5] International claims are cross-border claims denominated in all currencies; plus local claims denominated in foreign currencies.

[6] The data codes Q:GEWC:3P:09 and Q:GEUC:3P:00 represent international claims growth rates on the banking and non-banking sectors, respectively.

[7] We exclude Argentina, Aruba, Bangladesh, Bolivia, Hong Kong, Jordan, Kuwait, Macao, Malaysia, Singapore, Tunisia and Venezuela in our analysis, although data was available. The exchange rate to the US dollar did not change in many periods or hardly changed in these countries.

6   Global Liquidity and Uncovered Interest Rate Parity Puzzle

To obtain a sufficient sample size to consider changes in the relationship between global liquidity and deviation from UIP over time, we estimate correlation coefficients of 24 quarters for each country, such as the 1Q of 2000 to the 4Q of 2005, 1Q of 2002 to 4Q of 2007, 1Q of 2004 to 4Q of 2009, 1Q of 2006 to 4Q quarter of 2011, 1Q of 2008 to 4Q of 2013, and 1Q of 2010 to 4Q of 2015. We call the first three periods (1Q of 2000 to 4Q of 2005, 1Q of 2002 to 4Q of 2007, and 1Q of 2004 to 4Q of 2009) the former period and the last three periods (1Q of 2006 to 4Q of 2011, 1Q of 2008 to 4Q of 2013, and 1Q of 2010 to 4Q of 2015) the latter period.

6.4   Empirical Analysis

Figure 6.1 presents international claims on the banking and non-banking sectors expressed by growth rate of global liquidity indicators. Two international claims have upward trends from 2002 to the eve of the Lehman shock in September 2008. After the shock, they became extremely negative. They have been almost zero since 2010. In other words, global liquidity expressed by the growth rate is higher in the former period than in the latter period. Moreover, international claims on the banking and non-banking sectors are hardly different in the former period, but are clearly different in the latter period.

Figures 6.2 and 6.3 present scatterplots of the correlation coefficients between global liquidity and deviation from the UIP (correlation_X) and correlation coefficients between the expected rate of change in the exchange rate and bilateral interest rate differentials (correlation_Y) in developed and developing countries, respectively. In Fig. 6.2, the correlations based on international claims in the banking and non-banking sectors are −0.602 and −0.558 in the former period and −0.060 and −0.264

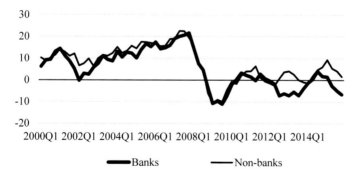

Fig. 6.1 International claims expressed by growth rate. *Note* "Banks" and "Non-banks" denote international claims on the banking and non-banking sectors, respectively. The vertical axis represents the percentages

---

Additionally, we exclude Swaziland, whose currency is fixed to the South African rand. If exchange rate to the US dollar does not change, the correlation between $s_{t+1} - s_t$ and $i_t - i^*_t$ will be zero.

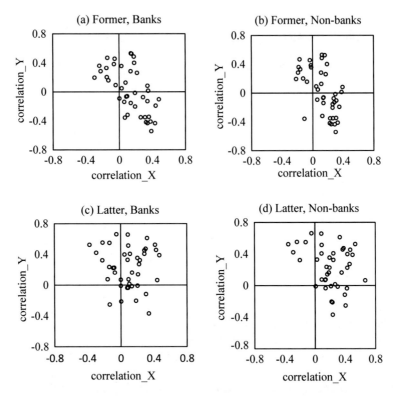

Fig. 6.2 Scatterplots for developed countries. *Note* Correlation_X in the horizontal axis is the correlation coefficient between global liquidity and deviation from UIP, and correlation_Y in the vertical axis is the correlation coefficient between the expected rate of change in the exchange rate and bilateral interest rate differentials. Former, Latter, Banks, and Non-banks indicate the former period, latter period, global liquidity based on the banking sector, and global liquidity based on the non-banking sector, respectively

in the latter period, respectively. The negative correlation in the former period is stronger than that in the latter period. In the former period, a strong negative correlation is observed for both cases of international claims, and in the latter, the correlation based on international claims in the banking sector is quite small. In Fig. 6.3, the correlations based on international claims in the banking and non-banking sectors are −0.340 and −0.260 in the former period and −0.071 and −0.376 in the latter period, respectively. The correlation based on international claims in the banking sector is quite small in the latter period. Moreover, in the former period, the correlation in Fig. 6.3 is less than that in Fig. 6.2.

Tables 6.2 and 6.3 present the regression results showing how much correlation_X can explain correlation_Y in developed and developing countries, respectively. If the coefficient of correlation_X is zero, global liquidity does not influence the UIP puzzle. In Table 6.2, the coefficient of correlation_X is almost −1 in the former period for both indicators of global liquidity. In the latter period, the coefficient is almost zero

6 Global Liquidity and Uncovered Interest Rate Parity Puzzle 149

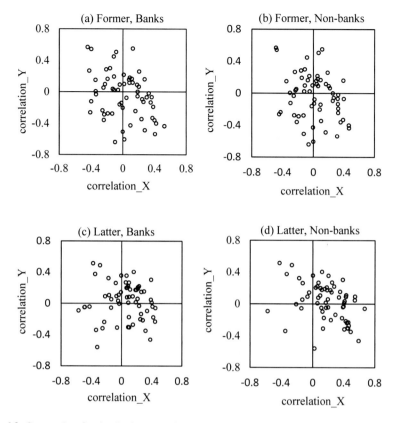

Fig. 6.3 Scatterplots for developing countries. *Note* See note to Fig. 6.2

Table 6.2 Regression results for developed countries

			Former	Latter
Banks	Correlation_X	Coefficients	−0.929[c]	− 0.077
		Robust S.E.	0.141	0.202
	Constant term	Coefficients	0.145[c]	0.241[c]
		Robust S.E.	0.040	0.044
	Adjusted R^2		0.346	−0.021
Non-banks	Correlation_X	Coefficients	−1.003[c]	−0.311[b]
		Robust S.E.	0.200	0.143
	Constant term	Coefficients	0.148[c]	0.297[c]
		Robust S.E.	0.046	0.043
	Adjusted R^2		0.294	0.046

Note Correlation_X is the correlation coefficient between global liquidity and deviation from the UIP. Global liquidity comprises international claims in banking and non-banking sectors. [c], [b], and [a] indicate significance at the 1, 5, and 10 percent levels, respectively

Table 6.3 Regression results for developing countries

			Former	Latter
Banks	Correlation_X	Coefficients	-0.392^c	-0.065
		Robust S.E.	0.130	0.129
	Constant term	Coefficients	-0.031	0.034
		Robust S.E.	0.035	0.032
	Adjusted R^2		0.101	-0.011
Non-banks	Correlation_X	Coefficients	-0.305^b	-0.336^b
		Robust S.E.	0.143	0.134
	Constant term	Coefficients	-0.031	0.090^b
		Robust S.E.	0.036	0.041
	Adjusted R^2		0.052	0.127

Note See note to Table 6.2

and is insignificant when global liquidity based on the banking sector is used. The coefficient is about -0.3 when global liquidity based on the non-banking sector is used. In Table 6.3, the coefficient of correlation_X is not significant when global liquidity based on the banking sector in the latter period is used. In other cases, the coefficients of correlation_X were approximately -0.3.

6.5 Conclusion

We hypothesize that global liquidity is one of the disruptive factors of UIP. We found that the correlation between the expected rate of change in the exchange rate and bilateral interest rate differentials is small when global liquidity and the deviation from UIP are highly correlated. According to our empirical results, when the correlation coefficient between global liquidity and the deviation from UIP is high, the correlation coefficient between the expected rate of change in the exchange rate and bilateral interest rate differentials is low. Moreover, this relationship is stronger: (i) in developed countries than in developing ones; (ii) in periods when global liquidity is high rather than when it is low; and (iii) the non-banking sector rather than in the banking sector in periods when global liquidity is low. The results of (i) and (ii) are consistent with those of Frankel and Poonawala [8], who point out that UIP is weaker in developed countries than in developing countries, and Lothian and Wu [11], who show that UIP does not hold in some periods. The results of (iii) relate to those of McCallum [12]. According to that study, UIP does not hold because of the monetary policy of governments that are included in the non-banking sector. Our results suggest that a high growth rate of global liquidity should be marked to avoid the negative effect of the volatility of exchange rate deviating from fundamentals on the real economy.

6 Global Liquidity and Uncovered Interest Rate Parity Puzzle

Acknowledgements I would like to thank Professor Akira Kohsaka for his critical comments. Furthermore, the constructive and valuable comments of Professors Yoichi Matsubayashi, Shigeto Kitano, and Shingo Iokibe are acknowledged.

References

1. Bekaert, G., Wei, M., & Xing, Y. (2007). Uncovered interest rate parity and the term structure. *Journal of International Money and Finance, 26*, 1038–1069.
2. Boudoukh, J., Richardson, M., & Whitelaw, R. F. (2016). New evidence on the forward premium puzzle. *Journal of Financial and Quantitative Analysis, 51*, 875–897.
3. Chaboud, A. P., & Wright, J. H. (2005). Uncovered interest parity: It works, but not for long. *Journal of International Economics, 66*, 349–362.
4. Chinn, M. D. (2006). The (partial) rehabilitation of interest rate parity in the floating rate era: Longer horizons, alternative expectations, and emerging markets. *Journal of International Money and Finance, 25*, 7–21.
5. Chinn, M. D., & Meredith, G. (2004). Monetary policy and long-horizon uncovered interest parity. *IMF Staff Papers, 51*, 409–430.
6. Committee on the Global Financial System (2011). Global liquidity – concept, measurement and policy implications. CGFS Papers No.45.
7. Flood, R. P., & Taylor, M. P. (1996). *Exchange rate economics, what's wrong with the conventional macro approach?* (pp. 261–301). The microstructure of foreign exchange markets. University of Chicago.
8. Frankel, J., & Poonawala, M. J. (2010). The forward market in emerging currencies: Less biased than in major currencies. *Journal of International Money and Finance, 29*, 585–598.
9. Froot, K., & Thaler, R. (1990). Anomalies: Foreign exchange. *Journal of Economic Perspectives, 4*, 179–192.
10. Lothian, J. R. (2016). Uncovered interest parity: The long and the short of it. *Journal of Empirical Finance, 36*, 1–7.
11. Lothian, J. R., & Wu, L. (2011). Uncovered interest-rate parity over the past two centuries. *Journal of International Money and Finance, 30*, 448–473.
12. McCallum, B. T. (1994). A reconsideration of the uncovered interest parity relationship. *Journal of Monetary Economics, 33*, 105–132.
13. Subrahmanyam, A. (1991). Risk aversion, market liquidity, and price efficiency. *The Review of Financial Studies, 4*, 417–441.

Yukio Fukumoto is a professor of economics at Osaka University of Economics. He received his Ph.D. from Kobe University, and his main research interest is open-economy macroeconomics.

Chapter 7
Bank Profitability in Europe Before and After the Global Financial Crisis: Leverage, Foreign Claims, and Monetary Policy

Agata Wierzbowska and Yoichi Matsubayashi

Abstract European banks played an important role in the origins and channels of the global gross capital flows and the prosperity of credit conditions prior to the global financial crisis. Their large exposition to the US assets made them vulnerable to the crisis. Moreover, many banks are in a vicious cycle of declining asset prices, non-performing assets, deleveraging, growing concerns about the quality of bank balance sheets, and economic recession, which have a negative impact on their performance. This chapter first describes the development of European banks' claims to the US and the world, bank profitability, leverage, and total assets and capital. Next, we base on the bank-level panel data analysis to study how these variables influence European bank profitability and how this impact changes between periods prior to and after the global financial crisis. The data show not only a post-crisis falls in banks' total international claims but also a slight upward trend in European banks' profits from 2011, occurring concurrently to area-wide deleveraging. The main results from empirical analysis reveal that the post-crisis bank deleveraging and shedding of claims to the US contribute to higher bank profitability. This notion points to the importance of the sound balance sheet and strong capital position for bank profitability in Europe in the post-crisis world. Although debt financing and higher leverage usually boost bank profits, in the post-crisis period, banks need to focus on strengthening capital positions and bank quality to reduce their risk-related barriers to expansion and ensure easier or cheaper access to funding to increase profitability.

Keywords Bank profitability · Bank leverage · Bank foreign claims · Global financial crisis

---

A. Wierzbowska (✉) · Y. Matsubayashi
Graduate School of Economics, Kobe University, 2-1, Rokkodai, Nada, Kobe 657-8501, Japan
e-mail: wierzbowska@econ.kobe-u.ac.jp

Y. Matsubayashi
e-mail: myoichi@econ.kobe-u.ac.jp

© The Author(s), under exclusive license to Springer Nature Singapore Pte Ltd. 2022
Y. Matsubayashi and S. Kitano (eds.), *Global Financial Flows in the Pre- and Post-global Crisis Periods*, Kobe University Monograph Series in Social Science Research,
https://doi.org/10.1007/978-981-19-3613-5_7

7.1 Introduction

European banks played an important role in the formation of the financial crisis through the origins and channels of the global gross capital flows and the prosperity of credit conditions. In particular, from the mid-2000s onward, claims by European banks on the US residents significantly increase. For instance, Borio and Disyatat [1] state that almost 50% of foreign-held US securities just before the crisis were held in Europe.

The large exposure of European banks to US securities made them extremely vulnerable to the housing market tensions that had begun to appear in the US in 2006. Following the collapse of Lehman Brothers, a full-fledged bust took place. The vicious cycle of declining asset prices, non-performing assets, deleveraging by banks, and growing fears of the quality of bank balance sheets and economic recession reinforcing each other occurred (e.g., [2]). The crisis also brought changes in the macroeconomic environment connected to the post-crisis monetary easing and changed the flow of international bank claims: European banks shedding their foreign claims, including US assets.

These developments did not stay without influencing bank performance in Europe, which is of high importance for bank sustainability, thereby affecting banks' ability and willingness to extend credit as well as stability of the whole banking system. From this perspective, bank profitability is particularly important in Europe, where banks are the main source of external finance for enterprises and consumers. Thus, their condition affects economic growth to large extent. Given this background, in this study, we aim at identifying the main factors that affect the profitability of the European banks prior to and after the global financial crisis. We are particularly interested in the impact of the bank deleveraging process, stock of bank claims to the US, and the influence of post-crisis monetary easing.

The main results show that bank deleveraging and shedding of claims to the US, which started after the crisis, helped banks achieve higher profitability. That is, in the post-crisis period, European banks needed to focus on strengthening capital positions and bank quality. Thus, their profitability is improved by reducing their risk-related barriers to expansion and ensuring easier or cheaper access to funding. Furthermore, the significant influence of net interest margin on bank profits is observed, again specifically in the post-crisis period. That is, banks are highly dependent on the interest rate environment, particularly in the post-crisis low-interest-rate environment, which pushed down bank profits.

The rest of the chapter is structured as follows. Section 7.2 conducts data observation to describe the trends in the international bank claims to the US, the performance and leverage of European banks, and their relevant balance sheet items. Section 7.3 describes the theoretical determinants of bank profitability, and Sect. 7.4 presents the model and results of the simple econometric analysis to identify the main determinants of the European bank performance. Section 7.5 concludes the study and provides implications.

7.2 Data and Stylized Facts

The country sample used for the analysis consists of 14 BIS-reporting European countries. Ten countries are from the euro area, namely, Austria, Belgium, France, Germany, Greece, Ireland, Italy, the Netherlands, Portugal, and Spain. Then, two are non-euro-area EU countries, that is, Denmark and Sweden. Furthermore, two are non-EU countries, namely, Switzerland and the UK.[1] The main data sources are BIS consolidated banking statistics and the Bankscope database. Here, we introduce the databases and the main data of interest used in the following econometric analysis.

7.2.1 BIS-Consolidated Banking Statistics

The BIS consolidated banking statistics provide data on banks' exposures, where multinational banks are aggregated by the country of headquarters location. Here, we focus on the data on each country's claims to the US.

Figure 7.1 shows the total claims to the US by country, where the data is scaled, such that the 2008Q4 value equals 100 after scaling. We observe that all the analyzed countries note an upward trend in claims to the US prior to the global financial crisis. The time of the peak exposure varies slightly across the countries but usually comes around the year 2007. The post-2007 situation is much more divergent. Most of the countries note a fall in claims to the US. McCauley et al. [3] consider this fall a part

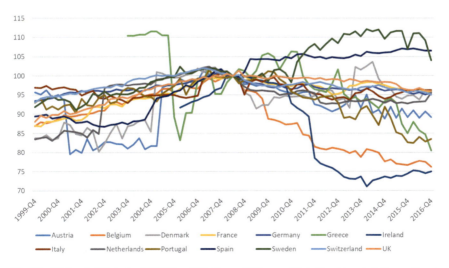

Fig. 7.1 Claims to US, index 2008Q2 = 100. *Source* BIS consolidated banking statistics, authors' estimations

---

[1] The UK left the European Union on 31 January 2020. Thus, during the time period considered in this chapter it was the non-euro-area EU country.

of the process of post-crisis deleveraging by European banks through the shedding of foreign assets. Moreover, the downward trend has notable exceptions. Particularly, Sweden and Spain show an increase in cross-border lending to the US in the post-crisis period. The extent of the post-crisis fall in external credit also varies greatly across the countries. The UK, France, Germany, and Switzerland, inter alia, note a small decrease. From another perspective, banks in Ireland, Belgium, Portugal, and Greece significantly cut their exposition to the US assets since 2012. These differences point at various responses to the crisis and divergent situations in the banking sector across European countries.

Notably, however, Fig. 7.2 shows not only the claims to the US but also the total foreign claims' decrease in most of the countries under analysis in the post-crisis period. In effect, the financial crisis has no evident influence on the share of US claims in the total country claims (Fig. 7.3). The share seems rather stable in many countries, and when the downward trend is visible, this trend usually starts before the outbreak of the full-fledged crisis. Thus, the European banks seem to cast off a wider range of foreign assets to strengthen their balance sheets. Given the decreasing share of US claims in total claims, US assets seem to make up a relatively large part of the shed foreign claims. Moreover, a part of the decreasing share in total claims may have originated from the will for diversification in bank foreign claims, as the downward trend often begins before the outbreak of the crisis.

Additionally, large cross-country differences in the share of US claims in the total claims can be observed. Therefore, large differences exist in the importance of US assets in banks' portfolios among the European countries.

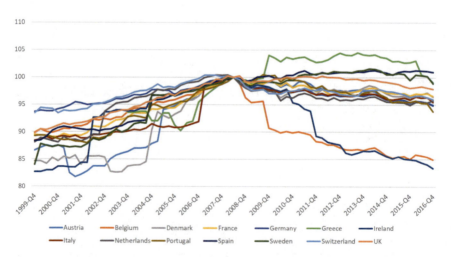

Fig. 7.2 Total foreign claims, index 2008Q2 = 100. *Source* BIS consolidated banking statistics, authors' estimations

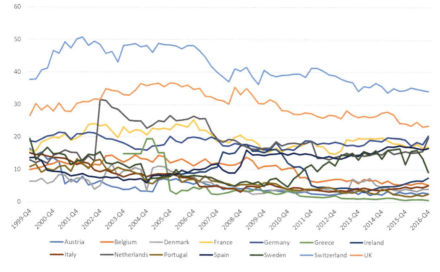

Fig. 7.3 Share of claims in US in total country claims. *Source* BIS consolidated banking statistics, authors' estimations

7.2.2 Bank-Level Data

The second important source of data for the analysis is the Bankscope database, which provides the bank-level information on, inter alia, the balance sheet and income statement items.

We take the annual bank-level data for the above-mentioned 14 European countries for the time period 2005–2015. The number of banks with available data varies considerably across countries. Thus, to slightly unify the sample sizes for each country, we choose the data on the top 100 banks in each country based on the average total assets ranking. The number of banks for each country-year pair depends on the exact data availability and ranges from 13 to 96. The total bank-year pair observations amount to 10,366. Table 7.1 presents the exact number of banks for each country.

The main point of our interest is the bank performance as measured by bank profitability. Bank profitability has important implications for banks and the real economy. The level of bank profits determines the ability of banks to fund their growth, raise new equity and debt, absorb the losses, implement recovery plans, and affect their sustainability in the medium term. Moreover, this level influences bank ability and willingness to finance the real economy; low profitability might be thus a cause of and a consequence of the weak economic environment [4].

We define bank profitability as a bank profit rate equal to the ratio of bank operating income to total assets. Figure 7.4 presents the average annual profit rates for all the countries under consideration (black thick line) and individual countries (thinner grey lines).

Table 7.1 Number of bank-year observations for each country

	2005	2006	2007	2008	2009	2010	2011	2012	2013	2014	2015
Austria	73	88	90	89	90	86	88	90	91	85	85
Belgium	71	74	66	72	72	76	77	71	72	70	72
Denmark	74	79	77	77	78	76	77	68	63	63	89
France	72	81	83	84	80	83	85	86	86	84	94
Germany	64	79	81	79	80	85	86	86	88	84	93
Greece	24	24	24	24	24	26	21	19	15	13	13
Ireland	47	52	53	46	42	44	47	42	37	35	26
Italy	78	83	77	75	73	70	70	70	65	64	84
Netherlands	61	61	61	63	64	64	64	69	68	64	65
Portugal	34	41	40	38	38	38	73	75	80	81	41
Spain	60	63	63	69	70	70	69	54	59	48	66
Sweden	59	67	67	68	70	74	76	81	84	83	88
Switzerland	76	74	73	72	68	70	71	74	79	82	96
UK	70	71	69	72	70	75	80	79	81	82	92

Note Based on the number of observations for which both data used for calculation of profit rates (operating income, total assets) are available

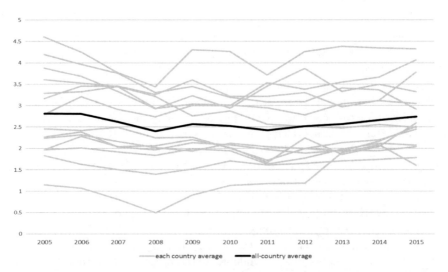

Fig. 7.4 Bank profit rates by country and year. *Source* Bankscope database, authors' estimations

We observe a decrease in average bank profit rates in Europe from 2005 to 2008 and again from 2009 to 2011. Since 2011, a slight upward trend can be observed. Most of the countries show rather similar developments with regard to the trend of changes but vary considerably concerning the magnitude of the change. At the same time, the average profits have a large cross-country dispersion, with the highest rates in Denmark and the lowest in Ireland and Germany.

Next, Figs. 7.5 and 7.6 present the developments in the median leverage and average total assets and capital of the European banks, respectively. The median leverage of European banks increases slightly between 2005 and 2008. Since 2008, however, this leverage decreases steadily, and this trend can be observed with few exceptions in most of the countries under analysis, most prominently in Germany, the UK, and Ireland.

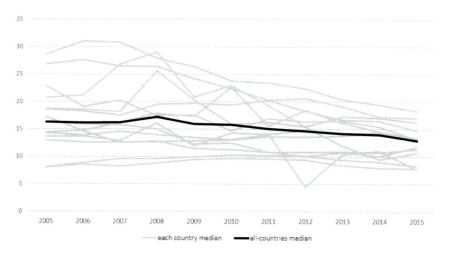

Fig. 7.5 Bank leverage by country and year. *Source* Bankscope database, authors' estimations

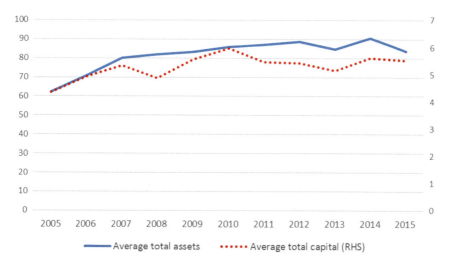

Fig. 7.6 Total assets and total capital of European banks (million euro). *Source* Bankscope database, authors' estimations

In addition, the average total assets of European banks increase at a very slow pace after 2007, which is slower than before 2007, noting slight falls in 2013 and 2015. Total capital is increasing, with a one-year break, in years 2005–2010 but then starts falling. Even after recovery from 2013, the total capital does not reach again the peak from 2010.

Thus, the data largely confirm the statement of McCauley et al. [3] that European banks are unable to raise enough capital in the post-crisis period and thus turn to deleveraging carried out mainly through lower asset growth and shedding assets with a considerable home bias—cutting down particularly foreign claims.

Overall, the data show that when the profits of European banks are increasing in the post-crisis period, the banks note a considerable fall in foreign claims and leverage and maintain rather stable levels of total assets and total capital. Thus, in the following sections, we consider theoretical determinants of bank profitability and check empirically the relationship among bank profitability in Europe, bank leverage, and country claims to the US.

7.2.3 Monetary Policy

The post-crisis period brings not only changes in the bank balance sheet and income statement but also a change in the macroeconomic environment connected particularly to a monetary policy easing across Europe. Figure 7.7 shows the yearly averages

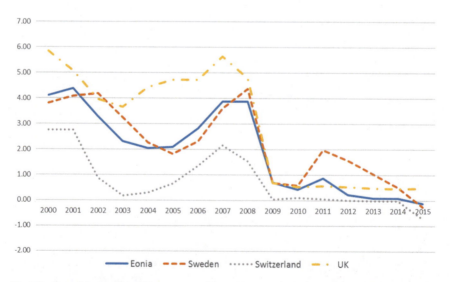

Fig. 7.7 Overnight interbank interest rates. *Source* Eurostat, each country central bank

of overnight interbank interest rates for the euro area, Sweden, Switzerland, and the UK.[2]

Central banks of all the countries were conducting interest rate hikes in few years prior to the crisis. After the crisis outbreak, large cuts took place, with interest rates reaching historically low levels. The easing trend has continued since 2009 with a short period of contraction in the euro area and Sweden around 2010–2011. Interest rates reached negative levels in Switzerland in 2013 and did so in the euro area and in Sweden in 2015.

7.3 Determinants of Bank Profitability

Having presented the developments in the main data of interest and before moving to the econometric analysis, we present the theoretical determinants of bank profitability. We describe the variables usually applied in the analysis of bank performance and their predicted impact on bank profits. Additionally, we consider possible impacts of bank claims to the US and monetary policy stance.

The literature studying the determinants of bank profitability usually points to the difference between interest income and interest expense of a bank (net interest margin), bank efficiency, bank size, bank liquidity, and capital strength as the main potential factors of influence.

Net interest margin is an important component of bank income, and thus, its increase will have a positive impact on bank profits [4]. The bank cost to income ratio provides information on the management efficiency regarding the level of expenses relative to the generated income. A higher ratio (meaning lower efficiency) has a negative impact on bank profits (e.g., [5]).

The impact of capital strength on profitability is ambiguous. The conventional risk-return theory implies the lower capital-to-assets ratio, indicating that lower capital strength and higher leverage should lead to higher bank revenues because of the lower cost of (debt) funding. From another perspective, empirical evidence shows the positive impact of higher capital ratios on bank profits (e.g., [6–8]). Berger [9] provides several potential explanations for the positive relationship between capital strength and profitability. A stronger capital position, meaning higher bank safety, might reduce costs of potential financial distress, serve as a means for signaling high bank quality, reduce risk-related barriers to expansion, diminish the need to issue off-balance-sheet guarantees, and borrow easier or cheaper uninsured funds. Here, we use the bank leverage measure as the inverse of the equity-to-asset ratio and thus expect either the positive coefficient because of positive effects of debt financing on bank profits or the negative coefficient because of any of Berger [9] arguments.

Similarly, bank liquidity, implying higher bank safety—an ability to meet unforeseen liquidity needs, might increase profits (e.g., [10]). However, bank liquidity might

---

[2] We use the EONIA rate for euro area countries and Denmark and each country interbank interest rates for Sweden, Switzerland, and the UK.

also work in the opposite direction because of lower returns from liquid assets and liquidity holdings as costs to the bank (e.g., [11]).

Bank size might also extend either a positive or negative impact on bank profits. On the one hand, the size might be related to higher profits because of the economies of scale, the exercise of market power, and the higher degree of product diversification (e.g., [8]). On the other hand, inefficiency problems of large organizations and diseconomies of the scale might diminish bank profitability (e.g., [12]).

The literature also points at the influence of macroeconomic conditions on bank profitability. Here, we use the real gross domestic product (GDP) growth rate as a measure of economic activity, in which the increase can have a positive impact on bank profits through higher demand for loans and deposits (e.g., [13]).

We also introduce in the analysis two other macroeconomic variables, namely, bank claims to the US and monetary policy stance. Bank foreign claims to the US might bring higher profits because of the higher profitability of US assets. In addition, however, higher riskiness of exposition to the US (e.g., because of asset risk and exchange rate risk) can mean diminished profits. Furthermore, as mentioned above, McCauley et al. [3] argue that European banks have lowered their expositions to the US as part of their post-crisis effort to fix the balance sheets. Thus, lower claims to the US might be associated with higher bank safety and stronger capital position in the environment of strained financial markets and thus extend positive effects on the profitability of European banks.

Finally, the impact of monetary policy stance on bank profitability stays ambiguous. Monetary contraction means, on the one hand, higher loan loss probability and lower non-interest income that contribute to lower profits. On the other hand, higher interest rates translate to higher net interest income that also increases bank profitability [14].

Table 7.2 presents a summary of the potential determinants of bank profitability used in the econometric analysis together with the definitions and the expected sign of relation.

7.4 Econometric Analysis

Here, we conduct a simple econometric analysis to determine the main contributors to bank profitability in Europe based on the panel data analysis.

7.4.1 Model

First, we estimate the benchmark panel model with fixed effects:

Table 7.2 Determinants of bank profitability—summary

Determinant	Proxy	Expected relation
Net interest margin	Net interest revenue/total assets	+
Bank efficiency	Cost to income ratio	−
Bank size	Logarithm of total assets	+/−
Bank liquidity	Liquid assets/total assets	+/−
Bank leverage	Total assets/equity	+/−
GDP	Real GDP growth (% annual)	+
Monetary policy stance	Overnight interbank interest rate	+/−
Claims to US	Logarithm of country claims to US Claims to US/total claims	+/−

$$y_{i,j,t} = \beta X_{i,j,t-1} + \delta GDP_{j,t} + \sum_{s=2006}^{2015} \theta_s year_{s,t} + f_i + \varepsilon_{i,j,t} \qquad (7.1)$$

for bank i, country j, time t, where $y_{i,j,t}$ is the bank profit rate, $X_{i,j,t-1}$ is a vector of bank-specific characteristics, $GDP_{j,t}$ is the real GDP growth rate, and $year_{s,t}$ are year dummies.

Then, to study the impact of the macroeconomic variables of interest–bank claims to the US and monetary policy stance in Europe, we estimate the regressions in which we first include the variables one at a time:

$$y_{i,j,t} = \beta X_{i,j,t-1} + \delta GDP_{j,t} + \vartheta claim_{j,t-1} + \sum_{s=2006}^{2015} \theta_s year_{s,t} + f_i + \varepsilon_{i,j,t} \quad (7.2)$$

$$y_{i,j,t} = \beta X_{i,j,t-1} + \delta GDP_{j,t} + \gamma r_{j,t} + \sum_{s=2006}^{2015} \theta_s year_{s,t} + f_i + \varepsilon_{i,j,t} \qquad (7.3)$$

where $claim_{j,t-1}$ is country j claims to the US, either size or share in total claims, and $r_{j,t}$ is the interest rate for country j. Then, we also put the size of bank claims to the US and a measure of monetary policy stance together in one model.

Table 7.3 Determinants of bank profitability—benchmark model estimations

	Full sample	Pre-crisis	Post-crisis
Cost to income ratio	−0.0001 (0.0001)	−0.0005* (0.0003)	−0.0001 (0.0001)
Net interest margin	0.3115*** (0.0470)	0.0979 (0.0767)	0.1809*** (0.0524)
Bank size	−0.0028*** (0.0007)	−0.0022* (0.0013)	−0.0020** (0.0010)
Leverage	−0.0002** (0.0001)	0.0030 (0.0332)	−0.0003* (0.0002)
Liquidity	−0.0022 (0.0016)	0.0042 (0.0036)	−0.0047* (0.0023)
GDP growth	0.0138** (0.0056)	0.0422* (0.0238)	0.0072 (0.0055)
N	8052	2372	5680
R-squared	0.094	0.112	0.037
Adj R-squared	0.092	0.109	0.035

Notes Authors' estimations. Standard errors are in the parentheses. ***, **, * indicate statistical significance at the level of 1, 5, 10%, respectively

7.4.2 Results

Table 7.3 presents the results of the basic regression model as described by Eq. (7.1). The estimation results for the whole period samples imply that the net interest margin plays the most important role in determining bank profitability—the coefficient is positive and statistically significant. Additionally, larger bank size and higher leverage seem to be related to lower profits. Moreover, we find no evidence on the role of bank efficiency in determining bank profitability.

Next, we divide the sample period into pre-crisis (2005–2008) and post-crisis (2009–2015) samples. Comparing the results of the two samples, first, we observe a considerable increase in the importance of net interest margin as a profit determinant after the outbreak of the financial crisis. The coefficient is statistically significant only since 2009.

Furthermore, higher leverage is associated with lower profits only in the post-crisis period, and prior to the crisis, the relationship is positive but not statistically significant. It seems that more debt-financed investment may not guarantee higher profits after the crisis, and that the opposite may even take place. The post-crisis environment of global financial tensions, European sovereign tensions, and strained banks might work as an exogenous factor that increases the risk of failure in the banking sector (and thus costs of bankruptcy), which increases the optimal capital ratio for banks. Such an environment might also considerably increase the need for banks to signal their high quality through increased capital ratios to increase their ability to access cheaper market funding and reduce risk-related barriers to expansion

[9]. Thus, the above-described deleveraging taking place in European banks, which was conducted to fix their strained balance sheets and regain credibility, might be one of the necessary ways to increase their profitability.

Additionally, higher bank liquidity seems to be associated with lower profits in the post-crisis period, implying the influence of lower returns from holding liquid assets. In the pre-crisis period, the profitability is influenced more by the cost to income ratio—more efficient banks achieving higher profits and by the GDP growth rate.

Next, we extend the benchmark estimation by including each country bank claims to the US and interest rates in the regression. Table 7.4 shows the estimated coefficients.

The results imply a great change in the influence of bank claims to the US with time. Prior to the crisis, in banks with higher claims to the US, higher profits are notable possibly because of higher profitability of US assets. After the outbreak of the crisis, the relation becomes negative. The fall in claims to the US seems to contribute to an increase in profits of the European banks. This result might be in part explained with the findings of McCauley et al. [3], who state that European banks have lowered their expositions to the US as a part of their post-crisis deleveraging effort to strengthen their balance sheets. Similar to deleveraging, shedding of US assets might also be a way to signal higher bank quality, which might be indispensable to restore profitability in the post-crisis environment, particularly when considering the fact of heavy pre-crisis investment in US assets prior to the crisis. Not only did European banks hold almost half of foreign holdings of US assets just before the crisis outbreak [1] but they were often high-risk assets. Milesi-Ferretti et al. [15] and Bertaut et al. [16] show that although East Asian countries focused their asset holdings on treasury securities and agency debt, highly leveraged banks in countries, such as France, Germany, Switzerland, and the UK, were important holders of private securities and other US "toxic" assets. To restore their balance sheets and credibility and thus boost profits, European banks might have no choice but to shed at least a part of their US exposure.

The impact of monetary policy stance on bank profitability also changes considerably with time. We observe a negative impact of higher interest rates in the whole sample and the pre-crisis period, and the latter is not statistically significant. The result is consistent with the assumption of monetary contraction contributing to lower profits through higher loan loss probability and lower non-interest income. In the post-crisis period, the situation changes entirely—the coefficient sign is positive and statistically significant, implying a positive impact of higher interest rates on the profits. The post-crisis low-interest environment seems to considerably push down bank profits because of lower net interest income. The supposition is corroborated by the importance of net interest margin as a profit determinant in the post-crisis sample.

At the same time, the results for other control variables change little with the introduction of new explanatory variables—net interest margin is still an important driver of profits, specifically in the post-crisis sample. The higher leverage ratio is associated with higher profits before the crisis outbreak, and with lower profits in

Table 7.4 Impact of claims to US and monetary policy stance on bank profitability

	Full sample	Pre-crisis	Post-crisis	Full sample	Pre-crisis	Post-crisis	Full sample	Pre-crisis	Post-crisis	Full sample	Pre-crisis	Post-crisis
Cost to income ratio	−0.0001 (0.0001)	−0.0005 (0.0003)	−0.0001 (0.0001)	−0.0001 (0.0001)	−0.0005 (0.0003)	−0.0001 (0.0001)	−0.0001 (0.0001)	−0.0005* (0.0003)	−0.0001 (0.0001)	−0.0001 (0.0001)	−0.0005* (0.0003)	−0.0001 (0.0001)
Net interest margin	0.3032*** (0.0466)	0.1035 (0.0808)	0.1817*** (0.0550)	0.3031*** (0.0474)	0.1076 (0.0790)	0.1777*** (0.0549)	0.3082*** (0.0464)	0.0975 (0.0770)	0.1812*** (0.0524)	0.2990*** (0.0458)	0.1029 (0.0811)	0.1826*** (0.0550)
Bank size	−0.0027*** (0.0007)	−0.0031** (0.0014)	−0.0018* (0.0010)	−0.0029*** (0.0007)	−0.0028** (0.0013)	−0.0018* (0.0010)	−0.0027*** (0.0007)	−0.0022* (0.0013)	−0.0021** (0.0010)	−0.0026*** (0.0007)	−0.0031** (0.0014)	−0.0018* (0.0010)
Leverage	−0.0003*** (0.0001)	0.0299 (0.0320)	−0.0004** (0.0002)	−0.0002** (0.0001)	0.0255 (0.0313)	−0.0004** (0.0002)	−0.0002** (0.0001)	0.0029 (0.0333)	−0.0003* (0.0002)	−0.0003*** (0.0001)	0.0298 (0.0321)	−0.0004** (0.0002)
Liquidity	−0.0026 (0.0018)	0.0029 (0.0038)	−0.0044* (0.0026)	−0.0029* (0.0018)	0.0028 (0.0037)	−0.0048* (0.0026)	−0.0022** (0.0016)	0.0043 (0.0036)	−0.0048* (0.0023)	−0.0026 (0.0018)	0.0029 (0.0038)	−0.0046* (0.0026)
GDP growth	0.0061 (0.0062)	0.0462** (0.0222)	0.0001 (0.0061)	0.0129* (0.0060)	0.0455** (0.0211)	0.0018 (0.0059)	0.0122 (0.0056)	0.0416* (0.0247)	0.0069 (0.0055)	0.0039 (0.0061)	0.0449* (0.0232)	−0.0004 (0.0061)
Claims to US—size	−0.1382*** (0.0432)	0.5355*** (0.1952)	−0.1275*** (0.0453)							−0.1441*** (0.0432)	0.5413*** (0.1914)	−0.1314*** (0.0452)
Claims to US—share				−0.0039 (0.0053)	0.0278** (0.0113)	−0.0212*** (0.0065)						
Interest rate							−0.1212*** (0.0367)	−0.0122 (0.0956)	0.1806*** (0.0525)	−0.1313*** (0.0373)	−0.0174 (0.0945)	0.1927*** (0.0525)
N	7397	2097	5300	7339	2117	5222	8052	2372	5680	7397	2097	5300
R-squared	0.091	0.105	0.0393	0.089	0.109	0.038	0.096	0.112	0.039	0.094	0.105	0.042
Adj R-squared	0.089	0.101	0.0370	0.087	0.105	0.036	0.095	0.108	0.037	0.092	0.101	0.039

Notes see Table 7.3

the post-crisis period, and higher liquidity lowers profits in the post-crisis period (although the result ceases to be statistically significant in most cases). Moreover, bank efficiency and GDP growth rate significantly influence profits before the crisis outbreak only.

7.5 Conclusions and Implications

This chapter analyzes the determinants of profitability of European banks before and after the global financial crisis against the background of the banks' heavy exposures to US assets prior to the crisis and post-crisis deleveraging, shedding of claims to the US, and monetary policy easing.

The data observation reveals a slight upward trend in European banks' profits from 2011, occurring concurrently to area-wide deleveraging. As European banks seem unable to raise enough capital in the post-crisis period—total capital holdings decrease from 2010, the deleveraging process seems to be carried out mostly through lower asset growth—bank total assets increase at a rather slow pace after 2007, falling in 2013 and 2015. Furthermore, a part of that slow asset growth might be connected to the post-crisis fall in banks' claims to the US and their total international claims.

The empirical analysis seeks the determinants of banks' profitability against this background and reveals that post-crisis bank deleveraging contributes to higher bank profitability. In a post-crisis environment, higher capital strength might be indispensable to increase bank credibility, ensure access to cheaper market funding, and thus boost profits.

Shedding of claims to the US in the post-crisis period might also play a similar role in the case of European banks. Prior to the outbreak of the global financial crisis, higher exposure of European banks to US assets boosted their profits, but in the post-crisis period, the relationship becomes negative. European banks might need to signal their improved bank quality with lower exposures after the pre-crisis heavy investments. Fall in claims to the US together with low total asset growth might also imply some home bias in the process of shedding assets to improve bank capital position.

Furthermore, the results point at the significant influence of net interest margin on bank profits in Europe, specifically after the crisis, thereby implying banks' high dependence on the interest rate environment. This fact is also confirmed by the result of interest rates showing that a low-interest-rate environment pushes down bank profits in the post-crisis period.

The analysis conducted in this chapter points at the importance of the sound balance sheet and strong capital position for bank profitability in Europe in the post-crisis world. Debt financing and higher leverage usually boost bank profits. However, in the post-crisis period, capital strength and bank quality, which reduce risk-related barriers to expansion and ensure easier or cheaper access to funding, have become conditions for increasing bank profitability. The question, how far this deleveraging is needed and will go, remains.

References

1. Borio, C., & Disyatat, P. (2011). Global imbalances and the financial crisis: link or no link? In *BIS Working Paper*, No. 346. Bank of International Settlements.
2. Noeth, B., & Sengupta, R. (2012). Global European banks and the financial crisis. *Federal Reserve Bank of St. Louis Review, 94*(6), 457–79.
3. McCauley, R. N., Benetrix, A. S., McGuire, P. M., & von Peter, G. (2017). Financial deglobalisation in banking? In *BIS Working Paper*, No. 650. Bank of International Settlements.
4. KPMG. (2016). *The profitability of EU banks: Hard work or a lost cause?* KPMG International Cooperative.
5. Dietrich, A., & Wanzenried, G. (2011). Determinants of bank profitability before and during the crisis: Evidence from Switzerland. *Journal of International Financial Markets, Institutions & Money, 21*, 307–327.
6. Goddard, J., Molyneux, P., & Wilson, J. O. S. (2004). The profitability of European banks: A cross-sectional and dynamic panel analysis. *Manchester School, 72*(3), 363–381.
7. Staikouras, Ch. K., & Wood, G. E. (2004). The determinants of European bank profitability. *International Business & Economics Research Journal, 3*(6), 57–68.
8. Pasiouras, F., & Kosmidou, K. (2007). Factors influencing the profitability of domestic and foreign commercial banks in the European Union. *Research in International Business and Finance, 21*, 222–237.
9. Berger, A. (1995). The relationship between capital and earnings in banking. *Journal of Money, Credit and Banking, 27*(2), 432–456.
10. Bourke, P. (1989). Concentration and other determinants of bank profitability in Europe, North America and Australia. *Journal of Banking and Finance, 13*, 65–79.
11. Molyneux, P., & Thornton, J. (1992). Determinants of European bank profitability: A note. *Journal of Banking and Finance, 16*, 1173–1178.
12. Berger, A., Hanweck, D., & Humphrey, D. (1987). Competitive viability in banking: Scale, scope, and product mix economies. *Journal of Monetary Economics, 20*(3), 501–520.
13. Petria, N., Capraru, B., & Ihnatov, I. (2015). Determinants of banks' profitability: Evidence from EU 27 banking systems. *Procedia Economics and Finance, 20*, 518–524.
14. Borio, C., Gambacorta, L., and Hofmann, B. (2015). The influence of monetary policy on bank profitability. In *BIS Working Paper,* No 154. Bank of International Settlements.
15. Milesi-Ferretti, G. M., Strobbe, F., & Tamirisa, N. T. (2010). Bilateral financial linkages and global imbalances: A view on the eve of the financial crisis. In *IMF Working Paper*, No. 10/257. International Monetary Fund.
16. Bertaut, C., DeMarco, L. P., Kamin, S. B., & Tryon, R. W. (2011). ABS Inflows to the United States and the Global Financial Crisis. In *International Finance Discussion Papers, No. 1028.* Board of Governors of the Federal Reserve System.

Agata Wierzbowska is an associate professor of economics at Kobe University, where she received her Ph.D. Her main research interests include analysis of banking systems and monetary policy.

Yoichi Matsubayashi is a professor of economics at Kobe University in Japan, where he received his Ph.D. His main research interest is international macroeconomics, especially external imbalances in the recent world economy. He has published many papers in refereed journals, such as the Japanese Economic Review and Japan and the World Economy. He is also the co-author of Financial Globalization and Regionalism in East Asia (Routledge 2013).

Chapter 8
Offshore Bond Issuance and Noncore Liability in BRICs Countries

Shugo Yamamoto

Abstract In BRICs countries, the use of offshore affiliates as financing vehicles for accumulating low-yield US dollar liability has become widespread to circumvent capital restrictions. To analyze this issue more deeply, we specifically examine noncore liability and analyze whether the increase of offshore bond issuance by offshore affiliates can be a source of the boom in noncore liability in BRICs countries. Finally, we analyze the Chinese shadow banking sector, which is similar to noncore liability. Because funds from offshore bond issuance are used, although financial restrictions are strict, shadow banking becomes increasingly vulnerable to turmoil in international financial markets. Furthermore, yuan depreciation will further amplify the damage of such a financial shock because of a currency mismatch.

Keywords Noncore liability · Offshore bond issuance · Shadow banking · Within-company loan

JEL classification F3 · F32 · F34

8.1 Introduction

The United States Federal Reserve Bank (FRB) implemented a monetary easing policy after the global financial crisis of 2008, which triggered and then sustained a considerable financial boom in economically developing countries through bond issuance. Shin [1] regards this as a "second phase of global liquidity." Regarding BRICs countries, two important characteristics are apparent: offshore bond issuance by offshore affiliates and within-company flows to repatriate offshore funds to headquarters in the home country

To circumvent capital restrictions in BRICs countries, the use of offshore affiliates as financing vehicles for accumulation of low-yield US dollar liability has become

---

S. Yamamoto (✉)
Rikkyo University, Tokyo, Japan
e-mail: shugo-y@rikkyo.ac.jp

© The Author(s), under exclusive license to Springer Nature Singapore Pte Ltd. 2022
Y. Matsubayashi and S. Kitano (eds.), *Global Financial Flows in the Pre- and Post-global Crisis Periods*, Kobe University Monograph Series in Social Science Research,
https://doi.org/10.1007/978-981-19-3613-5_8

widespread.[1] The purpose of having US dollar liabilities and of holding the proceeds in domestic funds might be to hedge export receivables, or simply to speculate on the appreciation of the domestic currency using a so-called carry trade strategy. In practice, the dividing line between hedging and speculation might be difficult to distinguish.

Bruno and Shin [2] report that non-financial corporations in emerging economies behave as financial intermediaries: co-movements in domestic financial assets and foreign liabilities have a positive sign. Therefore, offshore bond issuance might cause a financial boom in the domestic country. To assess this issue more deeply, using a method described by [3], we specifically examine noncore liabilities: an indicator of financial system vulnerability. During a financial boom, the pool of retail deposits will likely be insufficient for funding.[2] Therefore, the funding gap is filled by noncore liabilities, which include claims held by other financial intermediaries and liabilities to foreign creditors.

Using within-company flows to transfer funds from offshore affiliates to a headquarters in the home country to circumvent capital restrictions has become widespread. An important reason is that capital account transactions through banks can be regulated tightly, but the transactions of thousands of non-financial companies generated through international trade are expected to be much more difficult to monitor and regulate. This fact indicates that non-financial corporations act as surrogate intermediaries by issuing bonds at offshore affiliates and by transferring the funds to the headquarters in the home country [1, 4, 5].

Avdjiev et al. [6] explains an accounting convention in calculating the balance of payments (BOP) that classifies borrowing and lending between affiliated entities of the same non-financial corporate as "direct investment." Furthermore, such transactions are classified as "debt instrument" sub-items of direct investment. Therefore, in economies such as those of developing countries where capital flows are often restricted to some degree, FDI flow can turn out to be "hot" money that transmits global financial conditions to the segregated domestic economy. Consequently, this within-company flow will connect offshore bond issuance by offshore affiliates and noncore liabilities in the domestic economy.

Based on the two characteristics presented above, we would like to analyze whether the increase of offshore bond issuance by affiliates of non-financial corporate can be a source of the boom of noncore liability in BRICs countries. Financing of banks and nonbank financial institutions through noncore liabilities constitutes shadow banking [7–9], which has attracted attention particularly in China. Our analysis can clarify shadow banking in China with consideration of offshore bond issuance. The shortcomings of shadow banking in China are not merely confined to the domestic economy: they also constitute an important topic for international financial market stability.

---

[1] In Sect. 8.2, using detailed figures, we presented details of offshore bond issuance.

[2] Core liabilities are funds based on household retail deposits, for which growth is in line with household incomes.

8.2 Facts and Data Description

As described in detail below, offshore bond issuance by BRICs countries increased dramatically after the financial crisis in 2008. Because of low interest rate policies by the FRB after 2008, the cost of borrowing dollars became extremely low. However, because of the less-developed state of financial markets and strict financial restrictions, BRICs countries were unable to take advantage of easy external financing conditions domestically. Using the Chinn–Ito index [10], the financial openness of BRICs countries can be ascertained from Fig. 8.1. It is noteworthy that the increase shown by that number reflects a high degree of capital account openness. According to the figure, capital openness in China and India is the lowest among the four countries: both lines are overlapped. By comparison, although Brazil shows an inverted U-shaped trend, the index of Russia shows a rising trend. However, overall, one can reasonably infer that the capital openness of BRICs countries is not as high as in economically developed countries. Therefore, market imperfections that limit domestic borrowing options influence a firm's decision to issue bonds offshore.

The stream of offshore bond issuance by non-financial corporations can be portrayed as Fig. 8.2 [1, 11]. First, the offshore affiliate of a non-financial corporation issues US-dollar-denominated bonds. Then, through within-company flows, the offshore affiliates transfer funds to their headquarters in the home country. Subsequently the headquarters in the home country will deposit the funds in a domestic bank. Thereby using an offshore affiliate to circumvent capital controls and market

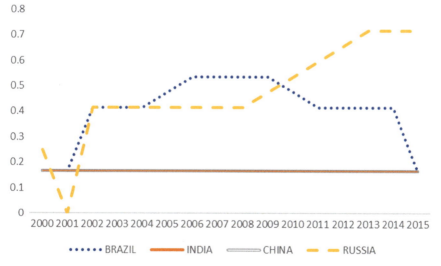

Fig. 8.1 Chinn–Ito Index of BRICs countries. *Note* Rising values represent increasing financial openness. *Source* Chinn and Ito (2016)

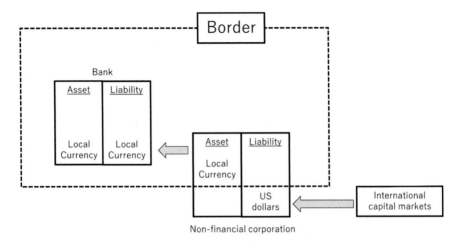

Fig. 8.2 Non-financial corporations as a surrogate intermediary. *Sources* [1 and 11]

imperfections, the headquarters in the home country will accumulate low-yield, US-dollar-denominated debt and high-yield claims of assets denominated in the domestic currency. The consequent increase of short-term assets might boost noncore liability.

Because no available data directly reflect characteristics or amounts of offshore bond issuance by foreign affiliates, one must conduct indirect estimation using existing data. As described herein, by referring to reports of earlier studies [1, 4, 12], we use statistics of two types related to the net issuance of international debt securities: nationality-based and the residence-based measures. The residence of the issuer is the country in which the issuer is incorporated, whereas the nationality of the issuer is the country in which the issuer's parent is headquartered.[3] Because the amount of international debt issued by foreigners within the borders of emerging countries is small, one can assume that the nationality-based measure is the sum of onshore and offshore measures. Furthermore, we use the residence-based measure as a proxy for the onshore measure. Consequently, the difference between nationality-based and the residence-based measures represents a proxy for the offshore measure.

In the following, we describe offshore US-dollar-denominated bond issuance by international debt securities of non-financial corporations using data from the Bank for International Settlements (BIS).[4] Figure 8.3 presents four variables: nationality or residence of the issuer and economically developing countries either including or excluding BRICs countries. It is noteworthy that the difference between the nationality and residence of the issuer reflects offshore bond issuance by offshore affiliates.

---

[3] For example, the debts of a Hong Kong subsidiary of a Chinese company might be guaranteed by the parent company. Therefore, debt securities issued by the Hong Kong subsidiary of a Chinese company would be allocated to the Hong Kong on a residence basis and China on a nationality basis.

[4] Hereafter, unless noted otherwise, all data of offshore bond issuance used in this paper are denominated in US dollars.

8 Offshore Bond Issuance and Noncore Liability in BRICs Countries 173

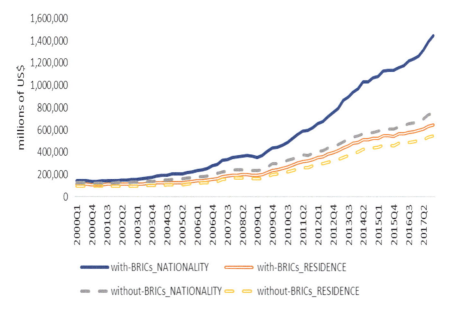

Fig. 8.3 Nationality and residence of issuer with and without BRICs countries. *Note* The difference between "NATIONALITY" and "RESIDENCE" is offshore bond issuance: "with-BRICs" are economically developing countries including BRICs countries; and "without-BRICs" are economically developing countries, not including BRICs countries. *Source* BIS securities statistics

From this figure, one can infer that offshore bond issuance increased in BRICs countries dramatically after 2010. Compared to this, offshore bond issuance of economically developing countries excluding BRICs is small. Therefore, the drastic rise of offshore bond issuance can be said to be a phenomenon that is specific to BRICs countries.

Next, we will find additional details related to offshore bond issuance of the four BRICs countries. In Fig. 8.4, offshore bond issuance of non-financial corporations in China, Brazil, Russia, and India are described. As this figure shows, the amounts for China outstanding are overwhelming. Brazil follows. The ratios of US-dollar-denominated bonds to total currency in 2017Q4 are 89.6% for China, 93.7% for Brazil, 72.7% for Russia, and 77.3% for India. Consequently, offshore issuance can be expected to mirror currency mismatches on the consolidated balance sheet. It is much more sensitive to US interest rates and exchange rate fluctuations.

After the issuance of offshore bonds by offshore affiliates, the funds must be repatriated to the headquarters in the home country. Avdjiev et al. [6] describe three channels: The company can lend directly to its headquarters (within-company flows), extend credit to unrelated companies (between-company flows), or make cross-border deposits in a bank (corporate deposit flows). As described herein, we exclusively examine within-company flows because no data directly indicate the remaining two channels described above. Therefore, we must estimate the amount using the combination of existing statistics such as BOP and banking statistics of BIS.

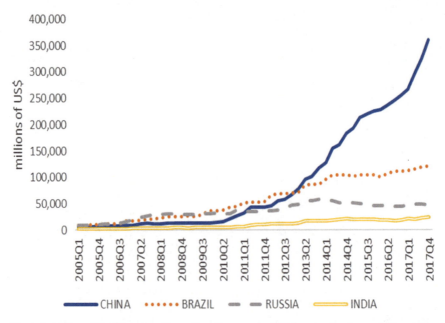

Fig. 8.4 Offshore US-dollar-denominated bond issuance by BRICs countries. *Source* BIS securities statistics

This procedure might decrease the accuracy of the estimation. In addition, according to Avdjiev et al. [6], between-company flows are described as "Trade credit" in "Other investments" of BOP. Consequently, a distinction of between-company related flows from "genuine" trade credit might be difficult to draw.

Following the explanation offered by Avdjiev et al. [6], data of within-company flows can be described as presented below. An accounting convention in the BOP deems borrowing and lending between affiliated entities of the same non-financial corporate to be "direct investment." Specifically, such transactions are classified under the "debt instruments" sub-item of direct investment. Furthermore, we use BOP data of the International Monetary Fund (IMF). Therefore, the foreign affiliate of a non-financial corporation can act as a surrogate intermediary by repatriating funds in economies such as those in emerging countries, where capital flows are often restricted to some degree. Moreover, even if capital account transactions through banks could be regulated tightly, the transactions of thousands of non-financial companies generated through international trade are expected to be much more difficult to monitor and regulate.

Before examination of the data of within-company flows, we describe noncore liability of BRICs countries here. During the financial boom, the pool of core liability such as retail deposits from an ultimate domestic creditor is insufficient to fulfill demand from the financial sector. Therefore, noncore liability from the wholesale market and the foreign sector is necessary: it serves as a useful indicator of financial procyclicality and as an early warning indicator. Funding sources of the financial sector consist of (1) liability because of an ultimate domestic creditor, (2) liability because of a financial intermediary, and (3) liability because of a foreign creditor [13]. Furthermore, they defined (1) as core liability and defined the remainder as noncore liability. Based on this knowledge, we construct a noncore liability of BRICs countries from an earlier report by [3] describing economically developing countries. Because of data limitations, they construct two alternative measures for noncore liability.

(A)   Liability of banks to the foreign sector + Liability of banks to the nonbanking financial sector

(B)   Liability of banks to the foreign sector + (M3-M2)

Although the priority is (a), if a data limitation does exist, then we adopt (B). The difference between M3 and M2 captures the market related financial instruments which is similar to wholesale bank funding.[5] For China, we adopt (A). From International Financial Statistics (IFS) of the IMF, we use the sum of "Monetary, Banking Institutions, Foreign Liabilities" and "Monetary, Banking Institutions, Liabilities to Other Financial Corporations." In the case of Brazil, because of data limitations, we adopt (B). From data of the Depository Corporations Survey and Broad Money Supply from Central Bank of Brazil, we use the sum of "Liabilities to Nonresidents" and M3-M2. For Russia, because of data limitations, we also adopt (B). From IFS, we use the sum of "Liabilities of Monetary, Depository Corporations to Non-residents" and M3-M2. For India, no data related to balance sheets of the banking sector are available. Therefore, we exclude India from our empirical analysis.

Finally, to clarify the object and hypothesis of our study, we describe trend behavior of three variables described earlier: within-company flows (FDI),[6] noncore liability (NONCORE), and offshore bond issuance by offshore affiliates (OFFSHORE). These three variables are expected to be mutually interacting. Therefore, it is worth presenting them together in the same figure. Figure 8.5 presents data for China. Figure 8.6 depicts data for Brazil. Figure 8.7 portrays data for Russia. Figure 8.8 shows data for India. For India, as explained earlier, because of data limitations in noncore liability, we described only OFFSHORE and FDI for reference. Because of data limitations, Figs. 8.5 and 8.6 are from 2005Q1 to 2017Q4. Figure 8.7 is from 2002Q1 to 2017Q1. Figure 8.8 is from 2007Q4 to 2017Q3. Furthermore, all data are expressed in US dollars.

From Fig. 8.5, one can confirm that the three variables of China exhibit similar trend behavior throughout the sample periods. As described later, because noncore liability is similar to shadow banking, one can infer that the boom in shadow banking

---

[5] Here, we briefly explain the meaning of M3-M2. First, M2 includes M1 plus short-term time deposits in banks. Therefore, M2 is similar to retail deposits. We can regard it as a liability because of an ultimate domestic creditor. Second, M3 includes M2 plus longer-term time deposits and money market funds.

[6] It is noteworthy that, because within-company flow is a flow of a new investment, to unify the terms used, we calculate the backward difference of stock variables of both offshore bond issuance and noncore liability.

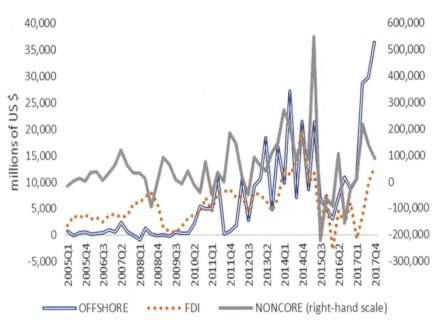

Fig. 8.5 China offshore bond issuance, within-company flow, and noncore liability. *Note* Because FDI represents a flow of a new investment, to unify the terms used, we calculate the backward difference of stock variables for both OFFSHORE and NONCORE. *Sources* OFFSHORE is from BIS securities statistics; FDI is from BOP of the IMF; and NONCORE is from IFS of the IMF

in China is fueled to some degree by offshore bond issuance by offshore affiliates. From Fig. 8.6, although offshore bond issuance and within-company flows in Brazil display similar trend behavior, noncore liabilities exhibit slightly different trend behavior. Therefore, empirical analysis must be conducted to elucidate this relation. From Fig. 8.7, the three variables for Russia exhibit similar trend behavior. Finally, from Fig. 8.8, it must be said that the trend behaviors of offshore bond issuance and within-company flow exhibit no similar trend behavior.

8.3 Shadow Banking and Offshore Bond Issuance in China

Shadow banking has been identified as one cause of the financial crisis of 2008. Therefore, it has attracted much attention in the United States. However, the term only recently came into widespread use. No single agreed definition exists. Since seminal work reported by [14], researchers and regulators have proposed different definitions for shadow banking. For example, the Financial Stability Board of United States broadly describes shadow banking as "credit intermediation involving entities and activities outside the regular banking system." Furthermore, financing of banks and nonbank financial institutions through noncore liabilities constitutes shadow banking

8 Offshore Bond Issuance and Noncore Liability in BRICs Countries

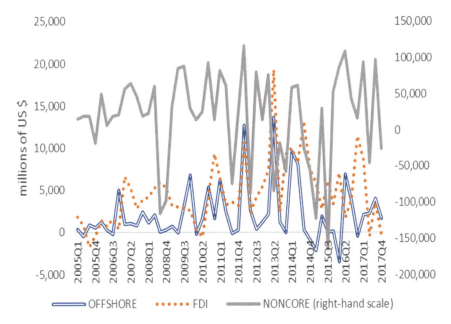

Fig. 8.6 Brazil offshore bond issuance, within-company flow, and noncore liability. *Note* Because FDI represents a flow of a new investment, to unify the terms used, we calculate the backward difference of stock variables of both OFFSHORE and NONCORE. *Sources* OFFSHORE is from BIS securities statistics; FDI is from BOP of the IMF; and NONCORE is from the Central Bank of Brazil

[7–9]. Because that definition of noncore liability is based on an idea presented by [13], we can associate our findings with shadow banking and can provide some policy implications. Among economically developing and BRICs countries, growth in shadow banking in China stands out [9].[7] Furthermore, as presented in Fig. 8.4, Chinese non-financial corporations issue overwhelming amounts of bonds in offshore markets compared to other BRICs countries. Therefore, we exclusively examine shadow banking in China associated with the empirical results described in an earlier section.

Ehlers et al. [16] regard the dominant role of commercial banks as one important feature of the shadow banking system in China. Contrary to this, securitization and market-based instruments playonly a minor role. Actually, that study compares shadow banking in China to a "shadow of the banks." To confirm similarity between noncore liability used in our empirical analysis and actual shadow banking data, we can examine the trend behavior of both data, as shown in Fig. 8.9. Using various statistics and indicators, several researchers and institutions have analyzed the volume and dynamics of shadow banking in China. Among them, we used "core shadow banking activity" from the Moody's quarterly China shadow banking monitor. This indicator is based on three sources: entrusted loans, trust loans, and undiscounted

---

[7] Regarding other BRICs countries, [15] presents a study of shadow banking in India.

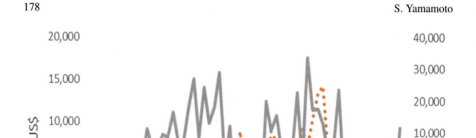

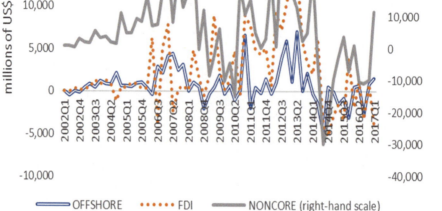

Fig. 8.7 Russia offshore bond issuance, within-company flow, and noncore liability. *Note* Because FDI represents a flow of a new investment, to unify the terms used, we calculate the backward difference of stock variables of both OFFSHORE and NONCORE. *Sources* OFFSHORE is from BIS securities statistics; FDI is from BOP of the IMF; and NONCORE is from IFS of the IMF

banker's acceptances.[8] As the figure shows, the core shadow banking indicator (CORE_SHADOW) and noncore liability in domestic currency can be confirmed as exhibiting similar trend behavior. Moreover, the outstanding amounts of the two variables are similar. Therefore, when assessing China, treating noncore liability as shadow banking is reasonable.

The sudden sharp increase in shadow banking in China in recent years represents an important difficulty for financial stability. To mitigate the financial vulnerability, monetary authorities in China such as the People's Bank of China and China Banking Regulatory Commission are making efforts to cut leverage in the financial system by issuing a flurry of regulations. These policies have pushed up corporate funding costs in the onshore market and have consequently suppressed shadow banking and interbank activities.

Although the FRB is set to raise interest rates, funding using US dollars will still be cheaper offshore. Therefore, Chinese non-financial corporations have strong demand to substitute low-yielding US dollar debt for higher-yielding yuan assets. As described in Sect. 8.2, compared to Brazil and Russia, China has strict capital controls. In spite of this attempt at management of the problem, within-company

---

[8] Data are from Aggregate Financing to the Real Economy of the People's Bank of China.

8 Offshore Bond Issuance and Noncore Liability in BRICs Countries   179

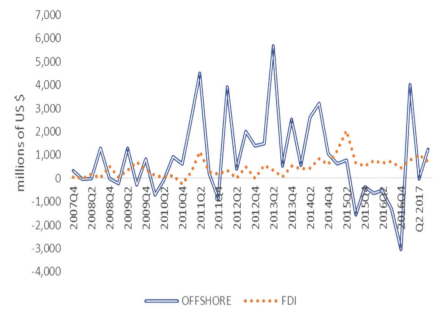

Fig. 8.8 India offshore bond issuance and within-company flow. *Note* NONCORE has a data limitation. We exclude this variable. Because FDI represents a flow of a new investment, to unify the terms used, we calculate the backward difference of stock variables of OFFSHORE. *Sources* OFFSHORE is from BIS securities statistics; FDI is from BOP of the IMF

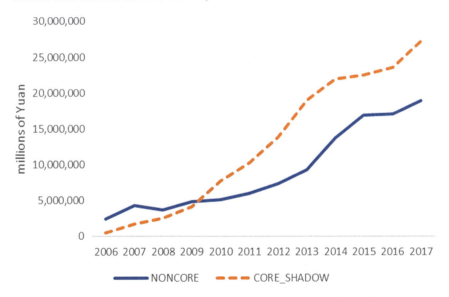

Fig. 8.9 Noncore liability and core shadow banking activity in China (millions of yuan). *Sources* NONCORE represents data from domestic currency from IFS of the IMF; CORE_SHADOW represents data from the People's Bank of China

flows between offshore affiliates and headquarters in the home country can circumvent financial restrictions. Therefore, using within-company flows, tight regulations and rising funding costs in China have pushed many Chinese firms to shift their fund-raising activities from the onshore to offshore markets during the past year, leading to a sharp drop in mainland bond issuance.[9]

Because funds from offshore bond issuance are used in shadow banking, a crisis occurring in the shadow banking system in China would spill over into international financial markets. Similarly, China has become more vulnerable to shocks arising in international financial markets. Furthermore, a currency mismatch persists because non-financial corporations in China are accumulating low-yielding US dollar debt and higher-yielding domestic investments. Consequently, yuan depreciation will amplify the damage caused by the financial shock further, not only to the domestic economy but also to international financial markets.

From the discussion presented above, comprehensive financial regulation targeting both offshore and onshore markets is necessary because of a search to circumvent financial regulation such as regulatory arbitrage by cash-hungry Chinese non-financial corporations.

8.4 Conclusions

In BRICs countries, to circumvent capital restrictions, the use of offshore affiliates as financing vehicles for accumulating low-yield US dollar liabilities has become widespread. Furthermore, funds are repatriated from offshore affiliates to headquarters in the home country via within-company flows. To analyze this issue more deeply, we specifically examine noncore liability, which is an indicator of financial system vulnerability. We analyze whether the increase of offshore bond issuance by offshore affiliates of non-financial corporations can be a source of the boom in noncore liability in BRICs countries.

Generally, earlier studies have included the assumption that FDI, compared to portfolio investment, is more stable and less prone to financial booms and sudden stops. Therefore, FDI flows into economically developing countries are often viewed as stable "cold" money generated and underpinned by long-term considerations. By contrast, portfolio flows are often regarded as unstable "hot" money that moves according to short-term considerations. Contrary to the conventional view presented above, in economies such as those of emerging countries where capital flows are restricted, the offshore affiliate of a non-financial corporation can act as a surrogate intermediary through fund repatriation. Because of within-company flows, which are classified as a debt instrument of FDI, FDI can turn out to be "hot" money, which transmits the global financial condition to a segregated domestic economy.

---

[9] Furthermore, this finding is consistent with news reports of [17], who reports that these tightening policies can be expected to shift Chinese firms from onshore to offshore bond issuance even as the FRB raises short-term interest rates.

Finally, we briefly analyze shadow banking in China, which is similar in terms of noncore liability. Because funds from offshore bond issuance are used for the boom in shadow banking sector, a crisis occurring in shadow banking in China would spill over into international financial markets. Moreover, China has become increasingly vulnerable to international financial market shocks. Furthermore, because of the currency mismatch of non-financial corporations in China, a declining value of the yuan can be expected to amplify the damage that a financial shock might cause.

References

1. Shin, H.S. (2013). The second phase of global liquidity and its impact on emerging economies. In *Proceedings* (pp. 1–10). Federal Reserve Bank of San Francisco.
2. Bruno, V., & Shin, H. S. (2017). Global dollar credit and carry trades: A firm-level analysis. *Review of Financial Studies, 30*(3), 703–749.
3. Hahm, J. H., Shin, H. S., & Shin, K. (2013). Noncore bank liabilities and financial vulnerability. *Journal of Money, Credit and Banking, 45*, 3–36.
4. McCauley, R. N., McGuire, P., & Sushko, V. (2015). *Dollar credit to emerging market economies.* BIS Quarterly Review, Bank for International Settlements.
5. Serena, J. M., & Moreno, R. (2016). *Domestic financial markets and offshore bond financing.* BIS Quarterly Review, Bank for International Settlements.
6. Avdjiev, S., Chui, M., & Shin, H.S. (2014). *Non-financial corporations from emerging market economies and capital flows.* BIS quarterly review (pp. 67–77). Bank for International Settlements.
7. Harutyunyan, A., Errico, L., Loukoianova, E., Walton, R., Korniyenko, Y., Amidžić, G., AbuShanab, H., Shin, H.S. (2014). *Mapping the shadow banking system through a global flow of funds analysis.* IMF Working Papers 14/10, International Monetary Fund.
8. Harutyunyan, A., Massara, A., Ugazio, G., Amidzic, G., Walton, R. (2015). Shedding light on shadow banking. IMF Working Papers 15/1, International Monetary Fund.
9. International Monetary Fund. (2014). *Global financial stability report: risk taking, liquidity, and shadow banking.* Chapter 2.
10. Chinn, M. D., & Ito, H. (2006). What matters for financial development? Capital controls, institutions, and interactions. *Journal of Development Economics, 81*(1), 163–192.
11. Chung, K., Lee, J. E., Loukoianova, E., Park, H., & Shin, H. S. (2015). Global liquidity through the lens of monetary aggregates. *Economic Policy, 30*(82), 231–290.
12. Gruic, B., & Wooldridge, P. (2015). BIS debt securities statistics: a comparison of nationality data with external debt statistics. IFC Bulletins chapters. In Bank for International Settlements (ed.), *Indicators to support monetary and financial stability analysis: data sources and statistical methodologies*, vol 39. Bank for International Settlements.
13. Shin, H.S., & Shin, K. (2011). *Procyclicality and monetary aggregates.* NBER Working Papers 16836, National Bureau of Economic Research, Inc.
14. Pozsar, Z., Adrian, T., Ashcraft, A.B., & Boesky, H. (2010). *Shadow banking.* Staff Reports 458, Federal Reserve Bank of New York.
15. Acharya, V. V., Hemal, K., & Öncü, T. S. (2013). The growth of a shadow banking system in emerging markets: Evidence from India. *Journal of International Money and Finance, 39*(c), 207–230.
16. Ehlers, T., Kong, S., & Zhu, F. (2018). *Mapping shadow banking in China: structure and dynamics.* BIS working paper No 701. Bank of International Settlements.

17. Chen, M. (2018). Chinese firms tipped to sell more dollar bonds despite Fed rate hike forecasts. Reuters, February 13, 2018. Retrieved June 18, 2018, from https://www.reuters.com/article/us-china-offshore-bonds/chinese-firms-tipped-to-sell-more-dollar-bonds-despite-fed-rate-hike-forecasts-idUSKBN1FX0EY.

Shugo Yamamoto is an associate professor at Rikkyo University in Japan. He received his Ph.D. from Kobe University, and his main research interest is international finance.

Chapter 9
Recent Developments in the Adoption of Capital Controls in Emerging Economies: Theory and Practice

Shigeto Kitano and Kenya Takaku

Abstract After the global financial crisis, policymakers and researchers have begun to discuss capital control policies—an option that attracted little attention in the past—as a real policy alternative for emerging economies looking to regulate capital flows properly. In this chapter, we first introduce the recent trends in theoretical research on capital control policies. Recent developments in theoretical analyses suggest that capital controls have greater potential for emerging economies as a regular policy instrument than previously thought. Next, we outline how emerging economies use these policies to regulate international capital flows. Recently created indicators of capital control provide a better understanding of changes in capital control policies that are difficult to capture with earlier indicators. The analysis using these new indicators suggests that emerging countries deploy capital control policies more intensively than previously assumed. We also find that significant heterogeneity exists even among emerging countries classified in the same subcategory of "wall," "gate," or "open" in terms of capital control policies.

Keywords Capital controls · Emerging economies · Financial frictions · Macroprudential regulation · Credit policy · Exchange rate system

9.1 Introduction

Developed countries responded to the global financial crisis with unprecedented quantitative easing measures. This massive quantitative easing program in developed countries had a significant impact on international capital flows. In particular, the

---

S. Kitano (✉)
RIEB, Kobe University, 2-1, Rokkodai, Nada, Kobe 657-8501, Japan
e-mail: kitano@rieb.kobe-u.ac.jp

K. Takaku
Faculty of International Studies, Hiroshima City University, 3-4-1, Ozuka-Higashi, Asa-Minami-Ku, Hiroshima 731-3194, Japan
e-mail: takaku@hiroshima-cu.ac.jp

© The Author(s), under exclusive license to Springer Nature Singapore Pte Ltd. 2022
Y. Matsubayashi and S. Kitano (eds.), *Global Financial Flows in the Pre- and Post-global Crisis Periods*, Kobe University Monograph Series in Social Science Research,
https://doi.org/10.1007/978-981-19-3613-5_9

lower interest rates in developed countries drove global capital into emerging countries in search of higher yields. This sudden influx of capital into emerging economies caused macroeconomic instability in these countries in the form of asset market bubbles, rising inflation rates, and declining international competitiveness due to the high valuation of domestic currencies. This macroeconomic instability caused great concern for policymakers. Since the phenomenon of lower interest rates in developed countries pushing capital into emerging and developing economies has been observed on a number of occasions in the past, many policymakers and researchers have considered some kind of policy intervention to be required. The International Monetary Fund (IMF) had previously opposed any policies that impede the free flow of capital; however, depending on the situation, it now recognizes that capital control policies are a valid alternative for emerging countries looking to manage excessive capital inflows.[1] For instance, Brazil, Thailand, South Korea, Indonesia, and Taiwan have implemented policies to manage large capital inflows because of concerns about the high value of their respective currencies, soaring asset prices, and rising inflation rates.[2]

Furthermore, history shows that after this kind of large-scale inflow of capital into emerging countries, capital flows tend to reverse sharply once interest rates in developed countries rise, siphoning capital out of emerging countries, and triggering currency and financial crises. This pattern has been repeatedly witnessed in developing and emerging countries.[3] Against this backdrop, policymakers and researchers now worry that if monetary policy normalization in developed countries materializes, emerging countries could experience a sudden outflow of capital that could spark another financial crisis. These concerns constituted a key policy agenda at the G20 summit in January 2016.

Capital flows between emerging and developed countries are a significant factor causing instability in both because the former have become increasingly important players in the global economy in recent years. For instance, while emerging and developing economies represented only about 37% of global GDP in 1980, this increased to about 59% in 2017.[4] A direct consequence of this is that instability in emerging economies can also pose a significant risk to developed countries, rendering the effective control of capital flows a major concern for policymakers in both emerging and developed countries.

In this environment, there has recently been a proliferation of theoretical and empirical research on capital control policies, a topic that has attracted little attention.[5] This chapter introduces recent trends in theoretical research on such policies

---

[1] For details, see Ostry et al. [53, 54].

[2] Nispi Landi and Schiavone [52] show that capital controls are generally effective and controls on portfolio inflows are more effective for emerging economies.

[3] For the capital inflow problem, see, for example, Agénor [1] and Agénor and Montiel [3].

[4] Data source: IMF, World Economic Outlook (April 2018), GDP based on PPP, share of world (Percent of World).

[5] Capital controls are not a new policy instrument, however. Even before the recent financial crisis, they have been discussed both theoretically and empirically. For the earlier literature on capital controls, see Kitano [42].

and shows that they may have significant potential as policy tools. In particular, we show that capital control policies could serve to stabilize the amplification mechanism in economies with financial frictions. We also elaborate on how emerging economies use capital control policies to regulate international capital flows.

Recently created indicators of capital control provide a better understanding of changes in capital control policies that are difficult to capture with earlier indicators. Our analysis using these new indicators suggests that emerging countries deploy capital control policies more intensively than previously assumed. In addition, we find that a wide variety of capital controls exist among emerging countries classified as the same subcategory of "wall," "gate," or "open" in terms of capital control policies.

9.2 Capital Controls in Theory

As we argue in the Introduction, the IMF used to oppose any policies that restrict the free flow of capital; however, it now recognizes that capital control policies are a valid alternative for emerging countries to manage volatile capital inflows. Ostry et al. [53, 54] argue that in limited circumstances, the use of capital controls is justified. Jeanne et al. [38] go further, arguing that "[p]roperly designed capital controls may even be effective as a regular instrument of economic policy" (p. 110). In this environment, theoretical research on capital control policies has recently proliferated.[6]

Jeanne and Korinek [37], Bianchi [10], and Brunnermeier and Sannikov [11] examine capital controls as a policy tool to internalize the pecuniary externalities associated with financial crises.[7] Farhi and Werning [25] and Schmitt-Grohé and Uribe [58] study the effects of capital controls under the peg. Davis and Presno [16] examine the effects of capital controls on the optimal monetary policy under the flexible exchange rate. De Paoli and Lipinska [17] examine the effects of using capital controls to manage an economy's terms of trade. Agénor and Jia [2] study the relationship between capital controls and reserve requirement rules. Liu and Spiegel [49] examine the relationship between capital controls and sterilization.[8,9]

Among the other related studies, we next explain several studies that explore the possibility of capital controls as a policy tool in a small open economy. The first study is Kitano and Takaku [43], which focuses on the relationship between capital controls

---

[6] Theoretical analyses of capital controls have mainly been related to the issue of currency crises and the capital inflow problem (e.g., Wyplosz [61], Park and Sachs [55], Auernheimer [6], Bacchetta [7], Dellas and Stockman [18], and Bartolini and Drazen [8], Kitano [40], and Kitano [41]).

[7] Harberger [33] also argues that externalities accompany foreign borrowing, and policymakers can internalize them through a corrective tax on foreign borrowing.

[8] Chang et al. [13] show that there exists a trade-off between inflation and sterilization costs under capital controls and pegs.

[9] In the aftermath of the financial crisis, the role of macroprudential regulation has also been discussed (Unsal [60], Ghilardi and Peiris [31], Engel [23], and Nispi Landi [51]). For details, see Kitano and Takaku [46].

and financial frictions. Second, we explain Kitano and Takaku [44], which shows that capital controls can be a credit policy tool to mitigate a crisis shock. The third example is Kitano and Takaku [45], which compares the welfare implications of an optimal monetary policy under flexible exchange rates and an optimal capital control policy under fixed exchange rates. The final example is Kitano and Takaku [46], which compares the effectiveness of capital controls and macroprudential regulation.

9.2.1 Capital Controls and Financial Frictions

Kitano and Takaku [43] examine the extent to which the welfare-improving effects of capital controls depend on the degree of financial frictions between banks and foreign investors. Financial frictions à la Gertler and Kiyotaki [30] are incorporated into a real business cycle model of a small open economy so that they exist between domestic banks and foreign investors. The small open economy consists of households, banks, non-financial firms, and the government. In this model, banks play a key role in causing the amplification effect due to financial frictions. Banks finance domestic non-financial firms by using their net worth, obtaining deposits from local households, and borrowing in international financial markets. Capital controls are imposed by the government to regulate banks' foreign borrowings.[10]

It will be shown that capital controls can be an effective instrument for addressing the amplification effect due to financial frictions. When the degree of financial frictions between banks and foreign investors is higher, the welfare-improving effect of capital controls becomes larger, and a more aggressive policy rule is thus appropriate. Banks also face the "liability dollarization" problem, and their foreign borrowing is denominated in the foreign currency. Emerging economies tend to face a mismatch in the currency denomination of their liabilities and assets, since they have difficulty borrowing abroad in their own currencies.[11] A comparison of the two economies, one with and one without "liability dollarization," reveals that the welfare-improving effect of capital controls is larger in the presence of "liability dollarization" and that the gap between the effects becomes larger as the degree of financial frictions increases.

Figure 9.1 shows the impulse responses of output (Y), the spread between the expected return on capital and that in the riskless rate ($E[R_k] - R$), consumption (C), and the real exchange rate (e) to an exogenous increase in foreign interest rates under different degrees of financial frictions. The initiating disturbance was set to a 1% unanticipated annual increase in foreign interest rates. In Fig. 9.1, a higher value of ω indicates a higher degree of financial friction between domestic banks and foreign investors. The thin, bold, and dotted curves represent the cases of a lower

---

[10] Shin [59] argues that "a tax on non-core liabilities has many advantages as a prudential tool in dampening the procyclicality of the financial system, especially for emerging economies" (p. 1).

[11] Eichengreen and Hausmann [20] refer to this incompleteness in financial markets as the "original sin."

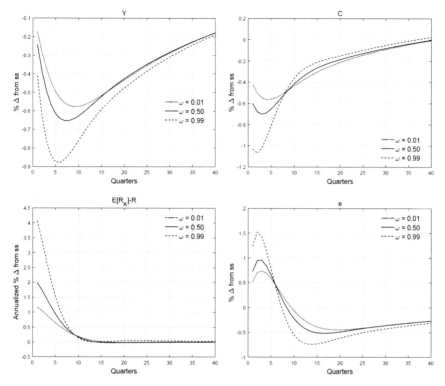

Fig. 9.1 Responses to an increase in the foreign interest rate: $\omega = 0.01, 0.5, 0.99$ (Y, C, $E[R_k] - R$, e). *Source* Kitano and Takaku [43]

degree of financial frictions ($\omega = 0.01$), a benchmark degree of financial frictions ($\omega = 0.5$), and a higher degree of financial frictions ($\omega = 0.99$), respectively.

These three curves show that the negative effects of an exogenous increase in foreign interest rates on (Y) and (C) become larger as the degree of financial frictions increases (i.e., ω increases). The increase in the spread ($E[R_k] - R$) also increases as the degree of financial frictions rises. Further, as the degree of financial frictions increases, the depreciation of the real exchange rate (e) increases, which raises the value of foreign debt in domestic currency terms and amplifies the negative effect on a bank's balance sheet. That is, as the degree of financial frictions expands, the economy's fluctuation increases.

Figure 9.2 shows the impulse responses of the same variables, with and without a low (not necessarily optimal) degree of capital controls. The dotted curve represents the impulse responses without the capital control rule, and the solid curve represents those with it. From Fig. 9.2, it is clear that the capital control rule mitigates the increase in the spread ($E[R_k] - R$) and dampens the decline in output (Y). This rule also reduces the size of the fluctuations in consumption (C) and the real exchange rate (e).

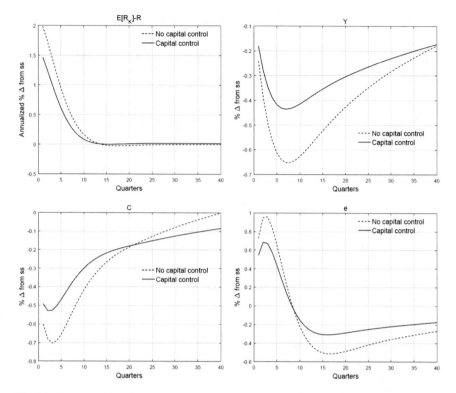

Fig. 9.2 Responses to an increase in the foreign interest rate, with and without capital controls: $\omega = 0.5$ ($E[R_k] - R_b$, Y, C, e). *Source* Kitano and Takaku [43]

Figure 9.3 shows the welfare curves corresponding to the three degrees of financial frictions ω. τ on the horizontal axis is the parameter associated with the capital control rule, and a higher value of τ implies that the capital control rule is more aggressive. The thin dotted curve, bold curve, and bold dotted curve represent the lower degree of friction case of $\omega = 0.25$, benchmark case of $\omega = 0.5$, and higher degree of frictions case of $\omega = 0.75$, respectively. The asterisk "∗" indicates the maximum welfare point for each of the three cases.

Figure 9.3 implies that capital controls may be welfare-improving. A range of τ improves welfare levels compared with the no-policy case. In addition, the welfare-improving effect of capital controls increases as the degree of financial frictions is higher. From the same comparison of the three cases, as the degree of financial frictions increases, the optimal value of τ becomes larger. This finding implies that a more aggressive policy rule is appropriate when the degree of financial friction increases.

Figure 9.4 plots the maximum welfare gain of capital controls under different degrees of financial frictions ω. The solid and dotted curves represent the welfare gain curves of capital controls in the "liability dollarization" economy and in the

9 Recent Developments in the Adoption of Capital Controls ...

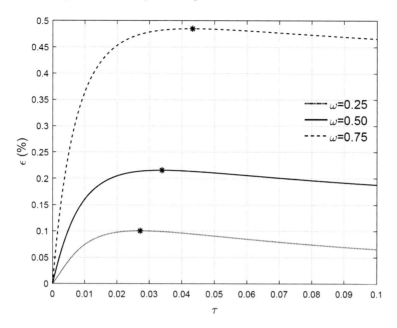

Fig. 9.3 Welfare curves with varying τ: Different degrees of financial frictions. *Source* Kitano and Takaku [43]

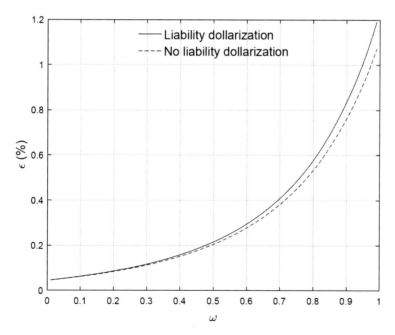

Fig. 9.4 Maximum welfare gains of capital controls under different degrees of financial frictions (ω): Liability dollarization vs. no liability dollarization. *Source* Kitano and Takaku [43]

"no liability dollarization" economy, respectively. In an economy where banks face the "liability dollarization" problem, their foreign borrowing is denominated in the foreign currency; by contrast, in the "no liability dollarization" economy, banks can borrow from abroad in their domestic currency terms.

In both cases, the maximum welfare gain of the optimal capital control rule increases as the degree of financial frictions increases. However, the maximum welfare gain of capital controls in the "liability dollarization" case is higher than that in the "no liability dollarization" case and the difference between the two cases becomes larger as ω increases.

When banks' liabilities are "dollarized," exchange rate behavior amplifies the effect of financial frictions through their balance sheets. In contrast, when banks' liabilities are not "dollarized," the exchange rate change has no direct valuation effect on a bank's balance sheet. Therefore, capital controls are more welfare improving in the "liability dollarization" case.

In this model, a higher degree of financial frictions means that domestic bankers are more likely to "divert" their assets financed by foreign investors, which implies a lower degree of financial development in an economy. If we follow this interpretation, our results suggest that capital controls are more appropriate for an economy with a less developed financial market.

9.2.2 Capital Controls as a Credit Policy Tool

Kitano and Takaku [44] examine whether capital controls can mitigate a crisis shock and fulfill the same role as the credit policy employed in advanced countries in the crisis period. The basic framework is a standard small open economy model (Faia and Monacelli [24]; Gáli and Monacelli [28]). However, financial frictions à la Gertler and Karadi [29] and liability dollarization are augmented with the sticky-price, small-open economy model. Financial frictions are due to the agency problem between foreign investors and domestic financial intermediaries in emerging economies. The small open economy comprises financial intermediaries, capital-producing firms, intermediate goods firms, retail firms, households, and the government. Along with traditional monetary policy, the government has two more policy tools. One is a direct credit policy that expands government credit intermediation. The other is capital controls that regulate the foreign borrowing of financial intermediaries.[12]

Figure 9.5 shows the impulse response to a negative shock that tightens the balance sheets of financial intermediaries. The response for the case without policy interventions is depicted by the thickest solid line ("No policy"). The response for the case with the direct credit policy rule is depicted by the thick solid line ("Direct policy"). As for the capital controls, we consider four alternative rules targeting the real exchange rate ("RER policy"), the current account level to output ratio ("CAY

---

[12] While Kitano and Takaku [44] investigate the role of capital controls as a credit policy tool, Mimir et al. [50] investigate the role of reserve requirements as a credit policy tool.

9 Recent Developments in the Adoption of Capital Controls ...

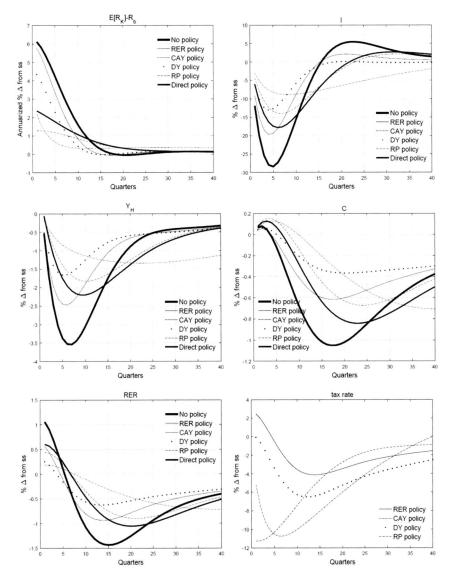

Fig. 9.5 Responses to a net worth shock (Y_H, $E[R_k] - R_b$, RER(e), C). *Source* Kitano and Takaku [44]

policy"), the debt level to output ratio ("DY policy"), and the risk premium level ("RP policy"). We set the coefficients in each of the capital control rules so that all the alternative rules yield the same level of welfare as under the direct credit policy rule. The solid line, dashed dotted line, dotted line, and dashed line depict the "RER policy," "CAY policy," "DY policy," and "RP policy," respectively.

Figure 9.5 confirms that the direct credit policy significantly mitigates the contraction (from the thickest solid line of "No policy" to the thick solid line of "Direct policy"), mainly because it moderates the rise in the spread $(E[R_K]-R_b)$ and then mitigates the drop in investment (I). As for the alternative rules, the "CAY policy" and "RP policy" produce an initial fall in tax rates and then dampen the initial rise in the spread as much as (or more than) the credit policy does. The "RER policy" and "DY policy" also dampen the initial rise in the spread compared with the no policy case but do not dampen it as much as the direct credit policy does. At the same time, however, in the cases of the "RER policy" and "DY policy," the fluctuation in the real exchange rate (RER) is more mitigated compared with that in the case of the direct credit policy. The stabilization of RER due to the "RER policy" and "DY policy" then stabilizes the output (Y_H) and consumption (C), which turns out to be welfare improving. In other words, in addition to the risk premium channel, capital controls can stabilize an open economy through a real exchange rate channel.

As we argue above, in the capital control rules, we first set the respective coefficients so that each rule yields a welfare level equal to that under the direct credit policy rule. By comparing the impulse responses for the respective rules with those for the direct credit policy, we can confirm that the capital control rules may serve as an alternative to the direct credit policy for mitigating the contraction.

Although central banks in advanced economies employed the direct credit policy in response to the financial crisis, few emerging economies followed suit [36]. On the contrary, in emerging economies, as we have already argued, capital controls have increasingly been recognized as a suitable policy for stabilizing economies against volatile capital flows. Thus, our results imply that capital controls can be a credit policy tool in crisis periods in emerging economies.

9.2.3 Capital Controls, Monetary Policy, and the Exchange Rate System

Kitano and Takaku [44] apply a Ramsey-type analysis and compare an optimal monetary policy under flexible exchange rates with an optimal capital control policy under fixed exchange rates. The welfare implications of both optimal policies are examined in a small open New Keynesian model with and without a financial accelerator mechanism. Broadly speaking, the welfare rankings of these two policies are markedly different in both cases.

We incorporate a financial accelerator a la Bernanke et al. [9] into a small open New Keynesian model, and there exist entrepreneurs, households, production firms, and the government in this model.[13] We then consider alternative policies in an economy with and without the financial accelerator.

In an economy without the financial accelerator (**No Financial Accelerator** in Table 9.1), we compare the welfare consequences of the following three cases: an

---

[13] In this sense, our model is close to those presented by Céspedes et al. [12], Devereux et al. [19], and Elekdag and Tchakarov [22].

9 Recent Developments in the Adoption of Capital Controls ... 193

Table 9.1 The welfare ranking of capital control and monetary policies

		No financial accelerator	Financial accelerator
Mon		1st	3rd
Cap.Con	ent. & hous	–	1st
	ent	–	2nd
	hous	2nd	4th
Peg		3rd	5th

Note **Mon.**: optimal monetary policy under flexible exchange rates, **Cap.Con.|ent.&hous.**: optimal capital control policies on households and entrepreneurs, **Cap.Con.|ent.**: optimal capital control policy on entrepreneurs, optimal capital control policy on households under fixed exchange rates **Cap.Con.|hous.**: optimal capital control policy on households under fixed exchange rates, and **Peg.**: peg regime without an optimal capital control policy

optimal monetary policy under flexible exchange rates (**Mon.**), an optimal capital control policy on households under fixed exchange rates (**Cap.Con.|hous.**), and a peg regime without an optimal capital control policy (**Peg.**).

In an economy with a financial accelerator, we compare the welfare consequences of the following five cases: an optimal monetary policy under flexible exchange rates (**Mon.**), an optimal capital control policy on households under fixed exchange rates (**Cap.Con.|hous.**), an optimal capital control policy on entrepreneurs (**Cap. Con.|ent.**), optimal capital control policies on households and entrepreneurs (**Cap.Con.|ent. & hous.**), and a peg regime without an optimal capital control policy (**Peg.**). Table 9.1 ranks the respective policies for the cases with and without the financial accelerator.

In the case without the financial accelerator, most welfare maximization is the optimal monetary policy under flexible exchange rates (**Mon.**). The optimal capital control policy under fixed exchange rates (**Cap.Con.|hous.**) significantly improves welfare under a fixed exchange rate regime without any policy (**Peg.**), but it is next to the optimal monetary policy under flexible exchange rates (**Mon.**).

In the case of a financial accelerator, however, the optimal capital control on both households and entrepreneurs under fixed exchange rates (**Cap.Con.|ent. & hous.**) is the most welfare-maximizing. The optimal monetary policy under flexible exchange rates (**Mon.**) is still better than the optimal capital policy on households (**Cap.Con.|hous.**), but the optimal capital control policy on entrepreneurs (**Cap.Con.|ent.**) is better than the optimal monetary policy (**Mon.**).

In summary, the ranking of welfare levels associated with the two policies depends on whether a financial accelerator mechanism exists in an economy. When it does not, the above results suggest that monetary policy may be a better tool than capital controls. In contrast, when a financial accelerator works, capital controls may be a better tool than monetary policy.

The intuition underlying our results is as follows. In a small open economy, entrepreneurs rely on foreign borrowing to finance their investments. In an economy with a financial accelerator, the borrowing rate of entrepreneurs includes an external finance premium due to a financial accelerator. The borrowing rate, which includes an external finance premium, can be more directly regulated with capital controls than monetary policy. Therefore, capital controls can be welfare improving in this environment.

9.2.4 Capital Controls and Macroprudential Regulation

Based on Kitano and Takaku [43], which incorporates banks into a small open economy model, Kitano and Takaku [46] compared the effectiveness of capital controls and macroprudential regulation. Following Korinek and Sandri [48], we differentiate between capital controls and macroprudential regulation. Capital controls regulate foreign lending and borrowing, whereas macroprudential regulation regulates domestic lending and borrowing. Focusing on the financial friction between banks and foreign investors, this study analyzes how financial friction influences the policy choice between capital controls and macroprudential regulation. Figure 9.6a, which is similar to Fig. 9.3 in Sect. 9.2.1, shows the welfare curves corresponding to three different degrees of financial frictions χ: the thin dotted curve ($\chi = 0.33$), the bold curve ($\chi = 0.43$), and the bold dotted curve ($\chi = 0.53$). A higher value of χ indicates a higher degree of financial friction between banks and foreign investors. The horizontal axis is the parameter τ_b associated with the capital control rule. A higher value of τ_b implies that the capital control rule is more aggressive. Figure 9.6b shows the equivalent welfare curves associated with the macroprudential regulation. A higher value of τ_k implies that the macroprudential regulation is more aggressive. In both cases, by comparing the three curves, we can see that their welfare-improving effect becomes larger as the degree of financial frictions increases.

Figure 9.7 shows the case where both capital controls and macroprudential regulation are employed at the same time. The maximum welfare gains from combining

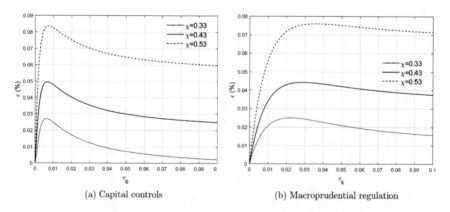

Fig. 9.6 Welfare curves with varying τ_b and τ_k. *Source* Kitano and Takaku [46]

9 Recent Developments in the Adoption of Capital Controls … 195

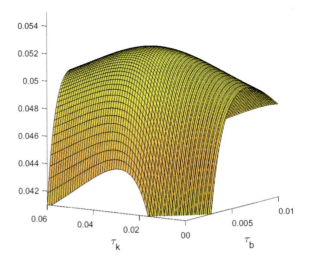

Fig. 9.7 Maximum welfare gains under both capital controls and macroprudential regulation ($\chi = 0.43$). *Source* Kitano and Takaku [46]

different values of τ_b and τ_k are plotted in Fig. 9.7. Compared to the case of optimizing either τ_b or τ_k, the optimal combination of τ_b and τ_k yields a higher level of welfare.

We again return to the case in which either capital controls or macroprudential regulation is employed. Figure 9.8 plots the maximum welfare gain of the two policies under different degrees of financial frictions (χ). The maximum welfare gain of

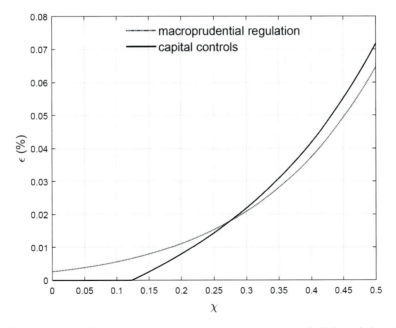

Fig. 9.8 Maximum welfare gains from capital controls and macroprudential regulation under different degrees of financial frictions (χ). *Source* Kitano and Takaku [46]

capital controls under different degrees of financial friction is plotted by the solid curve, and the maximum welfare gain of macroprudential regulation under different degrees of financial friction is plotted by the dotted curve. It is noteworthy that under low financial frictions (i.e., when χ is small), the maximum welfare gain from macroprudential regulation is higher than that from capital controls. Under high frictions (i.e., when χ is large), however, the maximum welfare gain from capital controls is higher than that from macroprudential regulation. In other words, when the degree of financial frictions is small, macroprudential regulation is more appropriate than capital controls. In contrast, when the degree of financial frictions is large, capital controls are more appropriate than macroprudential regulation.

So far, we have considered the welfare ranking of the two policies in an economy that suffers from liability dollarization. Whether an economy suffers from liability dollarization or not is likely to affect the ranking of the two policies. Next, we examine the welfare-improving effects of the two policies in the no-liability dollarization economy. Figure 9.9 shows the welfare gain curves of the two policies in the no-liability dollarization case. We can see that both the welfare-improving effects of the two policies become larger as the degree of financial frictions increases. However, it is noteworthy that the welfare-improving effect of macroprudential regulation is always equal to or greater than that of capital controls. This result implies that macroprudential regulation is likely to be more appropriate than capital

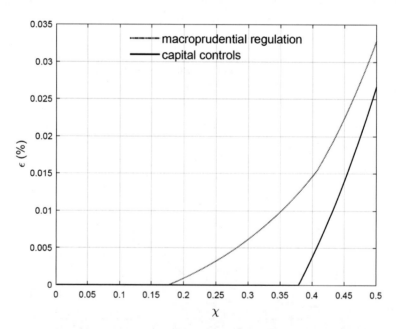

Fig. 9.9 Maximum welfare gains from capital controls and macroprudential regulation under different degrees of financial frictions (χ): No-liability dollarization case. *Source* Kitano and Takaku [46]

9 Recent Developments in the Adoption of Capital Controls ...

controls in the no-liability dollarization economy, such as advanced economies with a limited risk of exchange rate fluctuations.

9.3 Capital Controls in Practice

In Sect. 9.2, we briefly review the theoretical literature on capital controls and explain several studies that explore the possibility of capital controls as a policy tool in a small open economy. In this section, we elaborate on how emerging economies use capital control policies to regulate international capital flows. We first introduce indicators for capital controls to understand changes in capital control policies.

9.3.1 New Capital Control Measures

Many types of capital control measures exist (for example, Chinn and Ito [15], Schindler [57], Quinn et al. [56], Klein [47], Fernàndez et al. [27].[14] Many of these indicators are calculated by counting whether the controls exist in different categories. Therefore, as pointed out by Ahmed et al. [4], they may not always capture the detailed time variation in the intensity of capital controls.

9.3.1.1 India

For example, Figure 9.10 shows the capital control indicator for total inflows in India, which is produced from the data of Fernàndez et al. [27]. In this Figure, the vertical axis indicates the intensity of capital controls, and the value of one on the vertical axis represents that all categories of financial transactions have restrictions in India. According to Fernàndez et al. [27], India hardly changed its intensity of capital controls from 2002 to 2012. This is because India has some restrictions in most categories of financial transactions, which are greater than or equal to 90%.

However, according to Ahmed et al. [4]'s index, we obtain a different looking figure.[15] Figure 9.11 shows Ahmed et al. [4]'s capital control measures. In Fig. 9.11, "CUM" denotes the cumulative number of adopted capital control measures on inflows in each category. And "DIF" denotes the first difference of the cumulative series ("CUM"), which indicates the number of newly adopted measures in each quarter. In Fig. 9.11, "(a) Total," "(b) Equity," "(c) Bond," and "(d) Bank" indicate the number of changes in the categories of total inflows, equity inflows, bond inflows, and banking inflows, respectively. "(a) Total" is the sum of "(b)

---

[14] Quinn et al. [56] review numerous indicators of financial openness in detail.

[15] Ahmed et al. [4]'s data are available on their website: https://faculty.darden.virginia.edu/warnockf/research.htm.

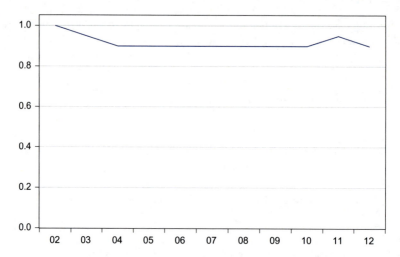

Fig. 9.10 Fernández et al. [27]'s capital control measures on total inflows in India. *Note* India's overall inflow restrictions index (kai). *Data Source* Fernández et al. [27]

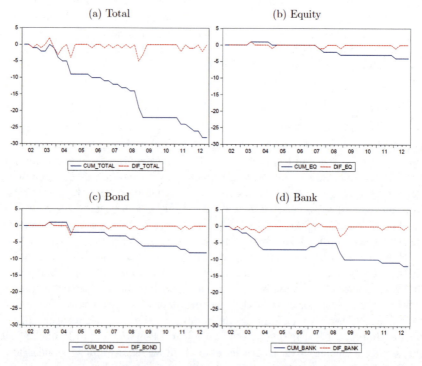

Fig. 9.11 Ahmed et al. [4]'s capital control measures on inflows in India. *Note* "CUM" denotes the cumulative number of capital control measures on inflows in each category. "DIF" denotes the first difference of the cumulative series, which indicates the number of new measures introduced in each quarter. *Data Source* Ahmed et al. [4]

Equity," "(c) Bond," and "(d) Bank." Ahmed et al. [4] count how often the authority has changed the measures of capital controls in each quarter by checking the qualitative narrative description in the "Changes during year" section of IMF (various years)'s AREAER.[16] By comparing Fig. 9.10 with (a) in Fig. 9.11, we can say that Ahmed et al. [4]'s index is more appropriate for capturing how the authority has changed the intensity of capital control measures.[17] Among the three categories of "(b) Equity," "(c) Bond," and "(d) Bank," Fig. 9.11 shows that India has changed the intensity of capital controls in the category of "(d) Bank" most frequently.

However, Ahmed et al. [4]'s index is also limited, as it does not capture the exact intensity of capital controls. Suppose that country A raises its tax rate on capital inflows by, for example, 1% in the first quarter of a year, while country B raises its tax rate by 0.25% in each quarter in the same year. If we follow Ahmed et al. [4]'s method, country B appears to increase its intensity of capital controls four times more than country A, even though both countries raise their tax rates by the same amount in that year (i.e., 1% in one year). However, Ahmed et al. [4]'s index is still more appropriate than Fernández et al. [27]'s index for capturing small changes in capital control policies.

9.3.1.2 Brazil

In the case of India, as argued above, Fig. 9.10 and (a) in Fig. 9.11 look different. However, this is not always the case. For example, Brazil is often referred to as a country that actively uses capital control measures.[18] Eichengreen and Rose [21] and Fernández et al. [26] argue that Brazil is exceptional, stating that emerging economies do not tend to respond to economic and financial cycles and that capital controls are generally acyclical. As shown in Figs. 9.12 and 9.13, in the case of Brazil, both indexes capture frequent fluctuations in capital control severity. Meanwhile, Fig. 9.13 indicates that, similar to India, Brazil has changed its intensity of capital controls in the category of "(d) Bank" most frequently.

9.3.1.3 Thailand

Another noteworthy case is Thailand. The imposition of capital controls in Thailand in 2006 is a well-known episode of the period of capital inflows to emerging economies (Jongwanich and Kohpaiboon [39]). Responding to a surge in capital inflows and the ensuing rapid exchange rate appreciation, Thailand drastically

---

[16] Chen and Qian [14] also compose a new measure that counts changes during specific time intervals by checking the AREAER data. Their data are specific to China, and are available on their website.

[17] By using Ahmed et al. [4]'s index, Ghosh et al. [32] show that emerging economies actually respond to capital inflows, whereas Eichengreen and Rose [21] and Fernández et al. [26] argue that capital controls are acyclical and that emerging economies do not respond to economic and financial cycles.

[18] See, for example, Alfaro et al. [5].

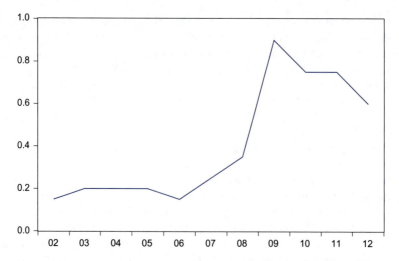

Fig. 9.12 Fernández et al. [27]'s capital control measures on total inflows in Brazil. *Note* Brazil's overall inflow restrictions index (kai). *Data Source* Fernández et al. [27]

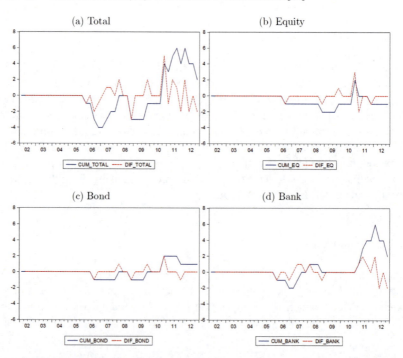

Fig. 9.13 Ahmed et al. [4]'s capital control measures on inflows in Brazil. *Note* "CUM" denotes the cumulative number of capital control measures on inflows in each category. "DIF" denotes the first difference of the cumulative series, which indicates the number of new measures introduced in each quarter. *Data Source* Ahmed et al. [4]

increased its capital control measures in December 2006. Figure 9.14 shows the changes in Fernández et al. [27]'s capital control indicator on total inflows in Thailand and Fig. 9.15 shows the changes in Ahmed et al. [4]'s indicator on total inflows in Thailand. By comparing Fig. 9.14 with (a) in Fi. 9.15, we note that the former misses the critical jump in Thailand's capital control measures in December 2006. Figure 9.15 also shows that in the imposition of capital controls in 2006, Thailand mainly used capital controls on bond and banking inflows.

9.3.1.4 Total of All 19 Sample Countries

Figures 9.11, 9.13, and 9.15 show Ahmed et al. [4]'s capital control indicators for India, Brazil, and Thailand. Our appendix presents the figures for the other 16 sample countries (Malaysia, the Philippines, Poland, Argentina, Taiwan, Indonesia, Korea, Turkey, Colombia, Romania, Chile, Czech Republic, Hungary, Mexico, South Africa, and Israel). These figures all show significant heterogeneity in the evolution of capital control intensity among these countries.

Figure 9.16 shows the evolution of capital control measures in all 19 sample countries. A prominent feature in Fig. 9.16a is the rapid decrease in the intensity of capital control measures during the period of the financial crisis (i.e., 2008) and ensuing increase after the crisis (i.e., 2010).

Figure 9.17 counts the number of capital control measures introduced in each quarter in different categories, namely "DIF EQ," "DIF BOND," and "DIF BANK" in Fig. 9.16b, c, and d, respectively. Figure 9.17 shows that the capital control measures

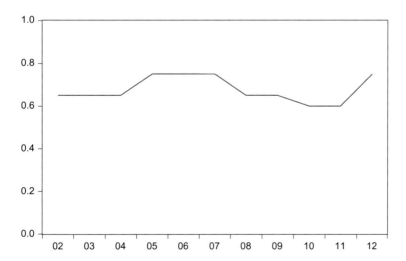

Fig. 9.14 Fernández et al. [27]'s capital control measures on total inflows in Thailand. *Note* Thailand's overall inflow restrictions index (kai). *Data Source* Fernández et al. [27]

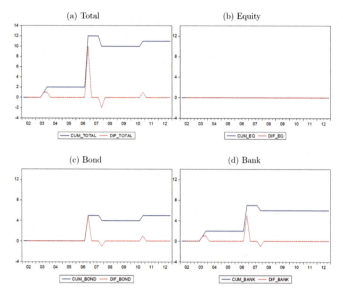

Fig. 9.15 Ahmed et al. [4]'s capital control measures on inflows in Thailand. *Note* "CUM" denotes the cumulative number of capital control measures on inflows in each category. "DIF" denotes the first difference of the cumulative series, which indicates the number of new measures introduced in each quarter. *Data Source* Ahmed et al. [4]

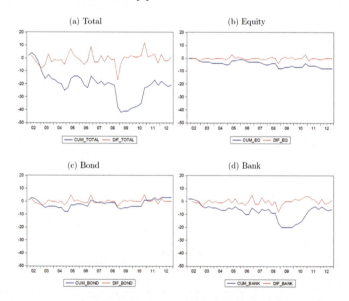

Fig. 9.16 Total of the 19 countries. *Note* The 19 countries included in Table 9.3. "CUM" denotes the cumulative number of capital control measures on inflows in each category. "DIF" denotes the first difference of the cumulative series, which indicates the number of new measures introduced in each quarter. *Data Source* Ahmed et al. [4]

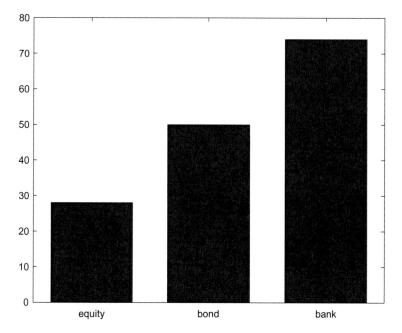

Fig. 9.17 Total number of capital control measures introduced in each quarter in different categories. *Note* The sample comprises the 19 countries over 2002Q1–2012Q4 as in Fig. 9.16

in the category of "DIF BANK" are the most often used, followed by "DIF BOND." The measures in "DIF EQ" are the least used.

9.3.1.5 Categorizing: "open," "Gate," or "Wall"

We next examine the heterogeneity among these countries more closely. Using data on inflow controls over 1995–2010 for five asset categories (money market instruments, bonds, financial credits, equities, and collective investments), Klein [47] divides 44 countries into three groups: "open" countries (persistently open to inflows), "wall" countries (persistently closed), and "gate" countries (i.e., episodic controls). Here, we also classify the 18 emerging countries in Table 9.2 into the three categories by using Fernández et al. [27]'s data on inflow controls over 2002–2012 based on the following Fernández et al. [27, page 558]'s classification criteria: *""Open" ("Walls") countries have, on average, capital controls on less than 15% (more than 70%) of their transactions subcategories over the sample period and do not have any years in which controls are on more than 25% (less than 60%) of their transaction subcategories. "Gate" countries are neither Walls nor Open."*

Table 9.2 shows our classification of the 18 emerging countries. The countries classified as "wall" countries are India, the Philippines, Malaysia, and Indonesia.

Table 9.2 Capital controls: Wall, gate, or open

	Overall inflow restriction index average	Wall/gate/open
India	0.92	Wall
Philippines	0.75	Wall
Colombia	0.72	Gate
Malaysia	0.72	Wall
Indonesia	0.71	Wall
Thailand	0.68	Gate
Argentina	0.57	Gate
Mexico	0.56	Gate
Poland	0.54	Gate
Brazil	0.41	Gate
South Africa	0.40	Gate
Turkey	0.33	Gate
Chile	0.21	Gate
Korea	0.20	Gate
Romania	0.20	Gate
Czech Republic	0.09	open
Hungary	0.07	Open
Israel	0.03	Open

Note 'kai' (overall inflow restrictions index)'s average over 2002–12. Following Fernández et al. [27], we classify a country as "open," "gate," or "wall." See Klein [47] and Fernández et al. [27] for details of the classification rule. Data source: overall inflow restrictions index (kai) Fernández et al. [27]

The "open" countries are Czech Republic, Hungary, and Israel and the "gate" countries are the remainder.[19] Table 9.2 shows that a high degree of heterogeneity exists among emerging countries. India's overall inflow restrictions index average is 0.92, while Israel's is only 0.03. The country-level figures presented earlier (i.e., Figs. 9.11, 9.13 and 9.15, and those in the Appendix) have already shown that significant heterogeneity in the evolution of capital control intensity exists among the sample countries. From this classification á la Klein [47] and Fernández et al. [27], we also confirm the high degree of heterogeneity among these countries.

Table 9.3 shows how each of the sample countries changed its capital control measures before and after the financial crisis based on our initial observations from the earlier figures (specifically, "(a) Total" in Figs. 9.11, 9.12, 9.13, 9.14, 9.15, 9.16, 9.17, 9.18, 9.19, 9.20, 9.21, 9.22, 9.23, 9.24, 9.25, 9.26, 9.27, 9.28, 9.29, 9.30, 9.31, 9.32, 9.33 and 9.34). The first column shows the classification of "open," "gate,"

---

[19] Although Colombia has an overall inflow restrictions index average above 0.70, it is still classified as a "gate" country. This is because Colombia has two years (i.e., 2011 and 2012) when the index is 0.50, which is below the critical level of 0.60.

9 Recent Developments in the Adoption of Capital Controls … 205

Table 9.3 Changes in capital control measures before and after the financial crisis

	Classification in Table 9.2	Ease	Ease before the crisis	Tighten before the crisis	Ease in the crisis	Tighten after the crisis
India	Wall	O			O	
Philippines	Wall	O			O	
Colombia	Gate		O	O	O	
Malaysia	Wall	O			O	
Indonesia	Wall		O	O	O	O
Thailand	Gate			O	O	O
Argentina	Gate		O	O		O
Mexico	Gate	O				
Poland	Gate	O			O	
Brazil	Gate		O	O	O	O
South Africa	Gate				O	
Turkey	Gate	O				O
Chile	Gate					
Korea	Gate		O	O	O	O
Romania	Gate		O	O	O	
Czech Republic	Open				O	
Hungary	Open	O				
Israel	Open					O
Taiwan	n.a		O			O

Note The first column comes from Table 9.2. The second to sixth columns are composed from "(a) Total" in Figs. 9.11, 9.12, 9.13, 9.14, 9.15, 9.16, 9.17, 9.18, 9.19, 9.20, 9.21, 9.22, 9.23, 9.24, 9.25, 9.26, 9.27, 9.28, 9.29, 9.30, 9.31, 9.32, 9.33 and 9.34, which are based on Ahmed et al. [4]'s data. Taiwan is not available in the first column, because the data for Taiwan are included in Ahmed et al. [4]'s data, but not in Fernández et al. [27]'s data

or "wall" in Table 9.2 for each country. The second column "Ease" means that the country gradually loosened its capital control measures throughout the sample period. The third column "Ease before the crisis" and the fifth column "Ease in the crisis" mean that the country loosened its capital control measures before and during the financial crisis, respectively. The fourth column "Tighten before the crisis" and the sixth column "Tighten after the crisis" mean that the country tightened its capital control measures before and after the financial crisis, respectively.

In Table 9.3, the "Ease in the crisis" cases are most often observed, consistent with the plunge in capital control intensity in all 19 sample countries observed in Fig. 9.16a. However, Table 9.3 shows that heterogeneity exists among emerging countries. While the "open" countries tend to be persistent, the "wall" and "gate" countries tend to adjust their degree of controls more often (i.e., the number of circles is larger) than the "open" countries. While this might be expected for the "gate"

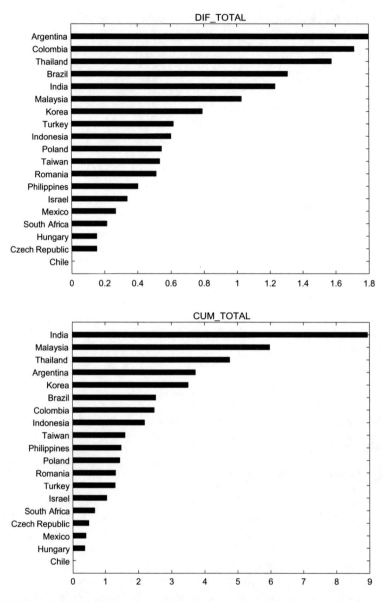

Fig. 9.18 Standard deviations of the capital control measures. *Note* The upper figure shows the standard deviations of DIF TOTAL in Table 9.4. The lower figure shows those of CUM TOTAL in Table 9.5

9 Recent Developments in the Adoption of Capital Controls … 207

Table 9.4 Standard deviations of the capital control measures introduced each quarter

	DIF TOTAL	DIF EQ	DIF BOND	DIF BANK
Argentina	1.798	0.551	1.011	0.498
Colombia	1.711	0.436	0.532	0.827
Thailand	1.574	0	0.793	0.804
Brazil	1.308	0.635	0.462	0.754
India	1.232	0.366	0.587	0.734
Malaysia	1.026	0.152	0.337	0.726
Korea	0.789	0	0.257	0.663
Turkey	0.615	0	0	0.593
Indonesia	0.600	0	0.213	0.478
Poland	0.543	0.213	0.152	0.213
Taiwan	0.532	0.257	0.152	0.366
Romania	0.511	0	0	0.511
Philippines	0.402	0	0.213	0.375
Israel	0.337	0	0.152	0.213
Mexico	0.266	0	0	0.218
South Africa	0.213	0	0	0.213
Hungary	0.152	0	0	0.152
Czech Republic	0.152	0	0	0
Chile	0	0	0	0
Average	0.7247	0.137	0.256	0.439

Note "DIF TOTAL," "DIF EQ," "DIF BOND," and "DIF BANK" respectively indicate the standard deviations of "DIF TOTAL," "DIF EQ," "DIF BOND," and "DIF BANK" in Figs. 9.11, 9.13, 9.15, 9.19, 9.20, 9.21, 9.22, 9.23, 9.24, 9.25, 9.26, 9.27, 9.28, 9.29, 9.30, 9.31, 9.32, 9.33 and 9.34.

countries, the "wall" countries such as Indonesia also tend to change their degree of controls more often than the "open" countries. There seems to be no reason to expect that the "wall" counties change their intensity of controls more often than the "open" countries.

Table 9.3 has offered a broad view of emerging countries' setting of capital control measures. To understand how often they change their capital control measures more precisely, we next calculate the standard deviations of the number of new measures introduced in each quarter in their countries. In Table 9.4, "DIF TOTAL," "DIF EQ," "DIF BOND," and "DIF BANK" respectively indicate the standard deviations of "DIF TOTAL," "DIF EQ," "DIF BOND," and "DIF BANK" in Figs. 9.11, 9.13, 9.15, 9.19, 9.20, 9.21, 9.22, 9.23, 9.24, 9.25, 9.26, 9.27, 9.28, 9.29, 9.30, 9.31, 9.32, 9.33 and 9.34. We arrange the sample countries from top to bottom in descending order of the standard deviation of DIF TOTAL. Table 9.5 also calculates the standard deviation, but that of the cumulative number of capital control measures in each country. "CUM TOTAL," "CUM EQ," "CUM BOND," and "CUM BANK"

Table 9.5 Standard deviations of the cumulative level of capital control measures

	CUM TOTAL	CUM EQ	CUM BOND	CUM BANK
India	8.940	1.697	2.974	3.340
Malaysia	5.973	0.254	1.109	4.295
Thailand	4.764	0	2.296	2.518
Argentina	3.720	1.634	2.205	1.470
Korea	3.501	0	0.949	2.637
Brazil	2.523	0.761	0.846	1.649
Colombia	2.478	0.561	0.659	1.481
Indonesia	2.191	0	0.753	1.478
Taiwan	1.593	0.927	0.408	1.635
Philippines	1.471	0	0.533	1.662
Poland	1.429	0.627	0.254	0.627
Romania	1.304	0	0	1.304
Turkey	1.290	0	0	1.322
Israel	1.044	0	0.347	0.707
South Africa	0.680	0	0	0.680
Czech Republic	0.497	0	0	0
Mexico	0.408	0	0	0.210
Hungary	0.369	0	0	0.369
Chile	0	0	0	0
average	2.325	0.340	0.702	1.441

Note "CUM TOTAL," "CUM EQ," "CUM BOND," and "CUM BANK" respectively indicate the standard deviations of "CUM TOTAL," "CUM EQ," "CUM BOND," and "CUM BANK" in Figs. 9.11, 9.13, 9.15, 9.19, 9.20, 9.21, 9.22, 9.23, 9.24, 9.25, 9.26, 9.27, 9.28, 9.29, 9.30, 9.31, 9.32, 9.33 and 9.34

respectively indicate the standard deviation of "CUM TOTAL," "CUM EQ," "CUM BOND," and "CUM BANK" in Figs. 9.11, 9.13, 9.15, 9.19, 9.20, 9.21, 9.22, 9.23, 9.24, 9.25, 9.26, 9.27, 9.28, 9.29, 9.30, 9.31, 9.32, 9.33 and 9.34.

Using Tables 9.4 and 9.5, we rank the standard deviations of the capital control measures in Fig. 9.18. The upper number of Fig. 9.18 indicates the standard deviations of DIF TOTAL in Table 9.4. The lower number of Fig. 9.18 indicates those of CUM TOTAL in Table 9.5. The first seven countries (Argentina, Brazil, Colombia, India, Korea, Malaysia, and Thailand) and the last six countries (Chile, Czech Republic, Hungary, Israel, Mexico, South Africa) are common in the upper and lower figures of Figure 9.18. Therefore, it would be appropriate to classify the sample countries into three groups: high-frequency countries (Argentina, Brazil, Colombia, India, Korea, Malaysia, and Thailand), medium-frequency countries (Indonesia, the Philippines, Poland, Romania, Taiwan, Turkey), and low frequency countries (Chile, Czech Republic, Hungary, Israel, Mexico, and South Africa).

9 Recent Developments in the Adoption of Capital Controls … 209

An interesting point is that the high-frequency group includes not only "gate" countries such as Argentina, Brazil, Colombia, Korea, and Thailand, but also India and Malaysia, which are identified as "wall" countries according to Fernández et al. [27]'s criteria.

In this section, we examine how emerging economies deploy capital control policies using Ahmed et al. [4]'s indicator, which provides a better understanding of changes in capital control policies than earlier indicators. Eichengreen and Rose [21] argue that capital controls are durable, and Fernández et al. [26] argue that capital controls are acyclical. However, Ahmed et al. [4]'s new indicator suggests that emerging market economies make more intensive use of capital control policies than previously assumed.

In addition, we find a high degree of heterogeneity in capital control policies among emerging countries. Even in the same group of "gate" countries, as shown in Table 9.3, the timing of increasing (or decreasing) the intensity of capital control measures varies. Countries categorized as "wall" also show a wide variety of capital control policies.

9.4 Conclusion

In this chapter, we introduce recent theoretical research on capital control policies. Recent theoretical research suggests that capital control policies may have significant potential as policy tools. In particular, we show that they can serve to stabilize the amplification mechanisms resulting from external shocks in economies with financial frictions. We also explain that emerging countries have been using capital control policies, which have attracted considerable interest in recent years, in the aftermath of the global financial crisis. The new capital control indicators created by Ahmed et al. [4] offer a better understanding of the small changes in capital control policies, which are difficult to capture with earlier indicators. These new indicators suggest that emerging market economies make more intensive use of capital control policies than previously assumed. Further, we find that significant heterogeneity exists among the emerging countries in our sample.

Many emerging economies have started to consider capital controls as a regular policy instrument to regulate massive international capital flows only after the global financial crisis, as we argue in Section 1. Therefore, it is not surprising that emerging economies did not tend to respond to their business cycles, and capital controls tended to be acyclical before the global financial crisis (Eichengreen and Rose [21], Fernández et al. [26]). It would be a good topic for future analyses to examine whether capital control policies in emerging economies changed after the global financial crisis.

Related to this, as developed countries continue to pursue monetary policy normalization, it remains to be seen whether capital will start to flow out of emerging countries, as it has in the past, and what policy measures emerging countries will adopt to mitigate this problem. These new trends in the global financial market are expected to spur significant development of empirical and theoretical research on capital flows in the future.

Finally, related to the COVID-19 pandemic, the massive credit expansion by central banks around the world, including both developed and emerging countries, surely mitigates the COVID-19 pandemic negative shocks. However, it also increases the potential risks entailed in the excess debt problem of the private sector around the world, which has already been a great concern for the world economy before the pandemic. From this point of view, as IMF [34] argues, capital controls could be deployed as a useful targeted macroprudential measure.

Acknowledgements This work was supported by KAKENHI (20K01744, 20H05633).

Appendix

Ahmed et al. [4]'s capital control measures for the remaining countries

In Figs. 9.11, 9.13 and 9.15 in the main text, we show Ahmed et al. [4]'s capital control indicators for India, Brazil, and Thailand. In this appendix, we present those for the other 16 sample countries (Malaysia, the Philippines, Poland, Argentina, Taiwan, Indonesia, Korea, Turkey, Colombia, Romania, Chile, Czech Republic, Hungary, Mexico, South Africa, and Israel).

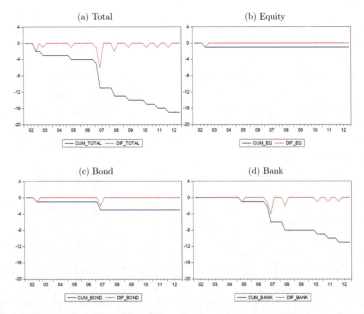

Fig. 9.19 Malaysia. *Note* "CUM" denotes the cumulative number of capital control measures on inflows in each category. "DIF" denotes the first difference of the cumulative series, which indicates the number of new measures introduced in each quarter. *Data Source* Ahmed et al. [4]

9 Recent Developments in the Adoption of Capital Controls … 211

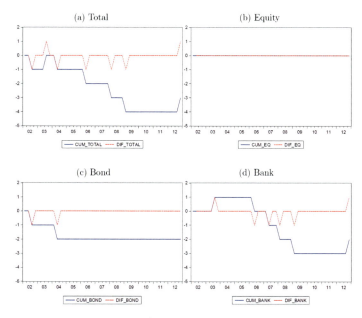

Fig. 9.20 Philippines. *Note* "CUM" denotes the cumulative number of capital control measures on inflows in each category. "DIF" denotes the first difference of the cumulative series, which indicates the number of new measures introduced in each quarter. *Data Source* Ahmed et al. [4]

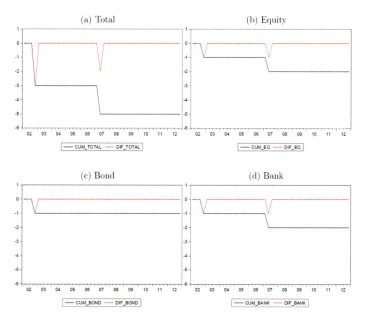

Fig. 9.21 Poland. *Note* "CUM" denotes the cumulative number of capital control measures on inflows in each category. "DIF" denotes the first difference of the cumulative series, which indicates the number of new measures introduced in each quarter. *Data Source* Ahmed et al. [4]

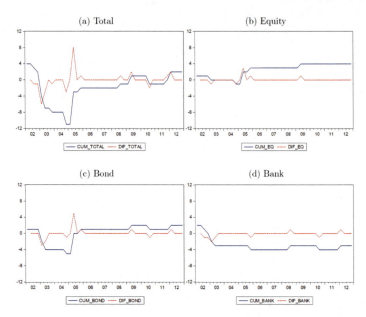

Fig. 9.22 Argentina. *Note* "CUM" denotes the cumulative number of capital control measures on inflows in each category. "DIF" denotes the first difference of the cumulative series, which indicates the number of new measures introduced in each quarter. *Data Source* Ahmed et al. [4]

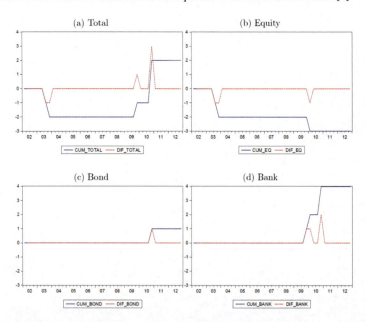

Fig. 9.23 Taiwan. *Note* "CUM" denotes the cumulative number of capital control measures on inflows in each category. "DIF" denotes the first difference of the cumulative series, which indicates the number of new measures introduced in each quarter. *Data Source* Ahmed et al. [4]

9 Recent Developments in the Adoption of Capital Controls ... 213

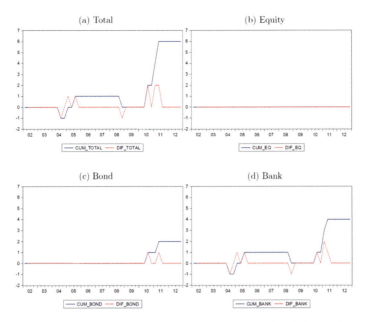

Fig. 9.24 Indonesia. *Note* "CUM" denotes the cumulative number of capital control measures on inflows in each category. "DIF" denotes the first difference of the cumulative series, which indicates the number of new measures introduced in each quarter. *Data Source* Ahmed et al. [4]

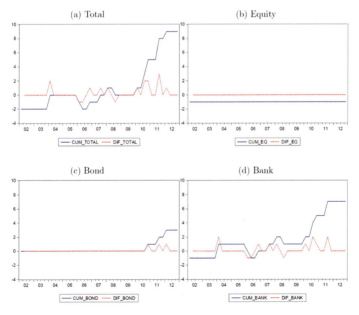

Fig. 9.25 Korea. *Note* "CUM" denotes the cumulative number of capital control measures on inflows in each category. "DIF" denotes the first difference of the cumulative series, which indicates the number of new measures introduced in each quarter. *Data Source* Ahmed et al. [4]

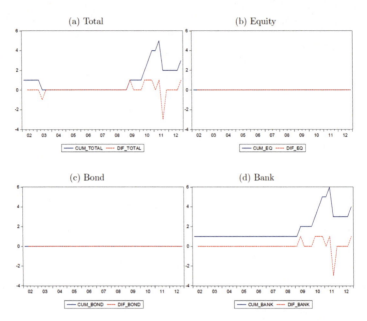

Fig. 9.26 Turkey. *Note* "CUM" denotes the cumulative number of capital control measures on inflows in each category. "DIF" denotes the first difference of the cumulative series, which indicates the number of new measures introduced in each quarter. *Data Source* Ahmed et al. [4]

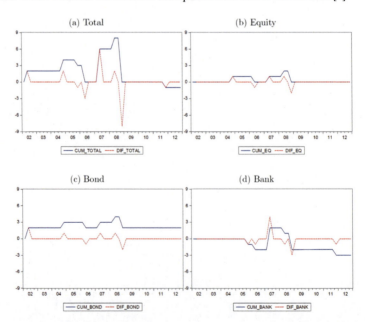

Fig. 9.27 Colombia. *Note* "CUM" denotes the cumulative number of capital control measures on inflows in each category. "DIF" denotes the first difference of the cumulative series, which indicates the number of new measures introduced in each quarter. *Data Source* Ahmed et al. [4]

9 Recent Developments in the Adoption of Capital Controls ...   215

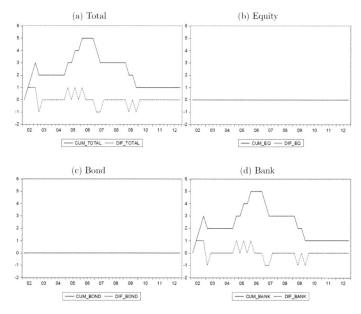

Fig. 9.28 Romania. *Note* "CUM" denotes the cumulative number of capital control measures on inflows in each category. "DIF" denotes the first difference of the cumulative series, which indicates the number of new measures introduced in each quarter. *Data Source* Ahmed et al. [4]

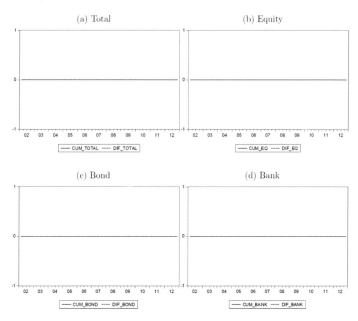

Fig. 9.29 Chile. *Note* "CUM" denotes the cumulative number of capital control measures on inflows in each category. "DIF" denotes the first difference of the cumulative series, which indicates the number of new measures introduced in each quarter. *Data Source* Ahmed et al. [4]

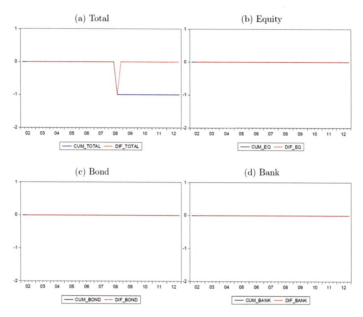

Fig. 9.30 Czech Republic. *Note* "CUM" denotes the cumulative number of capital control measures on inflows in each category. "DIF" denotes the first difference of the cumulative series, which indicates the number of new measures introduced in each quarter. *Data Source* Ahmed et al. [4]

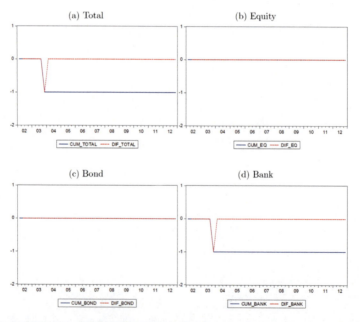

Fig. 9.31 Hungary. *Note* "CUM" denotes the cumulative number of capital control measures on inflows in each category. "DIF" denotes the first difference of the cumulative series, which indicates the number of new measures introduced in each quarter. *Data Source* Ahmed et al. [4]

9 Recent Developments in the Adoption of Capital Controls … 217

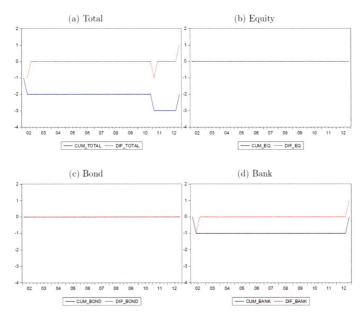

Fig. 9.32 Mexico. *Note* "CUM" denotes the cumulative number of capital control measures on inflows in each category. "DIF" denotes the first difference of the cumulative series, which indicates the number of new measures introduced in each quarter. *Data Source* Ahmed et al. [4]

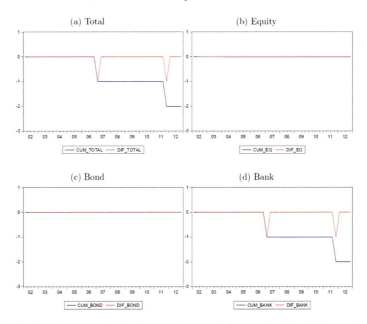

Fig. 9.33 South Africa. *Note* "CUM" denotes the cumulative number of capital control measures on inflows in each category. "DIF" denotes the first difference of the cumulative series, which indicates the number of new measures introduced in each quarter. *Data Source* Ahmed et al. [4]

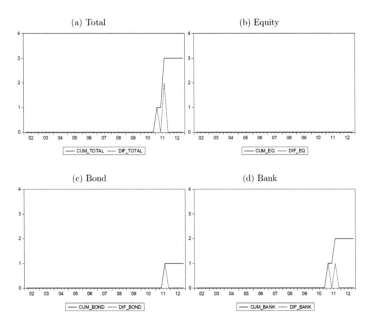

Fig. 9.34 Israel. *Note* "CUM" denotes the cumulative number of capital control measures on inflows in each category. "DIF" denotes the first difference of the cumulative series, which indicates the number of new measures introduced in each quarter. *Data Source* Ahmed et al. [4]

References

1. Agénor, P. R. (2004). *The Economics of Adjustment and Growth* (2nd ed.). Cambridge, MA: Harvard University Press.
2. Agénor, P. R., & Jia, P. (2015). *Capital Controls and Welfare with Cross-Border Bank Capital Flows*. Centre for Growth and Business Cycle Research Discussion Paper Series 212, Economics, The University of Manchester.
3. Agénor, P. R., & Montiel, P. J. (2008). *Development Macroeconomics: Third Edition*. Princeton University Press.
4. Ahmed, S., Curcuru, S. E., Warnock, F. E., & Zlate, A. (2016). Decomposing International Portfolio Flows. September, SUERF/PSE/CEPII Conference, Dataset on capital controls (2002Q1–2012Q4, 19 countries). https://faculty.darden.virginia.edu/warnockf/research.htm.
5. Alfaro, L., Chari, A., & Kanczuk, F. (2017). The real effects of capital controls: Firm-level evidence from a policy experiment. *Journal of International Economics, 108*, 191–210.
6. Auernheimer, L. (1987). On the outcome of inconsistent programs under exchange rate and monetary rules: Allowing the market to compensate for government mistakes. *Journal of Monetary Economics, 19*(2), 279–305.
7. Bacchetta, P. (1990). Temporary capital controls in a balance-of- payments crisis. *Journal of International Money and Finance, 9*(3), 246–257.
8. Bartolini, L., & Drazen, A. (1997). Capital-account liberalization as a signal. *The American Economic Review, 87*(1), 138–154.
9. Bernanke, B. S., Gertler, M., & Gilchrist, S. (1999). The financial accelerator in a quantitative business cycle framework. In J. B. Taylor, & M. Woodford (Eds.), *Handbook of macroeconomics*, Vol. 1 of Handbook of Macroeconomics, Chap. 21, pp. 1341–1393. Elsevier.

10. Bianchi, J. (2011). Overborrowing and systemic externalities in the business cycle. *American Economic Review, 101*(7), 3400–3426.
11. Brunnermeier, M. K., & Sannikov, Y. (2015). International credit flows and pecuniary externalities. *American Economic Journal: Macroeconomics, 7*(1), 297–338.
12. Céspedes, L. F., Chang, R., & Velasco, A. (2004). Balance sheets and exchange rate policy. *American Economic Review, 94*(4), 1183–1193.
13. Chang, C., Liu, Z., & Spiegel, M. M. (2015). Capital controls and optimal chinese monetary policy. *Journal of Monetary Economics, 74*, 1–15.
14. Chen, J., & Qian, X. (2016). Measuring on-going changes in China's capital controls: A de jure and a hybrid index data set. *China Economic Review, 38*, 167–182.
15. Chinn, M. D., & Ito, H. (2006). What matters for financial development? Capital controls, institutions, and interactions. *Journal of Development Economics, 81*(1), 163–192.
16. Davis, J. S., & Presno, I. (2017). Capital controls and monetary policy autonomy in a small open economy. *Journal of Monetary Economics, 85*(C), 114–130.
17. De Paoli, B., & Lipinska, A. (2013) Capital Controls: A Normative Analysis. staff reports, Federal Reserve Bank of New York.
18. Dellas, H., & Stockman, A. (1993). Self-fulfilling expectations, speculative attack, and capital controls. *Journal of Money, Credit and Banking, 25*(4), 721–730.
19. Devereux, M. B., Lane, P. R., & Xu, J. (2006) Exchange rates and monetary policy in emerging market economies. *The Economic Journal, 116*(511), 478–506.
20. Eichengreen, B., & Hausmann, R. (1999). Exchange rates and financial fragility. Working Paper 7418, National Bureau of Economic Research.
21. Eichengreen, B., & Rose, A. (2014). Capital controls in the 21st Century. *Journal of International Money and Finance, 48*, 1–16.
22. Elekdag, S., & Tchakarov, I. (2007). Balance sheets, exchange rate policy, and welfare. *Journal of Economic Dynamics and Control, 31*(12), 3986–4015.
23. Engel, C. (2016). Macroprudential policy under high capital mobility: policy implications from an academic perspective. *Journal of the Japanese and International Economies, 42*, 162–172.
24. Faia, E., & Monacelli, T. (2008). Optimal monetary policy in a small open economy with home bias. *Journal of Money, Credit and Banking, 40*(4), 721–750.
25. Farhi, E., & Werning, I. (2012). *Dealing with the trilemma: Optimal capital controls with fixed exchange rates* (Working Paper 18199). National Bureau of Economic Research.
26. Fernández, A., Rebucci, A., Uribe, M. (2015). Are capital controls countercyclical? *Journal of Monetary Economics, 76*, 1–14.
27. Fernández, A., Klein, M. W., Rebucci, A., Schindler, M., & Uribe, M. (2016) Capital control measures: a new dataset. *IMF Economic Review, 64*(3), 548–574.
28. Jordi, G., & Monacelli, T (2005) Monetary policy and exchange rate volatility in a small open economy. *The Review of Economic Studies, 72*(3), 707–734.
29. Gertler, M., & Karadi, P. (2011). A model of unconventional monetary policy. *Journal of Monetary Economics, 58*(1), 17–34.
30. Gertler, M., & Kiyotaki, N. (2010). Chapter 11-financial intermediation and credit policy in business cycle analysis. In Friedman, B. M. & Woodford, M. (Eds.), *Handbook of monetary economics* (Vol. 3, pp. 547–599). Elsevier.
31. Ghilardi, M. F., & Peiris, S. J. (2016). Capital flows, financial intermediation and macroprudential policies. *Open Economies Review, 27*(4), 721–746.
32. Ghosh, A. R., Ostry, J. D., Qureshi, M. S., (2017). Managing the tide; how do emerging markets respond to capital flows? (IMF Working Papers 17/69). International Monetary Fund.
33. Harberger, A. C. (1986). Welfare consequences of capital inflows. In Choksi, A. M. & Papageorgiou, D. (Eds.), *Economic liberalization in developing countries* (pp. 157–178). Basil Blackwell.
34. IMF (2021) *Global financial stability report.*
35. IMF (various years) *Annual report on exchange arrangements and exchange restrictions (AREAER).* Washington, D.C.: International Monetary Fund.

36. Ishi, K. o., Stone, M. R., Yehoue, E. B. (2009). Unconventional Central bank measures for emerging economies. *IMF working papers*, 1–42.
37. Jeanne, O., & Korinek, A. (2010). Excessive volatility in capital flows: a pigouvian taxation approach. *American Economic Review, 100*(2), 403–407.
38. Jeanne, O., Subramanian, A., Williamson, J. (2012). *Who needs to open the capital account?* Peterson Institute for International Economics.
39. Jongwanich, J., & Kohpaiboon, A. (2012). Effectiveness of capital controls: evidence from Thailand. *Asian Development Review, 29*(2), 50–93.
40. Kitano, S. (2004). Macroeconomic effect of capital controls as a safeguard against the capital inflow problem. *Journal of International Trade & Economic Development, 13*(3), 233–263.
41. Kitano, S. (2007). Capital controls, public debt and currency crises. *Journal of Economics, 90*(2), 117–142.
42. Kitano, S. (2011). Capital controls and welfare. *Journal of Macroeconomics, 33*(4), 700–710.
43. Kitano, S., & Takaku, K. (2017). Capital controls and financial frictions in a small open economy. *Open Economies Review, 28*(4), 761–793.
44. Kitano, S., & Takaku, K. (2018a). Capital controls as a credit policy tool in a small open economy. *The B.E. Journal of Macroeconomics, 18*(1), 1–19.
45. Kitano, S., & Takaku, K. (2018b). Capital controls, monetary policy, and balance sheets in a small open economy. *Economic Inquiry, 56*(2), 859–874.
46. Kitano, S., & Takaku, K. (2020). Capital controls, macroprudential regulation, and the bank balance sheet channel. *Journal of Macroeconomics, 63*, 103161.
47. Klein, M. W. (2012). Capital controls: gates versus walls. *Brookings Papers on Economic Activity, 43*(2), 317–367.
48. Korinek, A., & Sandri, D. (2016). Capital controls or macroprudential regulation? *Journal of International Economics*, vol 99. *Supplement, 1*, S27–S42.
49. Liu, Z., & Spiegel, M. M. (2015). Optimal monetary policy and capital account restrictions in a small open economy. *IMF Economic Review, 63*(2), 298–324.
50. Mimir, Y., Sunel, E., & Taskin, T. (2013). Required reserves as a credit policy tool. *The B.E. Journal of Macroeconomics*, 13(1), 823–880.
51. Nispi Landi, V. (2017). Capital controls, macroprudential measures and monetary policy interactions in an emerging economy. Temi di discussione (Economic working papers) 1154, Bank of Italy, Economic Research and International Relations Area
52. Nispi Landi, V., Schiavone, A. (2021). The effectiveness of capital controls. *Open Economies Review*, 32(1), 183–211.
53. Ostry, J. D., Qureshi, M. S., Habermeier, K., Bernhard, D., Reinhardt, S., Chamon, M., & Ghosh, A. (2010). Capital inflows: the role of controls. IMF Staff Position Notes 2010/04, International Monetary Fund.
54. Ostry, J., Ghosh, A., Korinek, A. (2012). Multilateral aspects of managing the capital account. IMF Staff Discussion Notes 12/10, International Monetary Fund.
55. Park, D., Sachs, J. (1987). Capital controls and the timing of exchange regime collapse (Working Paper 2250). National Bureau of Economic Research
56. Quinn, D., Schindler, M., Maria Toyoda, A. (2011). Assessing measures of financial openness and integration. *IMF Economic Review, 59*(3), 488–522.
57. Schindler, M. (2009). Measuring financial integration: a new data set. *IMF Staff Papers*, 56(1), 222–238.
58. Schmitt-Grohé, S., Uribe, M. (2016). Downward nominal wage rigidity, currency pegs, and involuntary unemployment. *Journal of Political Economy*, 124(5), 1466–1514.
59. Shin, H. S. (2010). Non-core liabilities tax as a tool for prudential regulation. Policy Memo. http://online.wsj.com/public/resources/documents/NonCoreLiabilitiesTax.pdf
60. Unsal, D. F. (2013). Capital flows and financial stability: monetary policy and macroprudential responses. *International Journal of Central Banking, 9*(1), 233–285.
61. Wyplosz, C. (1986). Capital controls and balance of payments crises. *Journal of International Money and Finance, 5*(2), 167–179.

Shigeto Kitano is a professor of economics at Kobe University. He received his Ph.D. from Nagoya University in Japan. His main research interest is international macroeconomics. He has published many papers in refereed journals, such as the *Journal of Macroeconomics, Economic Inquiry, Open Economies Review, Pacific Economic Review, International Review of Economics and Finance, Review of Development Economics, International Journal of Economic Theory, Journal of Economics,* and *Applied Economics Letters.*

Kenya Takaku is an associate professor of economics at Hiroshima City University in Japan. He received his Ph.D. from Nagoya University, and his main research interest is international macroeconomics.

Index

A
Advanced countries, 127, 190

B
Bank foreign claims, 156, 162
Banking sector, 22, 29, 30, 67, 71, 77, 81–83, 92, 156, 164, 169, 175, 181
Banking system, 19, 22, 23, 27–30, 32, 34–36, 39, 41, 42, 44, 45, 48, 50, 51, 53, 55, 56, 58, 60, 62, 154, 176, 177, 180
Bank leverage, 159–161, 163
Bank profitability, 153, 154, 157, 160–165, 167
Brazil, 8, 31, 70, 72, 127, 171, 173, 175–178, 184, 199–201, 204, 207–210
BRICs, 169–175, 177, 180

C
Capital controls, 15, 171, 178, 183–211
Capital inflow, 27, 30, 31, 43, 67–69, 71, 73–77, 81–83, 92, 94, 95, 128
China, 8, 31, 36, 92, 107, 127, 170–173, 175–178, 180, 181
Cointegration, 101, 108, 109
Correlation coefficients, 35, 45
Credit default swap (CDS), 113, 114, 117, 126–128, 139, 140
Credit policy, 186, 190–192
Cross-border bank flows, 19, 21, 23, 24, 30, 32, 42, 48, 61

Cross-border capital flows, 16, 25, 92
Current account, 3, 190

D
Demand deposits, 99–102, 105–108, 110, 111
Demand for the dollar, 102, 103, 108, 110–112
Destination of capital flows, 20, 77, 82
Developed countries, 61, 62, 171, 183, 184, 209
Developing countries, 29, 61, 102, 169, 170, 172, 173, 175, 180
Dollar liquidity, 2, 5, 8, 9, 11, 13, 16, 21, 71
Domestic credit, 36, 48, 68, 69, 71, 73, 74, 92
Dynamic panel, 69, 76

E
Emerging economies, 29, 67, 71, 73, 76, 83, 92, 94, 95, 113, 114, 117, 126, 127, 139, 140, 170, 183–186, 190, 192, 197, 199, 209
European debt crisis, 20, 116
European Union, 22, 39, 155
Exchange rate system, 3, 4, 192

F
Financial account
Financial frictions, 186, 190

© The Editor(s) (if applicable) and The Author(s), under exclusive license to Springer Nature Singapore Pte Ltd. 2022
Y. Matsubayashi and S. Kitano (eds.), *Global Financial Flows in the Pre- and Post-global Crisis Periods*, Kobe University Monograph Series in Social Science Research, https://doi.org/10.1007/978-981-19-3613-5

Index

Financial institutions, 1, 3, 4, 8, 9, 11, 13, 15, 16, 21, 25, 99, 100, 103, 105, 108, 170, 176
Foreign assets, 156
Foreign banks' penetration, 22, 27, 28, 30, 34, 36, 42, 48, 56

G
Global financial crisis, 1, 11, 15, 16, 19, 20, 68, 69, 71, 72, 76, 79, 99–105, 108, 111, 113, 114, 153–155, 167, 169
Global liquidity, 1, 2, 8, 9, 11, 13, 15, 16, 19, 21–31, 33, 34, 39, 42–45, 48, 51, 56, 61, 62, 67–69, 95, 100, 169
Global risk, 113
Gross capital flow, 153

I
India, 8, 31, 92, 171, 173, 175, 177, 179, 197–199, 201, 203–205, 207–210
International capital flow, 1, 7, 15, 24, 25
International currency, 99–103, 107, 108, 110–112
International finance, 2
International financial market, 2–4, 6, 8, 11, 13, 68, 169, 170, 180, 181
International liquidity, 2–4, 8, 9, 16

L
Large-scale asset purchases, 114
London Interbank Offered Rate (LIBOR), 11

M
Macro-prudential policy, 74–76, 83, 92
Macroprudential regulation, 185, 186, 194–196
Monetary policy, 3, 11, 21, 27, 114, 128, 160–163, 165–167, 184–186, 190, 192–194, 209

N
Noncore liability, 169, 170, 172, 174–181

O
Offshore bond issuance, 169–173, 175–181

R
Regulatory arbitrage, 19, 22, 23, 29, 32, 45, 51, 56, 61, 62, 180

S
Shadow banking, 169, 170, 175–181
Sovereign CDS spreads, 114, 117, 126–128, 139, 140
Subprime mortgage crisis, 1

T
Thailand, 8, 31, 70, 127, 199, 201, 202, 204, 205, 207–210

U
Uncovered Interest Rate Parity (UIP) puzzle, 143
United States (US), 1–5, 8, 21, 31, 92, 99, 100, 102, 103, 108, 126, 169, 176
U.S. economic policy uncertainty, 113, 114, 117, 126–128, 139, 140

V
Volatility index (VIX), 13, 14, 21, 113, 117, 126–128, 139, 140

W
Within-company loan, 169

Printed in the United States
by Baker & Taylor Publisher Services